Additional Praise for
The Power of We

"What a great idea to write *The Power of We*. This is exactly how great companies are built."

Bill Marriott
Chairman and CEO
Marriott International, Inc.

"Organizations these days are all becoming more permeable. Strategic alliances and partnerships are key to success in the public, private, and not-profit sectors. Drawing from his own experience in both business and public service, Jonathan Tisch offers great advice and guidance to those seeking to enhance their ability to work with others for mutual gain. Everyone can learn something from this book."

Lawrence S. Bacow
President
Tufts University

"Jon Tisch is one of America's most imaginative and forward-looking business leaders. *The Power of We* provides some unique insights into the philosophy that has helped make Jon—and his company—both highly successful and widely admired. And it's great reading, too!"

Thomas J. Donohue
President and CEO
U.S. Chamber of Commerce

"Gone is the 'go-it-alone' era. Our increasingly complex and inter-woven world favors those who know how to connect the dots and con-nect people to harness the creativity and energy of multiple minds. That's the idea behind the power of partnership, of which Jonathan Tisch is a master practitioner."

Marilyn Carlson Nelson
Chair and CEO
Carlson Companies

THE POWER OF WE

SUCCEEDING THROUGH PARTNERSHIPS

JONATHAN M. TISCH

WITH KARL WEBER

WILEY

JOHN WILEY & SONS, INC.

Published by John Wiley & Sons, Inc., Hoboken, New Jersey.
Published simultaneously in Canada.

For general information on our other products and services, or technical support, please contact our Customer Care Department within the United States at 800-762-2974, outside the United States at 317-572-3993 or fax 317-572-4002.

Wiley also publishes its books in a variety of electronic formats. Some content that appears in print may not be available in electronic books. For more information about Wiley products, visit our web site at www.wiley.com.

Library of Congress Cataloging-in-Publication Data:

Tisch, Jonathan M.
    Succeeding through partnerships / Jonathan M. Tisch with Karl Weber.
      p. cm.
    Includes bibliographical references and index.
    ISBN 0-471-65282-2 (cloth)
  1. Partnership.   2. Management.   3. Cooperativeness.   4. Strategic alliances (Business).   I. Weber, Karl.   II. Title.
    HD69.S8.T57 2004
    658′.042—dc22

                                      2004007927

Printed in the United States of America.

10 9 8 7 6 5 4 3 2

To Charles and Henry . . .
my most cherished partners of all.

CONTENTS

ACKNOWLEDGMENTS

FOR ME, AS FOR MANY FIRST-TIME AUTHORS, THE EXPERIENCE OF WRITing a book has been filled with fear, trepidation, frustration, and eventually, joy.

Over the past two years, I've found myself constantly thinking about how I got to this point.

The journey would never have been completed if not for the valuable input, support, counsel, and advice of so many individuals. Some I've known forever, others I've met only in the past few months while struggling to write an interesting and informative book about business and community in the context of today's world.

My family has always been at the center of my existence. They've afforded me so many opportunities, allowing me to explore my own thoughts and ideals, but also always forming a support group filled with love and humor. My parents, Joan and Bob, are certainly at the heart of this tight-knit group. So are my two sons, as well as my siblings, Laurie and Steve, their families, and the larger Tisch clan I grew up with including my late Uncle Larry, Aunt Billie, and their wonderful four sons and families. Today, we are stronger than ever, and for that I credit my parents and my aunt and uncle. I'd also like to thank my two cousins, Andrew and Jim, with whom I'm honored to serve in the office of the president of Loews Corporation.

There are two friends whose early prodding and continued support were essential to the existence of this book. My agent, Wayne Kabak of the William Morris Agency, was the first to read copies of the speeches I had been giving around the country, and then boldly comment, "There is a book in this." I thank him for his confidence and sage input. Jeffrey Stewart, vice president of communications and public affairs for Loews Hotels, has not only been invaluable for his advice, input, and ability to keep everything on track, but also for his friendship that has made this process enjoyable.

At Loews Hotels, we have more than 7,500 dedicated and hard-working employees. I want to thank them for their ongoing commitment to all of our partnerships. I also appreciate our board of directors, whom I continue to learn from on a daily basis: Jack Adler, president and chief operating officer; Vince Dunleavy, executive vice president of finance and chief financial officer; Sherrie Laveroni, executive vice president of operations; Alan Momeyer, vice president of human resources; and Charlotte St. Martin, executive vice president of marketing. I'm also grateful for the wise advice of Gary Garson, general counsel of Loews Corporation, and Glenn Zarin for his legal assistance. I also want to acknowledge and thank my personal assistant, Vicki Alfonzetti, who keeps me focused, on time, and may be the most organized person I have ever met, as well as her assistant, Loren Vecchio, who is helpful in so many ways.

The Power of We could have made it this far only with the help of an exceptionally talented literary team. It has been a true pleasure working the past two years with my co-author, Karl Weber. He is an extremely intelligent and well-read writer, whose years of experience have been invaluable. I have enjoyed the process of working with Karl, and I'm grateful for his help and skill in capturing my ideas on paper.

Also, I want to thank the team at John Wiley & Sons, including my publisher, Joan O'Neil; my editor, Debra Englander; Mary Daniello, my production manager; Peter Knapp from the marketing team; and all the others who contributed to the creation of this book. Thanks also to Jennifer Jue-Steuck, my diligent fact-checker.

As you will read in the pages that follow, the lessons in *The Power of We* are applicable to a broad and diverse group—businesses and organizations of all kinds and sizes, executives, managers, entrepreneurs, and individuals from all walks of life. I am honored that a number of remarkable people that I admire and respect took time to share their own examples of the power of partnerships in this book. My sincere thanks to Kate Carr, president and chief executive officer of the Elizabeth Glaser Pediatric AIDS Foundation; Rodney Carroll, president and chief executive officer of the Welfare to Work Partnership; President Jimmy Carter; Chef Emeril Lagasse; former Mayor Marc Morial, president and chief executive officer of the National Urban League; David Neeleman, founder, chairman and chief executive officer of JetBlue Airways; film producer Jane Rosenthal, co-founder of the Tribeca Film Festival; Sir Howard Stringer, chairman and chief executive officer of Sony Corporation of America and vice chairman of Sony Corporation; Commissioner Paul Tagliabue of the National Football League; and Jeff Zucker, president of NBC Universal Television.

My sincere thanks also to Don Ziccardi and his wonderful team at Ziccardi Partners Frierson Mee Inc., and Marian Succoso of Loews Hotels for their creativity in designing the book jacket; and to my good friend, Don Epstein, who has helped me spread the word about the power of partnerships.

To all the above, and so many more, I simply say, thank you for your confidence, support, and love.

JONATHAN M. TISCH

New York, New York
July 2004

CHAPTER 1

The Power of Partnerships

Getting from Me to We

Coming together is a beginning.
Keeping together is progress.
Working together is success.

—Henry Ford (1863–1947)
American industrialist

THIS BOOK IS ABOUT A PRINCIPLE OF LEADERSHIP THAT I CALL THE *POWER of Partnerships.* It's a simple philosophy based on putting aside our individual concerns in order to work together toward a greater good. For business people like me, the Power of Partnerships can produce dramatic benefits for the bottom line. Whenever managers, employees, communities, shareholders—and even competitors—join forces in pursuit of shared goals, *everybody* wins.

It's an approach to leadership that is not divisive, but unifying; not competitive, but collaborative; not based on a zero-sum philosophy of scarcity, but on abundance—the economic, intellectual, and spiritual abundance that human beings can produce when their talents and energies are unleashed. The Power of Partnerships has worked for our company, Loews Hotels, benefiting our employees, our owners, and the communities we serve. And as I'll explain in this book, it's also working for many individuals, businesses, and other organizations in almost every field of human endeavor.

1

This isn't the standard approach to business. Most of the heralded CEOs you see on the cover of *Fortune* magazine or being interviewed on CNBC didn't get there by talking about partnerships. Some of them pride themselves on their ability to squeeze, manipulate, and exploit other people. Of course, they probably don't use those words. Management gurus have developed plenty of euphemisms. But in the end, the classic hard-driving business leader most Americans are familiar with achieves results through power and fear—not through collaboration. It's a model of leadership that dates back to the robber barons of the nineteenth century and survives today in the newest dog-eat-dog reality TV show, *The Apprentice.*

Yet, history shows that the power of intimidation is often short lived. As the master manipulators of the 1990s are discovering, one by one, the effectiveness of leading through fear eventually fades. And when your ethical lapses eventually come back to ruin you, few of those who once flattered you are really sorry to see you go.

Deep down, I believe, most business people—most people from any walk of life—are idealistic. They'd like to believe that it's possible to succeed by appealing to the best in their fellow humans . . . that the Power of Partnerships is real and not a naïve fantasy. But many people find it hard to break away from cynical assumptions about human nature. I see the skepticism on their faces when I talk about the amazing things that real partnerships can achieve. I can almost hear them thinking:

> This all sounds very nice. And it probably works, up to a point. When times are good, people are willing to work together and share the rewards. But it's a different story when times are bad. When the crunch comes, it's everyone for himself! The law of the jungle rules. That's just the way people are.

This attitude is very hard-nosed, realistic, and cold-blooded—and *dead wrong.* I can tell you that, when the crunch comes, the vast majority of people will respond to an appeal for cooperation, mutual support, and teamwork. If a few leaders show by their own attitudes, words, and actions that they *really* believe in the Power of Partnerships, most people around them will rise to the occasion and join in the effort for the good of all.

The Power of Partnerships isn't a brand-new idea. Smart leaders in business, politics, and nonprofit organizations have long operated through partnerships. But it's an idea that has become more timely than ever.

In today's complex world, no one can be all things to all people; no single organization is capable of mobilizing all the resources required to accomplish everything it needs to do. Therefore, we *must* work with and through other organizations. For businesses, the organizations we need to partner with include other companies as well as industry associations (which advocate for us in the public arena), educational institutions (which provide us with skilled employees), civic groups (which help shape a society in which we can work and do business comfortably), and government agencies (which provide a framework of laws, regulations, and infrastructure that allows business to operate).

The Power of Partnerships begins with the recognition that no organization exists in a vacuum; we can achieve success and prosperity only by working effectively with others. But managing by partnership means more than this. It also means redefining the terms of traditional business relationships and transforming them from adversarial to cooperative. In essence, it means shifting your philosophy of relationships from *Caveat emptor* ("Let the buyer beware") to the Golden Rule: "Do unto others as you would have others do unto you."

As this book demonstrates, managing in accordance with the Power of Partnerships offers you and your organization enormous benefits:

- The Power of Partnerships eliminates or reduces obstacles by converting potential adversaries and enemies into allies and friends.
- The Power of Partnerships expands your reach into markets and suppliers by giving you contacts, connections, and channels of communication beyond those you own.
- The Power of Partnerships gives you access to resources, talents, and strengths controlled by other companies and organizations, thereby multiplying your capabilities and compensating for your limitations.
- The Power of Partnerships aligns the interests of your organization with those of a broader community, so that anything that benefits one of your partners benefits you.
- The Power of Partnerships reduces the amount of time, energy, and money that must be devoted to conflict resolution and stress management, freeing up resources for more productive pursuits.
- The Power of Partnerships makes your organization a more positive, ethical, and friendly place to work, which attracts better employees.
- And because one partnership tends to beget further partnerships, the Power of Partnerships produces a positive spiraling effect. By contrast, when conflict and division dominate, they lead to increasing isolation and a negative, downward spiral.

You can enjoy these benefits only if you make a serious commitment to address the challenges involved in partnership:

- You can't fake partnership. Unless you are genuinely prepared to treat your partner's concerns as equal in importance to your own, don't expect to forge a real or lasting partnership.
- Partnership demands creativity. It is usually easy to see how the interests of partners conflict or clash; it is not so easy to find a new way of doing business that allows you to transcend the conflict and meet both partners' needs.
- Partnership requires compromise. If the idea of leaving a single dollar on the table drives you nuts, you may not be cut out for management by partnership.

- Partnership demands commitment and consistency. When you enter a partnership, you are inviting other people and organizations to rely on you. In effect, you are saying, "I will follow through on my promises; I will be here tomorrow, and the day after that, and the day after that." This doesn't mean that a partnership-oriented company can never change; it does mean that you can't change arbitrarily or capriciously, without considering the impact on your partners.
- Partnership requires flexibility. A control freak is unlikely to be comfortable in a true partnership. One of the main benefits of partnership is that it mobilizes the talents of two or more partners to benefit them all; but this can't happen unless you are willing to let your partners unleash their talents—even if they make choices that are different from the ones you would have made.
- Partnership requires openness. Partners need to understand one another as well as their businesses. This means sharing information—not necessarily in every detail, but in enough depth so that every partner is equipped to manage appropriately for everyone's mutual benefit. You can't expect to keep a partner in the dark.
- Above all, a partnership requires fairness. Everyone must benefit from a partnership; otherwise, it's not a true partnership. If you try to use a partnership as an opportunity to exploit or take advantage of other people or organizations, the partnership will soon collapse.

The chapters of this book provide illustrations of these challenges, along with stories about how smart leaders are tackling those challenges and turning them into opportunities.

Some in the business world who resist the idea of partnership do so because of a "libertarian" philosophy that emphasizes the supposedly absolute moral right of each person to the fruits of his or her labor. Libertarianism has many variations, each with its favored theorists and vocabulary. Some libertarians consider themselves devotees of the novelist Ayn Rand, others of economists like F. A. Hayek and Milton Friedman, still others of philosophers such as Hume, Locke, and Mill; they describe themselves using terms ranging from "libertarian" to "objectivist" to "anarcho-capitalist." I'm not trying to write a philosophical treatise. My quarrel is with the loosely defined, often ill-considered form of libertarianism that some business people use to criticize most forms of collective enterprise.

According to this form of libertarianism, the idea that business accomplishments grow out of cooperation among individuals and groups is for wimps. "Real" business people believe in going it alone, with no reliance on government or social institutions, which are viewed as parasites or leeches draining resources and energy from the only true creators of wealth—the entrepreneurs.

At its worst, this philosophy can be egotistical and mean-spirited. It's also factually inaccurate. The reality is that virtually every business relies on social and governmental resources for part of its success. The myth of the go-it-alone business hero is just that—a myth.

Where would the entrepreneur be without the infrastructure provided by American government and society?—the roads, harbors, water supply, sewage systems, airports, and railroads, all of which were built partly or entirely with government funding, planning, and resources. Where would businesses get trained employees without the public systems of education at the elementary, secondary, and college levels? How could business survive without the basic guarantees of law and order, enforceable contracts, and elemental rules of fair business established and maintained by governments?

And within the memory of some living Americans, we've seen instances of how dependent capitalism is on a vibrant and effective public sector. During the Great Depression of the 1930s, when tens of millions of Americans lost their jobs and their homes, faith in free enterprise sank to historic lows. Many joined extreme political parties—the socialists, communists, and various right-wing groups—that promised to fix the failures of capitalism through dictatorial methods.

How was capitalism saved? In significant measure through the creative efforts of Franklin D. Roosevelt (FDR) and the "brain trust" in his government, which created a safety net for citizens through Social Security and related programs; stimulated the economy through spending programs like the TVA, CCC, and WPA; and created mechanisms to correct the excesses and abuses of capitalism, such as the SEC, FDA, and FTC. The era of partnership between government and private enterprise that FDR launched—and into which some business people had to be dragged kicking and screaming—may have kept America from going the way of Germany, Japan, Italy, and Russia.

Some young entrepreneurs in the high-tech arena echo the "libertarian" idea that business and the broader community are two completely separate and unrelated spheres. For example, they lobby against regulation of commerce on the Internet by saying that government contributes nothing to their success and can only harm them. They overlook the fact that the Internet wouldn't exist without the government. It originated in the 1960s in a Defense Department research program known as Arpanet, and its successful protocols and systems owe much to ongoing government programs.

The point is not that regulation of the Internet is necessarily a good idea; it's a complex question with good arguments on both sides. But for the young denizens of Silicon Valley to imagine that they created today's high-tech industries from scratch, with no help from the rest of society, is very naïve.

If you think your business today has been operating successfully without partnerships, you are probably fooling yourself. Look again at your operation and think seriously about how you rely on help or cooperation from other businesses, community groups, civic and educational institutions, government, social agencies, and individual citizens.

TISCH'S TIPS

What role do partnerships play in the success of your business or other organization? To answer this question, begin by jotting down a list of the outside businesses, associations, nonprofit or civic groups, public agencies, and other organizations your business interacts with. For each, note what they contribute to your organization, as well as how your organization contributes to them. You may be surprised at the number, complexity, and importance of the partnerships your organization relies on.

In today's complex world, operating without partners is not really an option for any but the simplest of businesses. The real choice is whether you will partner deliberately or inadvertently, effectively or ineffectively, thoughtfully or carelessly.

HERE'S A STORY THAT ILLUSTRATES THE ROLE OF PARTNERSHIPS IN creating prosperity for people, companies, and communities. It also reveals more than a little about my personal leadership style—and how my company, Loews Hotels, manages to succeed in a highly competitive business arena through skillful use of partnerships, creativity, and sometimes a bit of *chutzpah.*

The story begins in 1993, a time when the hospitality industry was in the midst of some very tough times. The late 1980s had seen tremendous overdevelopment, leading to a glut of hotel rooms, just in time for the prolonged recession of the early 1990s to send demand into a tailspin.

We at Loews Hotels were fortunate. We'd watched the feeding frenzy of the 1980s from the sidelines rather than contributing to the overbuilding. (The conservative investment philosophy for which our parent company, Loews Corporation, is noted served us well then, as it has so many other times.) Thus, as other hotel chains were licking their wounds, we were preparing for a period of controlled growth, hoping to take advantage of the improving business climate.

We were looking for opportunities. A big one came along in 1993 when the city of Miami Beach announced it was seeking a business partner to build a new hotel geared both to upscale family travelers and to groups, associations, and businesses holding meetings.

Famous for its sunny climate and beautiful seashore, Miami Beach also boasts a magnificent convention center, which in 1990 had been renovated and nearly doubled in size to over 500,000 square feet. But because of the lack of large, upscale beachfront hotels to house convention-goers, the city-owned center was underutilized, costing Miami Beach millions of dollars in lucrative convention contracts and saddling the city government with an expensive asset that was losing money year after year. And with the economy still stagnant, no hotel company was ready to launch any major development in Miami Beach on its own.

To remedy the problem, the city had decided to initiate a competitive search to find a partner that could work with the local government to develop, build, and operate a new 800-room luxury hotel near the convention center.

The deal wouldn't be a slam-dunk by any means. The lingering slump in the hospitality business meant that investment funds for hotel building were hard to find. The city soon discovered that no developer was willing to take on the risk alone. In response, the City Commission developed a well-thought-out plan for a private/public partnership. It included some carefully targeted tax breaks and loan guarantees that would make a profitable development project possible at minimal cost to taxpayers.

The result: Every major hotel company in American responded to the request for proposals, touching off an intense bidding process. Names like Sheraton, Hyatt, Marriott, Peabody, and Ritz-Carlton topped the list. The relatively small Loews Hotel chain was a distinct underdog in this competition against the nation's biggest hospitality firms.

Nonetheless, we at Loews believed we had a special feeling for the project. One reason was our history. The Tisch family would not be newcomers to the Miami area. The very first hotel we'd ever built from scratch had been the Americana in neighboring Bal Harbour, a magnificent 400-room beachfront resort that became an icon of modernist architecture in the 1950s, the heyday of Miami Beach.

The Americana was designed for us by Morris Lapidus, the creator of such renowned Miami Beach landmarks as the Fountainebleau and Eden Roc hotels. Lapidus was aptly described by *The New Yorker* as "a fearless manipulator of colors and materials [who] dares to juxtapose them in a way that would make poor, timid Mother Nature blanch." He'd gone all out on the Americana, designing a lobby of Italian travertine marble, a rock pool with live alligators, and a glassed-in garden of tropical flowers with an open roof to capture rain.

The hotel was opened in December 1956, with five days of nationally televised publicity. Stars like Groucho Marx and Gina Lollabrigida attended the opening ceremonies, and NBC's *Today, Tonight,* and *Perry Como* shows were all broadcast live from the Americana.

Loews Hotels eventually sold the Americana in 1972, seemingly closing the Miami chapter in our family's history. During the subsequent decades, Miami fell on hard times. The Mariel boatlift of the 1970s, the Liberty City riots of 1980, and the drug and crime problems of the 1980s all helped to scare away travelers. Now, 20 years after the departure of Loews, the city was ready for a comeback. Miami's South Beach district was beginning to become a hot spot favored by artists, photographers, fashion models, musicians, and others from the hip young crowd. Loews Hotels was determined to be a part of the city's renaissance.

In response to the call for hotel proposals, we pulled together a team that worked 14-hour days through January and February of 1994. We crafted an impressive package that included architectural concepts, financial projections, environmental protection plans, and much more. We worked hard to make the best possible use of the proposed location for the hotel—a five-acre site at Collins Avenue and 16th Street in the heart of Miami Beach's historic Art Deco district. It included the historic St. Moritz Hotel, a long disused property dating to 1927 that the winning firm would be expected to renovate and include in the new facility.

Back in the late 1930s, up to one hundred small hotels were built in this neighborhood every year, most of them designed in the glamorously rhythmic, colorful, playful art deco style. Our plans, developed by architects John Nichols and Bernard Zyscovich, called for a hotel on a grand scale that would harmonize with rather than fight this magnificent artistic heritage.

This approach was a natural for Loews Hotels. We're unusual in that we pride ourselves on the uniqueness of each property we own or operate. Every Loews Hotel echoes the special style of the city it adorns. The only thing they all have in common is a high level of amenities and service as well as a warm, unpretentious quality of casual elegance that is distinctly Loews. Our insistence on developing properties that complement their surroundings is another aspect of our belief in treating the communities we serve not merely as customers, but also as partners.

During the spring of 1994, the very public competition for the Miami project began to heat up. In March, six developers submitted their conceptual plans to the city government. Reaction to these plans, we knew, would be an important first hurdle. The Loews design quickly won kudos. In the *Miami Herald,* architecture critic Peter Whoriskey observed that two of the six plans "actually fit" the challenging beachfront site—ours and that submitted by the Marriott team. The Loews plan, Whoriskey wrote, succeeded "by respecting the peculiar urban/beach blend of the neighborhood." He even preferred our design to that developed for Hyatt by none other than Morris Lapidus himself (in partnership with his son Alan)—a handsome concept, Whoriskey acknowledged, but one that "adapts less successfully to the pedestrian character of South Beach streets" than the Loews design.

This was a good omen. But we knew that esthetics alone wouldn't win the competition. Loews Hotels needed another edge. Four months before we were scheduled to present our final plans to the Miami City Commission, we gathered for a crucial brainstorming session.

As the meeting began, I laid down the challenge as I saw it. "We're an underdog in this competition," I said. "Loews Hotels doesn't have as extensive a distribution network like some of the chains we're up against. But we know that we're the right company for this project. We understand the kind of public/private partnership Miami Beach is seeking. We'll manage our end in a way that will enrich the whole community, from the hundreds of local employees we'll hire to the nearby businesses who will benefit from our presence. But how can we convey that sense of commitment? How can we design our presentation so that it shows, not just our professionalism and our intelligence, but our *heart*?"

The meeting began to percolate. We filled a pad with notes. There were many clever ideas, but none of them struck the right chord. Then an offbeat notion occurred to me. "Have you been watching the Winter Olympics on TV? David Letterman's mom is over in Lillehammer, and her video reports are really wacky and fun. Maybe we could do something like that."

"What do you mean?" someone else responded. "Get David Letterman's mom to make a video for our presentation?"

"No, no," I replied. "Not David Letterman's mom—we'll use *my* mom!"

Suddenly everyone around the table was excited. This might be the difference-maker we'd been seeking. But there was just one problem. My mother, Joan, is a very private person. I wasn't so sure she'd be willing to join our road show company.

When our team next met, I had to report that my mom wouldn't be serving as our spokesperson in Miami. The truth is, I'd been afraid to ask her.

The table fell silent. You could feel the disappointment in the room. My mind was racing, scrambling for an alternative. Suddenly it hit me. "I have an idea," I announced. "It may be crazy. But here it is. I'll appear in the video myself—*playing my mom.*"

One thing I've always said is that no leader should ever consider himself too important for any job, no matter how big or how small. Or how embarrassing. Now, I'd decided, it was time for me to walk the walk.

The reactions around the table ranged from shock to disbelief to disapproval. "You're right about one thing—it *is* crazy," someone commented. "It's embarrassing," "It'll make you look silly," "Don't do it!" others declared.

But a few people warmed to the idea. "This is South Beach we're talking about," someone noted. "Not Boston or Chicago. It's a free-spirited place. People will get it—and they'll like it."

The more we talked, the better the idea began to sound. It was gimmicky, yes. But maybe this gimmick could help us stand out from our rivals in a positive way. As the competition had unfolded over the previous two years, I'd spent a lot of time in Miami. I'd come to know the community well. I had a pretty good feeling as to how they'd respond. A few moments of self-deprecating humor, I suspected, might make our audience feel comfortable with Loews Hotels, maybe even help them bond with our company emotionally. "It'll work," I decided. "Let's do it."

So it came to pass that, on a sunny May morning, I found myself strolling the streets of Miami Beach with a camera crew, interviewing passers-by about the prospects for a new hotel—decked out in a dress, high heels, lipstick, rouge, a curly wig, and even a set of Lee Press-On Nails.

The resulting videotape was unique, to say the least. Nearly all of the interviewees I spoke to expressed enthusiasm about the idea of the new hotel. They could also be seen eyeing the interviewer with expressions ranging from incredulity to confusion to barely suppressed laughter. You couldn't blame them. My wig and makeup didn't do a very good job of hiding my five o'clock shadow, and it was probably obvious from the way I tottered that I'd never been in high heels before. My greatest triumph was simply managing to keep a straight face.

Later, with a little deft editing, we produced a short video that we felt sure would help Loews Hotels stand out from our competitors. At the very least, it would demonstrate to the people of Miami Beach our eagerness to become their partners, and our willingness to do anything reasonable—or even unreasonable—to earn the assignment.

The day before the big meeting with the Miami City Commission, our team flew down to Miami and set up shop in the Alexander Hotel. We spent the day honing and rehearsing our presentation. Our first run-through took three hours. This was a problem—a big one. The city had set a strict one-hour time limit and had warned us, "If you run long, we'll turn off your microphone and shut off the lights." So we knew they meant business.

We went to work on cutting the presentation down to size. We eliminated exhibits, trimmed financial details, simplified our explanation of the design. The second run-through was better, but it still ran two hours. By now it was late in the afternoon; we were scheduled to open the morning session at nine o'clock sharp. We had no choice but to fuel up on coffee, pizza, and sandwiches, and keep working.

Now we started eliminating entire sections of the presentation. Some scheduled speakers, such as representatives of our bank and project consultants who'd traveled to Miami specifically for the occasion, were scratched from the agenda. The remaining items were reduced even further. Finally, we thought we were ready for our last run-through.

It was after midnight. All of us were exhausted, our nerves frayed. Just then, my father, Bob Tisch, walked in. We'd invited him to join us in Miami, not only as one of the founders of Loews Corporation and our company's spiritual leader but also as a business person with a long history of success in Florida. Dad was with Armando Codina, a friend and local business partner. "You're just in time to watch our dress rehearsal," I told them. "Grab a seat."

The final run-through went smoothly. Everyone presented their segments crisply, hitting the key ideas and then quickly handing the microphone to the next team member. We were delighted—being forced to drastically trim our presentation had made it far more forceful and compelling. When the last PowerPoint slide was shown, exactly 55 minutes had elapsed. Perfect timing.

Charlotte St. Martin, our executive vice president of marketing, rose to her feet. "We have a final surprise," she announced in her usual southern drawl. "Our CEO's mom was very excited when she heard about this project. In fact, she was so excited, she flew all the way down to South Beach to talk to some local people about it. Now here's a video in which Joan Tisch shares what she heard."

Bob was perplexed. He turned to me. "I didn't know your mom flew down to Miami. When did this happen?"

"Just watch, Dad," I said. In silence, we watched the video of me in drag. My stomach was churning. Bob's sense of business decorum is a little more traditional than mine. I had no idea how he'd react to my stunt.

When the video ended and the lights went up, my dad looked at me. "What was *that*?" he asked. Before I could respond, he continued, "You are *not* going to show that video."

I took a deep breath. "Last time I checked, my business card said, 'Jon Tisch, President of Loews Hotels.' It's my decision, and I say we're showing it."

"Have it your way," he replied. "But don't say I didn't warn you."

If the next day's showdown hadn't already been producing butterflies in my stomach, now I had one more reason to be nervous. No one wants to give his father an opportunity to say, "I told you so"—even though I knew that after-the-fact recriminations have never been my dad's style.

Our team members exchanged some final handshakes and scattered to their rooms to catch a few fitful hours of sleep before the next morning's showdown.

At 9 A.M., the Loews Hotels team made its presentation before the City Commission. Because of Florida's so-called "sunshine law," virtually all government meetings are open to the public, and this competition had captured the interest of the city. Over 400 people, including members of the rival hotel teams, local lobbyists, lawyers, business people, and interested citizens had crammed the auditorium.

We reviewed our architectural, financial, and other plans, and talked about our readiness to partner with the city and the entire Miami community. The presentation went smoothly, just like the dress rehearsal. The final five minutes arrived. We ran the videotape.

The first few moments were greeted with dead silence. The audience was clearly puzzled: Who *was* this homely dame in the tape? And why did she look so suspiciously like the CEO of Loews Hotels?

As the silence dragged on for what seemed an eternity, we on the Loews' team were becoming increasingly nervous. Would no one get the joke? Would the concept bomb? Would the Commission members decide that the CEO of Loews Hotels had a few screws loose? Maybe we'd all made fools of ourselves and blown the project in the process. I began thinking, *Well, if I have to, I can probably get a job at some other hotel company . . .*

Finally, after an agonizing 90 seconds, one member of the audience chuckled. Then a second person suddenly burst out laughing. The dam broke. Within seconds, the room was awash with laughter. *We did it!* I thought. *We've got them on our side!*

Sure enough, little Loews won the contract.

We later learned that one of our major competitors had been so sure of winning the deal that it had printed thousands of brochures proudly listing its forthcoming Miami Beach property—a hotel that was never to be.

Did we beat out our bigger competition just because we made the commissioners laugh? Not really. If our proposal hadn't been absolutely first rate, they'd have laughed at the video—then picked another company. Fortunately, the Loews Hotel plan had captivated the experts. Vincent Scully, the noted architectural historian who served on the selection committee, described our design as "a wonderful example of using history in the present. There is a sense that the architects care about Miami Beach." Our company structure and

le also played a part in the decision. According to the
the selection committee liked the relatively small size
otel chain, believing that "a smaller outfit would mean
nark Miami property would garner more attention
from ..., e headquarters." On both points—the quality of our
design and the importance Loews Hotels attached to the project—
our readiness to create a true partnership with the city helped push
us over the top.

Nonetheless, I'm convinced that our video stunt also made a difference. The fact that we were willing to go the extra mile—even to
do something unorthodox in pursuit of the project—underscored
the depth of our commitment. The message of our video was: *We
want to be your partners—and we'll stop at nothing to make our partnership work.*

SOON AFTER THE ANNOUNCEMENT THAT LOEWS HAD WON THE BID,
future bookings at the Miami Beach Convention Center increased dramatically. We set to work restoring one hundred rooms at the St. Moritz
to their original art deco splendor and constructing our new hotel
tower on the adjacent property, complete with restaurants and 65,000
square feet of meeting space.

The Loews Miami Beach Hotel opened with much fanfare on December 24, 1998. It's expected to generate a billion dollars in economic
activity within 10 years, attracting conventions and trade shows to the
city and revitalizing a formerly depressed neighborhood in the process. In fact, in April 2001, less than two and a half years after the
hotel's opening, the City of Miami Beach issued a press release proudly
noting that the hotel had already become profitable—far faster than
projected—and that, as a result, the city's Redevelopment Agency had
already earned extra rental revenues of $3.3 million.

Furthermore, the Loews project had helped to trigger a domino effect
for the entire neighborhood. As the release noted, "Over $700 million in
private and institutional investment in 2,950 hotel rooms has transformed Collins Avenue into one of the most prestigious hotel corridors in

the world." It's a great example of how partnerships can benefit the bottom line, not just for one business but for an entire community.

And the hotel is much more than simply a financial success. In return for the city's willingness to make us their partner in revitalizing the neighborhood, Loews Hotels has also gone the extra mile in operating as a real partner to the community and all its people.

Our idea of partnership includes programs and activities both big and small. For example, we pitched in to refurbish the boardwalk and launched a continuing program of giving to Miami Beach charities, all part of a company-wide program we call the Good Neighbor Policy. (I'll explain this policy in more detail in Chapter 6.) Perhaps most important, we helped launch a major local initiative to provide hospitality jobs for Miami-area welfare recipients, a program that ultimately helped transform hundreds into tax-paying citizens.

First, a bit of background: The opening of the Loews Miami Beach Hotel took place about two years after President Bill Clinton signed the historic Personal Responsibility and Work Opportunity Reconciliation Act—often called, in shorthand, the *welfare reform law*. It was a much-needed initiative to overhaul a welfare system that had become costly, unwieldy, and ineffective. But many Americans were understandably worried about how families who depended on welfare would be affected. In Florida's Dade County alone, up to 28,000 people were scheduled to lose their welfare eligibility. That could translate into thousands of kids without a place to live or food to eat—as well as a host of worsened social problems, from crime to drugs.

Nearly everyone in America was rooting for the success of the welfare reform law. But there was no way the government could create jobs for so many people in need. Only business could do that. What was needed was a private/public partnership—one of the most ambitious and important partnerships in our nation's history.

In response to the challenge, five companies—Burger King, Monsanto, Sprint, United Airlines, and UPS—formed an organization called the Welfare to Work Partnership. Headed by Eli Segal, a close associate of President Clinton, the Partnership was a nonprofit organization charged with working with business and government agencies at all levels to help welfare-dependent individuals become independent.

When the Partnership was founded, I'd read about it in the *New York Times,* and I'd noticed that no companies from travel and tourism were included. That bothered me for several reasons. First, travel and tourism (including restaurants) probably employs more entry-level workers than any other industry in America. Second, by the mid-1990s, our business was booming, and we were desperate for reliable employees. So the time was perfect for us to become involved in the new welfare reform movement. I called Eli Segal right away, and Loews Hotels became one of the earliest companies to sign on to the program.

By the time Loews Miami Beach Hotel was nearing completion, Welfare to Work had already created jobs for thousands of welfare recipients around the country. We wanted to bring Dade County into the process. So we sent our vice president of human resources, Alan Momeyer, to Florida to see what we could do to organize the hospitality community around this effort.

Alan began making phone calls to our fellow hoteliers in the area. He met with the leaders of the Miami Beach and Dade County Hotel Associations, Mayor Alex Penelas, the leaders of a community organization called WAGES (Work and Gain Economic Self-Sufficiency), as well as executives from Lockheed and America Works, two so-called *third-party providers*—for-profit firms that specialize in helping welfare recipients become job-ready applicants. These companies help people clear out the clutter from their lives, solving problems concerning transportation, clothing, and child care, and arranging many other details that you and I take for granted but that can overwhelm a person who is trying to break the cycle of welfare dependence.

By the time Loews Miami Beach was ready to open its doors, we'd pulled together a consortium of 45 hotels in the Miami area that had made a commitment to hire welfare recipients. All in all, we estimated that hotels in Miami Beach could provide 800 jobs for welfare recipients—in many cases, the first jobs these folks had ever had. The largest single group would work for Loews—about 45 of the 800 employees we hired for our opening day would come from the local welfare rolls.

According to the latest figures (fall, 2003), 25 of those 45 are still working for us, some of them having received two or three promotions. Statistically, we've found that our welfare-to-work employees actually have a better track record than our average entry-level employees—better rates of attendance, retention, loyalty, and so on. It is an experiment that has proven to be a success, both for our business and for the workers involved. And Loews Hotels has continued to partner with welfare-to-work organizations in locations around the country.

THE MIAMI STORY IS A CLASSIC ILLUSTRATION OF THE POWER OF Partnerships, on several levels.

First of all, Loews Miami Beach Hotel would not exist at all if not for the partnership between private and public sectors that made its development and construction possible. When an area has become economically depressed over a period of decades, the obstacles to new growth are often enormous. Frequently, businesses will scrutinize the opportunities for expansion in the area but shy away, preferring lower risk investments elsewhere. The only solution may be for government to kick-start development by creating one-time incentives to attract private money—a form of pump-priming that often stimulates a steady flow of cash without further intervention.

It's important to distinguish this kind of public/private partnership from what's sometimes called "corporate welfare"—handouts to big business that produce no new growth or benefits to the community. If you can't turn a profit without taxpayer handouts, you ought to get into another line of business. An effective public/private partnership pays for itself within a reasonable time and then begins generating economic benefits for all partners, including the taxpayers.

That the Miami Beach partnership was properly conceived and managed is indicated by the fact that our hotel quickly made it into the black; that government coffers have grown as a result, thanks to increased revenues from the city's resort tax, convention development tax, utility tax, and other sources; and that other businesses soon followed us into the Collins Avenue area, from restaurants and souvenir shops to clothing stores and movie theatres—and even other hotels—all generating still more jobs and tax revenues.

Welfare to work is another aspect of the partnership story in Miami Beach, and another example of how *everyone* benefits from a true partnership. The business community favors welfare reform for many obvious reasons: It increases the tax rolls, transforms people from dependents into potential consumers, strengthens communities, and reduces the tax burden on businesses. As a result, business leaders have long been lobbying for welfare reform.

But real welfare reform isn't a job for government alone. Instead, a coalition of leaders from government, social agencies, and business must work together to help solve the problems that welfare recipients face in making the transition to independence. That's the genius of the Welfare to Work Partnership: Rather than simply gripe about the problem, the business leaders who support the Partnership are choosing to make a difference through action, helping thousands of people make the difficult transition from the dependence of a welfare check to the independence of a paycheck.

At Loews Hotels, we're as profit-driven as anybody is. But as the Miami story illustrates, we do things a little differently. We've found that when we manage in accordance with the Power of Partnerships, everybody wins. Loews Hotels' reputation as a caring corporate citizen means that political leaders and community activists welcome Loews Hotels into their neighborhoods, that local organizations and businesses like to choose Loews Hotels for their own gatherings because they think of us as "their" hotel, and that the best employees—the most caring, committed, and creative people in our industry—rank Loews high on the list of companies they want to work for. The ultimate impact on our bottom line is hugely favorable.

If you're a leader in a business or any other organization, I hope what you've read so far has captured your interest in the Power of Partnerships. But it's only fair to warn you that leading and managing according to this philosophy isn't always easy. In fact, a real commitment to the partnership principle may land you in some unexpected adventures—as you'll discover in the next chapter.

PORTRAIT IN PARTNERSHIP

Rodney Carroll

Rodney Carroll, current president and CEO of the Welfare to Work Partnership, has a personal story that's as remarkable in its own way as the story of the organization he heads. Growing up in low-income housing in North Philadelphia, Rodney and his siblings were forced onto welfare after Rodney's alcoholic and abusive mother was declared unfit to raise her children. Though lured by the local gangs to join their life of drug dealing and crime, Rodney clung instead to his wise and loving grandmother and his desire to somehow find a better way of life.

A part-time job as a truck loader for United Parcel Service (UPS) changed Rodney's life forever. For the first time, Rodney had the opportunity to be recognized and rewarded for his hard work and accomplishments. He rose to a management position at UPS. Then, putting his own job on the line, Rodney created a program to employ welfare recipients at UPS, a plan that would become a model for other firms around the country. His intimate personal knowledge of what it takes to make the transition from welfare to work, along with his enormous skills as an organizer, communicator, and leader, made Rodney a natural choice when the national Welfare to Work Partnership sought its president.

When we spoke to Rodney in spring 2004, we asked him to update us about the current direction and status of the Partnership.

"Today the Partnership and its fifty-odd employees are supported primarily through federal funds," Rodney explained. "That's something new. Originally our main source of income was donations from companies. But after 9/11, many companies were facing huge financial challenges and had to cut back on philanthropy. So one of my challenges has been to reshape our strategy so as to move the Partnership toward economic self-sufficiency. To do this, we're working to develop a competitive federal contract

(Continued)

strategy, partnering with both government agencies and with private companies in search of reliable workers.

"For example, we're currently running a demonstration project for the Department of Labor which involves working with businesses to hire, retain, and advance—18- to 25-year-old youths—who are either at risk or previously incarcerated. In the first eight months, our business clients hired about 300 young people.

"The process has several steps. We start by going to employers and learning about their business needs, including their workforce needs. Then we partner with service providers—churches, social service agencies, and so on—to identify project participants and get them job-ready. In some cases, the main factor is attitude—we have to provide tough love to help these young people understand the kind of commitment to work that they need to make. In other cases, we leverage community resources to help with housing, child care, and other practical problems. The average hourly wage for the entry-level jobs that we link the participants to is about $10.50, which is almost twice the minimum wage. And 81 percent of the jobs have growth potential.

"Over the next two years, our goal is to continue to work as a business-driven intermediary and help move 800 youths in Washington, DC, Miami, and Chicago into jobs. We're currently applying for further contracts with the federal government and also with the Ford Motor Company, which would expand our efforts into 12 cities as well as beyond the youth population."

We asked about the difficulty of finding jobs for ex-offenders—particularly in today's security-conscious era. "It's tough," Rodney acknowledged, "since most people don't realize that about three-quarters of ex-offenders were arrested for nonviolent offenses—crimes like passing a bad check. So hiring persons with criminal records is really not very risky. In Washington, DC, having an ex-offender background makes it hard to find a job because of security rules imposed on government jobs and even on jobs with private companies that have government contracts.

"On the other hand, in the post-9/11 era, the security industry is booming, which helps produce some jobs for our participants. We've helped a handsome young guy whose ultimate goal is to be a fashion model. We just got him a security job at Ralph Lauren. He hopes to bump into Ralph Lauren one day and audition for him!"

We asked Rodney to talk about the challenges of partnering with the government. Is it hard to secure funding for employment-related programs in an era of tight budgets and government deficits? "Actually, there's so much money being misspent by government that there would be more than enough to train and employ the underemployed—if only the money was channeled to projects like ours. Ours is the only demand-side project of its type in the country that is actually focused on getting people jobs. Most offer counseling and job preparation programs, but no actual employment—they get people all dressed up, but they still have no date!"

Rodney Carroll has little patience for programs that fail to deliver meaningful change. "My business background makes me results-oriented. And I think all nonprofit organizations are finding they have to evolve in the same way, toward being self-supporting and being paid only for delivering measurable outcomes. Historically, the nonprofit world has been living on welfare—relying on handouts for survival. Now that's changing, which is a good thing."

The gradual shift of the Welfare to Work Partnership to contract work reflects an important truth about partnerships in general: As economic and social conditions change and the needs of partners evolve, partnership organizations must be prepared to evolve as well. Today, Rodney's organization receives relatively few corporate contributions. "We're not really soliciting corporate funds any longer. We eventually hope to support our efforts

(Continued)

by providing businesses with qualified employees on a fee-for-service basis. We've already had some arrangements of that kind—an $80,000 contract with Home Depot, for example."

It's clear that Rodney's job at the Welfare to Work Partnership is both challenging and rewarding. But we wondered whether he misses the competitive energy of the for-profit arena. "I really don't," he told us. "Back in 2000, after I got a little nice publicity for appearing at a town hall meeting about welfare reform with President Clinton, I got lots of attractive offers, including an offer for what used to be my dream job at UPS. There are 400,000 talented people at UPS, and each of them would have loved this rare shot at a top executive slot. But I turned it down. The more I thought about it, the more I realized that I'd found my true niche here at the Partnership.

"I'm doing what I was destined to do. And that's a fantastic feeling."

CHAPTER 2

Now Who's Boss?

Lessons in Partnership from the CEO's Desk to the Housekeeper's Cart

As they say on my own Cape Cod, a rising tide lifts all the boats. And a partnership, by definition, serves both partners without domination or unfair advantage.

—John F. Kennedy

WHEN I'M ASKED TO SPEAK TO A GATHERING OF LOEWS HOTELS' employees, I generally stress the crucial role of our front-line workers. "After all," I like to say, "you're the ones who touch the lives of our guests every day. I'm back in my office on 61st Street in New York. I'm not behind the front desk checking in guests, making beds, serving coffee in the dining room, toting bags, or washing linens in the laundry. You are."

It's a pretty good line, and it's usually true. But not always. In June 2003, I actually spent a week doing all the things those front-line employees usually do.

As a bellman, I escorted guests to their rooms, helping with their bags, showing them where to find the thermostat and the hair dryer (and trying hard to remember to smile through it all).

As a room service waiter, I delivered coffee and juice, omelets and pancakes, trying to remember all the complicated steps in handling an order correctly (and to use the guest's name throughout the process).

As an engineer, I replaced light bulbs, adjusted blinds, and even fixed a recalcitrant ice machine. As a pool attendant, I raced to collect towels and stack up lounge chairs as a thunderstorm approached. And as a housekeeper, I changed beds, scrubbed toilets, and vacuumed carpets.

None of this was my idea. It all came about when Loews Hotels was approached by Matt Gould from New York Times Television. Matt had enjoyed a stay at the Loews Vanderbilt Hotel in Nashville while filming nearby, and after reading a little about our hotel chain and my background, he thought I might be an appropriate subject for a new series being created for TLC (formerly known as The Learning Channel).

"We're calling it *Now Who's Boss?*" he said. "We plan to have CEOs from various industries try their hand at jobs done by their own entry-level workers. They'll be trained by front-line employees, then thrown into the fray. We think viewers will enjoy seeing the tables turned on a few corporate big shots. And we'd love to have Jon Tisch be our first victim—er, subject."

Now Who's Boss? is an intriguing new twist on the recent reality TV trend. It's fun to list the CEOs, past and present, you'd like to see on the program. (Can you picture Steve Wynn working as a croupier in one of his casinos? How about Lee Iacocca welding parts on a Chrysler assembly line? Or Carly Fiorina on the phone in a help center, fielding tricky questions from customers about their new HP computers?) Most working people have exclaimed at one time or another, "I just wish that, for once, the big boss could see the things I have to put up with!" *Now Who's Boss?* makes that fantasy come true.

In most companies, I suspect, the TV producer's proposal wouldn't have gotten very far. At Loews Hotels, it quickly landed on my desk. I'm known as someone who is willing to take a few risks in public—for the good of the company, naturally. (I guess roaming the streets of Miami Beach in drag for our presentation video earned me that reputation.) In addition, I suspect that the members of our corporate team relished the idea of watching me lugging suitcases, sponging down bathrooms, and clearing dirty dishes on national TV.

In any case, just a week after Matt's initial call, I met with the members of the production team, and I agreed to appear in the show's premiere episode. We arranged for me to spend a week at Loews Miami Beach Hotel learning and then tackling several of the toughest entry-level jobs in the business . . . with a camera crew on hand to capture every embarrassing mishap.

It was quite a week.

The hardest job, I soon learned, is housekeeping. For one thing, it's physically challenging. Just pushing that cart laden with sheets, towels, and cleaning supplies down hotel corridors that are long, narrow, and winding was enough to make me red-faced and winded. Then you have to clean every surface in each room—countertops, baths and showers, sinks and toilets, and so on—set out fresh towels and washcloths, strip and remake the bed, vacuum the rugs . . . for about 14 rooms per day. I guarantee that spending a day as a housekeeper would fill any hotel guest with a profound sense of respect for the dedication—and strength—of the people who make our travels comfortable and pleasant.

Furthermore, housekeeping is psychologically tough. You work by yourself all day except for the morning team meeting and your lunch break. It can get very lonely. And as with any service occupation, you sometimes have to deal with the worst traits of human beings. While the great majority of hotel guests are thoughtful and mature, some seem to think that having housekeeping services gives them license to go wild. You wouldn't want to hear about some of the appalling messes hotel housekeepers have to clean up. I like to think that I've always been a reasonably considerate guest. But after my week on the front lines in Miami, I find that I am extra careful to pick up after myself when I stay in a hotel. Knowing the kind of back-breaking work the housekeepers have to do makes me appreciate them more than ever.

Under the watchful eye of supervisor Sara Roiz, a dark-haired, bright-eyed bundle of energy, I struggled to finish my set of rooms. (One of the housekeepers who observed my struggles suggested that I might be able to finish a full day's load of 14 rooms—if I had a whole week to work at it.) Later, watching on videotape as my work was critiqued by room inspector Maria Atassi was a humbling experience. Maria quickly spotted the dust bunnies I missed with my vacuum: "This room isn't clean!" she declared, sounding highly indignant (and rightly so).

The other jobs I tackled were almost equally demanding. I was a short-order cook in the kitchen, whipping up breakfast orders like pancakes and *huevos rancheros.* Sounds simple? Not really; I burned myself three times in the process. (When I retreated to my bedroom at the end of the day, I found that the hotel staff had taken pity on me: They'd sent me a basket laden with band-aids, lotions, pain medicines, and "Get Well Soon" balloons.)

Another day, I served drinks and canapés at cocktail receptions in the banquet hall and delivered meals for room service. (Think that's easy? Try bending over that room service cart as you roll it down seemingly endless corridors, and see what *your* back feels like after a few hours.)

And working in the laundry, I discovered, is a little like tending the boiler of a battleship from an old war movie: Imagine spending a day in a hot, dark room in the bowels of the hotel, roaring with the sound of huge washers and dryers tumbling tons of sheets, towels, and tablecloths.

None of the jobs I tackled proved to be as easy as you might assume. I felt reasonably self-confident when I was assigned to work the front desk, checking in guests, because I'd done the same job as a teenager, working in our Americana Hotel on the west side of New York City. (We later sold the property, which is now run by Sheraton.) But even this relatively familiar task had its pitfalls. My first challenge was to master the computerized check-in system. (When I was a teenager, hotels were still using old-fashioned registration cards in quadruplicate.) I refused to start work until I was assured that there was no key I could press that would cause the entire hotel to grind to a halt.

Later, when Star Service manager Mahernosh Jehangir critiqued my taped performance, he found plenty of room for improvement. I'd failed to button my jacket, I'd pointed my finger at something (a strict no-no), and I'd even slumped wearily onto the desk top. ("That's not acceptable body language when behind the front desk!" Mahernosh sniffed.)

Then there were the small challenges. I found some of the uniforms that came with the jobs uncomfortable. (Frankly, I've never gotten used to dress codes of any kind. I'm happiest when I can wear jeans and a

T-shirt.) My least favorite get-up was the room service waiter's outfit, which included a yellow vest and a little bow tie—not exactly my best look. And I was startled by how uncomfortable the polyester pants and shirts got to be after a couple of hours of sweaty work (though I guess I shouldn't have been; after all, this *was* Miami Beach). There's a good reason for using polyester: The uniforms have to be laundered every day, and no other fabric would stand up to that kind of treatment. Still, I'm glad my regular job doesn't require a uniform. I'd find it hard to do my job dressed that way and keep smiling—as we ask all our employees to do.

Perhaps the most disturbing experience of my week on the front lines was the least obvious. It involved something that *didn't* happen, something that not one person in a hundred would be likely to notice.

One day, I was working as a banquet waiter, dressed in the appropriate uniform: the hated bow tie, white shirt, and black pants, all in polyester. It happened that, on my way to the ballroom, I was riding in an elevator along with two executives from our home office, who were dressed, of course, in ordinary business attire. We stopped at the fourth floor where a guest was waiting for the elevator. That's when it happened: The guest stepped into the elevator, made eye contact with my colleagues Jeff and Emily, and smiled slightly; then glanced at me, noticed my uniform, and looked away. It was as if I wasn't even there.

Of course, the guest didn't mean anything by it. But I was shocked at how demeaned I felt. Putting on the waiter's uniform hadn't made me any less of a human being. But to some people, apparently, it

---

TISCH'S TIPS

Have you ever experienced work—or life—from the point of view of someone at the bottom of your organization's totem pole? If not, give it a try. You may be surprised by the lessons you'll learn . . . lessons that can make you both a better leader and a more thoughtful, compassionate human being. As a result, the crucial partnership between yourself as leader and the people you lead will be greatly strengthened.

transformed me into a nonentity. The experience reinforced my determination never to *ignore* another person in my presence, no matter what that person's role or status.

My week in Miami also gave me a renewed appreciation for the remarkable degree of coordination it takes to run a full-service hotel. It's like a miniature city with a complex network of operating systems, all of which must work together seamlessly. Think of this as another vital form of partnership—one that no hotel could manage without.

Consider what needs to happen when a banquet is scheduled—let's say for the opening night of a business gathering. The event is usually booked well in advance, sometimes years before the scheduled date. Three to four months prior to the event, the client has several meetings with the hotel's conference and banquet department at which a series of crucial decisions are made, from the number of guests to the kinds of foods to be served and the entertainment to be arranged. All of these orders must then be written up properly and distributed well in advance so that dozens of necessary preparatory steps can take place, from printing programs and arranging flowers on 60 tables to setting up and testing the appropriate sound system for the band.

On the day of the event, hundreds of details need to be coordinated among employees at all levels in several departments of the hotel, from the kitchen staff to the stewarding department to the front desk. Every change in plans has a domino effect. If the sponsoring organization decides they'd like to serve white wine along with the red, the banquet department must order 10 cases of chardonnay, 600 more glasses must be ordered, set, and cleared, and waiters and stewards must be notified.

Now multiply this complexity by 200 meetings and throw in hundreds of weddings, thousands of ordinary pleasure trips, and a host of unpredictable complications, and you have some idea of the logistical and managerial challenges involved in running a hotel.

Most important, if these complexities aren't handled in the spirit of partnership, the process will collapse. Sure, someone near the top of the organizational pyramid could try to keep tabs on all the details and hand out orders to compliant underlings. But there's really no way for any one person to understand, track, and coordinate the thousands of elements involved (and it doesn't matter how fancy a computer system you own). The city-within-a-city that is a modern hotel can only be

> ## TISCH'S TIPS
>
> How do the processes of communication and coordination work in your organization? Which way does information generally flow? When employees get together, is all the talking done by a few leaders, while everyone else only listens? An organization in which communication is strictly a one-way affair is likely to miss vital clues as to what is happening at the ground level, where interaction with customers is most intense. Partnering with employees includes listening to their concerns, paying attention to the information they provide, and including them in the processes of planning and decision making.

managed effectively if hundreds of employees are using their eyes, minds, and hearts to share information, exchange ideas, develop plans, allocate responsibilities, and adjust to constant changes. That means that everyone in the organization must be treated as a partner—not just a cog in a corporate machine.

While I knew all this before my week in Miami, watching the operations of our hotel from the perspective of an employee on the front line gave me a deeper appreciation for the importance of the many hundreds of links that go to make up each piece of the hospitality business—and how crucial it is for top management to give the front-line people the tools, resources, and freedom they need to carry out their demanding jobs. Another word for it is *empowerment*—a word that has taken on greater meaning for me than ever.

Maybe Sara Roiz, who'd undertaken the possibly hopeless task of trying to turn me into a capable housekeeper, offered the best lesson of all. When Sara showed me how to squirt purple cleaning goo all over the tiled bathtub walls, I remarked, "It's like finger painting!"

Sara smiled and agreed. "Exactly, Jon. *You have to find the joy in every job.*"

The next time I'm having a tough day back in my office on 61st Street, I hope I remember the wisdom of Sara Roiz.

So why did I give up a week of my life in the home office to work on the front lines of Loews Hotels? Like most of my business decisions, it had several purposes.

First of all, I admit I have a soft spot for the TV business. My first job after graduating from Tufts University was working at WBZ-TV in Boston as a cinematographer and producer. I helped put on the air kids and sports shows, public affairs programs, and documentaries. I loved the work and developed a bit of an instinct for visual communication; I was even nominated for two local Emmy awards.

To this day, there's still show business in my blood. It's a sensibility I try to apply to the hotel business every day. Because I think of hospitality as a segment of the entertainment business, when I have an opportunity to partner with a media company like New York Times Television or TLC, I'm happy to do it.

In addition, all of us at Loews Hotels are continually looking for appropriate publicity opportunities. It's part of the unconventional approach by which we market our image around the country.

Loews currently operates 20 properties, all in the United States and Canada. That makes us one of the industry's smaller hotel chains. Compare our 20 hotels with the 55 Ritz-Carltons, the 209 Hyatts, the 479 Hiltons, and the over 2,600 Marriotts. By any measure, we're a small fish in a pretty big pond. Yet surveys show that experienced travelers *think* of Loews as a large chain; in fact, when asked to guess, they often imagine that Loews owns 50 or more hotels.

The reason is that Loews Hotels doesn't conduct itself like a small-time operation. Our executive team devotes an unusual amount of time and effort to industry organizations—mostly because we believe it's appropriate to contribute to the betterment of our business, but partly because we want to position Loews as a leader in the field. And although we don't have an advertising budget to match those of our larger competitors, we use shrewdly designed publicity efforts to partner with the media, thereby gaining print and electronic coverage out of proportion to our size. As a result, the Loews Hotels name is more widely known and better respected than a company of its size would normally be.

Here's a small example. In 2003, *Parenting* magazine named Loews Hotels the best hotel chain for families. (Our special "Loews Loves

Kids" offering, part of our ongoing customers-as-partners program, was a big reason why.) This was great news in itself, but typical of Loews Hotels was the way we moved quickly to expand on the opportunity it presented. We got together with the people at *Parenting* to brainstorm ways we could serve their constituency even better. Today we are partnering with the experts at *Parenting* to develop a "kids' concierge" program for our hotels. It'll include a special manual and a training program that we'll use to turn at least one staffer at each Loews Hotel into a specialist in serving the needs of kids traveling with their parents.

This is the kind of promotion we love. The cost is modest, the benefits for every partner potentially great. Parents and kids will have more fun when they travel together; *Parenting* magazine will gain recognition and prestige for their efforts to improve the travel experience for families; and Loews Hotels will capture a larger share of the family traveler market.

In a similar way, the opportunity to participate in *Now Who's Boss?* was a perfect fit for our partnership-based, publicity-friendly approach to marketing. It was also a great learning opportunity for me—a chance for me to refresh and reinforce my understanding of the challenges that confront our staff members at all levels, which will help me to strengthen our employee partnership in the future.

When the show aired in March 2004, the reactions from inside and outside the Loews Hotels' family were all we'd hoped. An employee from Loews Le Concord e-mailed me, "My father (my mentor) has spent 35 years in the hotel business as a bell captain, and he enjoyed every second of the show." Another wrote, "I watched it with my 15-year-old son who said, 'I thought CEOs were all like those Enron guys!'" And a third wrote, "I think you should keep your day job, but if it doesn't work out, you could either be a chef's assistant or work for room service. But please please never come to make my bed—we might have to send you to a masseuse."

In fact, I was so impressed by the value of my week on the front lines that I have asked all the members of our Loews Hotels' executive team, as well as the executive committee members at each hotel in the chain, to go through a similar experience during the next year. As I write these words, the members of our board are busily trying to decide whether they want to work in the kitchen or behind the front desk, toting luggage or vacuuming floors. Wherever they end up, I guarantee they'll learn a lot.

But the biggest reason I liked the idea was that slipping into the role of a front-line employee was such a good fit for the Loews Hotels' philosophy—and for my personal approach to business.

It's disturbing to me when I see businesses being run primarily to benefit the privileged few at the top of the organization. It's an approach I believe is counterproductive in the long run—especially in a people-oriented industry like hospitality, where the face of your business *is* your front-line employees. If you treat them badly, the unhappiness they experience will be passed along to your guests. In time, your hotel will get a reputation as an unhappy place, and the guests will stop coming.

In hospitality, the vast majority of employees hold entry-level jobs. Most are high school grads or holders of GED certificates; the work they do is hands-on, sometimes physically strenuous, always demanding. You might consider these routine jobs, but they're integral to the success of the hotel. So it's important that we treat the people who hold these jobs with the dignity they deserve, including providing them with opportunities for training and the chance to become managers—all aspects of the partnership philosophy that's central to our success.

None of this is any different from what a college graduate or MBA would expect when going to work for Loews Corporation—or, for that matter, for General Electric or IBM. That's the point. If you work for us, no matter what your level of education or your entry-level salary, you deserve to be treated with respect . . . because without mutual respect, there can be no true partnership.

Leading and managing in accordance with the Power of Partnerships can be tough. A business executive who wants to enlist employees, members of the community, and other stakeholders as true partners must learn to treat their problems, needs, and dreams as seriously as his own. And that means really *knowing* and *understanding* their concerns—not just paying lip service to them in a speech or an annual report, but spending enough time in the trenches with them so that you can personally share their feelings, empathize with their needs, and celebrate their successes. This is the lesson my week on the front lines in Miami reinforced for me.

It would be easier to conduct business as usual, simply looking out for Number One rather than struggling to find the creative solution that balances diverse objectives. It would be easier—but it would also be a lot less fun, less rewarding, and less profitable. As I've learned through my own experiences as well as through my observations of other corners of the business world, managing through partnerships is the *only* way to build lasting success.

To fully understand what my career has taught me about the Power of Partnerships, you need to know a little more about the company I help to run, the arena in which we compete, and the important role played by our industry—travel and tourism—in the broader economic and social fabric of today's world. We'll explore those topics in the next chapter.

PORTRAIT IN PARTNERSHIP

Jeff Zucker

Jeff Zucker, president of NBC Entertainment, holds one of the most powerful and demanding jobs in show business.

Jeff made his name as executive producer of *The Today Show* from 1992 to 2000, helping to shape the format and style of the nation's most-watched morning news program. Among other innovations, he helped make the show's glass-enclosed set, which brings the New York City street scene right into the broadcast, into one of the most recognizable images in broadcasting.

Jeff also served as executive producer of NBC's coverage of such major events as the 2000 election night broadcast, the 1996 and 2000 political conventions, the 1996 bombing of Centennial Olympic Park in Atlanta, and the Persian Gulf War. For his remarkable creative work, Jeff has won five Emmy Awards.

(Continued)

Most people tend to think of creativity as emanating from one person at a time (a "creative genius"). This raises the question: How can a partnership be managed so as to promote creativity? So we started our conversation with Jeff Zucker in March 2004 by asking him about how he develops and maintains a spirit of creativity in the collaborative environment of a major television network.

"Creativity is such an important differentiating factor," he told us, "that you have to do whatever it takes to foster it. I try to promote the attitude that it's okay to try new things and even to make mistakes—so long as you don't make the same mistake twice.

"It's not easy to bring a fresh perspective to a business that's already very successful. It takes a degree of courage. When I joined *The Today Show*, it had a history of 40 years of success. So people were naturally resistant to change. When I suggested a new approach, they'd say, 'We don't do it that way.' That bothered me. I think it's important to understand the history of an organization and to respect it—but not to let history dictate your future."

Jeff is famous as a network *wunderkind*: He was just 26 when he became the executive producer of *Today,* and he is still one of the youngest high-level leaders in the business. We asked how such a youthful personality is able to hold his own in the tough world of show business.

"It's true that you must be aggressive to succeed in the world of entertainment," he told us. "But it isn't necessary to be a predator. It's no secret that an entertainment executive must learn to deal with some very powerful egos. Juggling and balancing the conflicting agendas of the various players is an important key to success.

"One secret is simply making everyone involved feel important. With the people at the top of the pyramid, that's fairly obvious. Less obvious is the need to connect with the people whose names don't appear in big lights. Taking the time to call the person who is second or third or fourth on the totem pole may be even more important in the long run.

"It's also important never to take success for granted. When I was at *The Today Show,* we finished first in the morning ratings something like 250 weeks in a row. It bothered me when I felt the network ignored us. I try not to do that now. With long-running hits like *Friends* and *ER,* which have been so important to the success of our network, I try not to let a week go by without a phone call to the executive producer, even if the only purpose of the call is to let him or her know they are still appreciated.

"And when a project is struggling, the call is also important—to encourage people without being misleading. We've all been through hard times, and it means a lot to know that there is someone out there who understands. I know from personal experience how meaningful these gestures of support can be."

Of course, success creates its own challenges. One test for any high-level executive is his ability to maintain a balanced two-way relationship with partners who've achieved enormous success, and with it, a degree of fame and power that might appear intimidating. For Jeff Zucker, who works on a weekly basis with such celebrities as Katie Couric, Jay Leno, and Tom Brokaw, it's a vital question.

"You mustn't let yourself be intimidated by the stars in your organization. They're important people who've earned respect. But at bottom, they're human beings, with the same needs we all have. They want to hear from you, to have you call and visit, to be able to share their worries, concerns, and dreams. If you reach out to them, they'll appreciate it, and any disagreements that arise can usually be handled amicably.

"Above all, never let problems fester. Don't let things go unspoken. Be willing to confront problems—not in a spirit of confrontation, but of partnership. Knowing the right time to raise the tough issue is a challenge—but it's one you mustn't try to avoid. The key is to have no unpleasant surprises."

CHAPTER 3

A Family Business

It All Started with Sayde and Al

"Do you like being a parent—you know, being a father, having children and all?" Linnet once asked me. "Yes," I said, after a moment. "It's like dancing with a partner. It takes a lot of effort to do it well. But when it's done well it's a beautiful thing to see."

—Gerald Early
U.S. writer, specialist in African-American studies

MANY PEOPLE ARE BORN INTO FAMILIES THAT RUN A BUSINESS—A FARM, a grocery store, a restaurant. They grow up watching their moms and dads at work—planting crops, stocking shelves, waiting on tables. Some of these kids start helping out as soon as they're able to walk. It's a natural extension of the oldest form of partnership—the family—into the world of business. When the kids grow up, they have to decide whether to take a share in the family concern or strike out on their own.

That familiar American experience is my story, too. By the time I came along, our family business had grown quite a bit bigger than most. This isn't the place for a detailed history of my family or of the growth of Loews Corporation, but I need to share a bit of the story with you as a backdrop for the ideas and experiences I'll be recounting in the rest of this book.

The Tisch family business got its start in 1935, when my grandfather Al Tisch, who ran a clothing company on New York's Union

Square, decided to buy a couple of kids' camps in the Kittatinny Mountains of New Jersey. For the next few years, Al and his wife Sayde ran the camps with the help of their two sons, Laurence and Preston Robert (better known as Larry and Bob). Everybody pitched in, whether running the canteen, waiting on tables in the dining hall, or picking up campers at the train station. That style of a working partnership became a family tradition—one that persists to this day.

By 1946, Sayde and Al had done well with their camps and were looking for a new investment opportunity. Young Larry, fresh from his World War II service in the U.S. Army, spotted an ad in the *New York Times:*

> For sale: 300-room Kosher winter resort hotel,
> Laurel-in-the-Pines, Lakewood, New Jersey.

When the family investigated, they found that Laurel-in-the-Pines was a premier lakeside resort, a lavishly appointed property sometimes called "The Grand Hotel of New Jersey."

This looked like a risk worth taking. They sold the summer camps, pooled the money with some profits from Al's clothing business, and purchased Laurel-in-the-Pines for $375,000, betting everything on the postwar prospects of the hospitality business. A year later, they co-leased the 350-room Monterey Hotel in Asbury Park, New Jersey.

Other hotels followed. In 1950, the Tisch family leased the historic Traymore Hotel in Atlantic City. (They bought it two years later.) It was the first of several properties the family would own or manage in Atlantic City, then the convention capital of the world. (Perhaps you've seen the 1981 Louis Malle film *Atlantic City;* the opening sequence of the picture includes newsreel footage of the Traymore's demolition to make way for a casino soon after the 1978 legalization of gambling in the city.) In 1956, we built the Americana in Bal Harbour, Florida—a high-risk enterprise that paid off magnificently—followed by the Summit in New York (1961), the first new hotel built in Manhattan in 30 years.

The family company grew to include a variety of other businesses, purchased with the profits from the increasingly successful hotel operations. Along with it grew the role played by the two smart, ambitious Tisch brothers—my father Bob, and my Uncle Larry.

In 1959, Bob and Larry invested in the famous Loews Theatres chain, founded in the early years of the twentieth century by entrepreneur Marcus Loew. Shortly thereafter, Larry and Bob joined the board of directors and became president and chairman of the executive committee, respectively. Eventually, Loews Corporation became the parent of Loews Theatres. The theatres were sold in 1985 to become part of Loews Cineplex Entertainment, one of the world's largest movie exhibition companies. The Loews name was kept for the corporation.

During the years 1986 to 1995, Loews Corporation had a sizeable stake in the venerable CBS Inc. broadcasting firm. Loews was hailed as a corporate "white knight" when it made its investment in CBS, thereby saving the company from a hostile takeover. However, when CBS was forced to cut costs and downsize some of its operations (just as the other networks did during the same time period), some criticized Loews— unfairly, in my view—for damaging the reputation of the so-called "Tiffany network." CBS was sold to Westinghouse Electric in 1996, garnering an overall profit of more than a billion dollars for Loews.

During the 1990s, founders Bob and Larry Tisch gradually gave up direct responsibility for running the corporation on a day-to-day basis, formally handing over the reins to my two cousins, Andrew and James, and me in 1998. My uncle Larry passed away in November 2003, leaving behind not only the great business he and his brother built but also a generous philanthropic legacy to organizations in and around their beloved New York City.

IN RETROSPECT, IT'S EASY TO SEE HOW MY FAMILY BACKGROUND HELPED to shape my commitment to the partnership philosophy.

Observing the dynamic of a family business teaches many lessons about the connection between human relationships and success. We sometimes hear about family businesses run in a tyrannical style by an autocratic founder. Companies like that rarely succeed for long. Other family members eventually tire of being treated thoughtlessly—if they won't put up with mistreatment, why should "outsiders" without flesh-and-blood connections to the boss? By the second generation, most family businesses managed in this fashion fall apart.

Bob and Larry Tisch set a very different example. Larry was a brilliant investor; he could look at a column of numbers and instantly spot the crucial trend that gave them meaning. Bob is a people person with an instinctive understanding of human motivations. Recognizing the complementary nature of their talents, the two founders treated one another with deep respect, forging a true partnership that served both their friendship and the business well. The tradition of trust, integrity, and civility they established has helped make Loews Corporation an attractive place to work for thousands of employees—including several members of the Tisch family.

My approach to life and work has been shaped by the unique personalities of my mom and dad. A moment ago, I referred to my father Bob as a *people person*. No one works a room like Bob Tisch. He connects with people on every level—intellectually, emotionally, personally—and enjoys nothing more than making a new friend for whom he can do something thoughtful.

Charlotte St. Martin, now the executive vice president of marketing for Loews Hotels, likes to tell this story about the first time she met my dad, some 25 years ago. At the time, she was working for the Anatole Hotel in Dallas, which had just become part of the Loews' chain.

"We were all a little nervous the first time Mr. Tisch visited our offices," Charlotte explains. "He was such an important man, after all. But he was very friendly and pleasant to talk to. It so happened that my secretary at the time was a big movie fan. Hanging in her office was an antique poster for *Gone with the Wind,* which mentioned a Loews theatre. She showed it to Mr. Tisch and commented, 'I always wondered what theatre this is.'

" 'Well,' Mr. Tisch replied, 'I don't know, but I'll find out.' Then he said good-bye and flew back to New York City. I doubted we'd ever hear back from him; I figured he was just being polite. But three days later, we got an airmail letter from Bob Tisch answering my secretary's question and enclosing a complete history of the theatre, which turned out to be the Atlanta Loews where *Gone with the Wind* premiered in 1939."

Charlotte laughs. "That's when I made up my mind I wanted to stay with the Loews Corporation as long as I could."

My dad is still the same way. As a co-owner of the New York Giants football team, he literally works the stadium at a Super Bowl; he brings a list of 50 friends and their seat numbers so he can visit every one of them during the course of the game.

Then there's my mom, Joan, an independent, opinionated person who is never shy about speaking her mind. She's also one of the most generous and open-minded people I know.

Mom has been at the forefront of issues like the prevention and treatment of AIDS since long before it was fashionable. The story goes that 20 years ago Mom dropped into the little office of the Gay Men's Health Crisis in downtown Manhattan. "I'm Joan and I'd like to volunteer," she told them. They put her to work licking stamps, making photocopies, brewing pots of coffee, and so on, just like any of the (very few) volunteers they had at the time.

One day, she heard the manager of the office bemoaning the fact that the photocopier was constantly breaking down. "Why not buy a new one?" she asked.

"Why else? No money," was the answer.

"How much would it cost?"

"We just got a price quote of $475," she was told.

My mom promptly wrote a check for $475 and handed it to the manager. He looked very dubious. "How do I know this check won't bounce?" he asked her.

She replied, "Trust me, it won't bounce."

He looked at the check . . . and that's when he realized she was Joan Tisch. Soon she became a member of the board of directors of the Gay Men's Health Crisis, a position she proudly held for close to a decade.

Today, every member of our family has one or more social or community causes to which we donate time, energy, and money. Interestingly, there's little overlap among the groups we support. I suppose that each of us uses pro bono work as a way of expressing a personal interest or passion as well as contributing to society. The causes currently supported by Tisch family members include such diverse organizations as the Museum of Modern Art; Take the Field, which partners with the New York City Board of Education to refurbish sports facilities at

> ### TISCH'S TIPS
>
> How has your own family history affected your style as a leader and manager? What lessons about life and work did you learn from observing your parents and other family members as a child? What values did you absorb from those around you as you were growing up? Answering questions like these can help you discover more about your strengths and weaknesses and help you distinguish the personality traits you want to pass on to others from those you want to change.

public high schools all around city; the Center for Arts Education, a partnership between the New York Board of Education and the Annenberg Foundation that raises money for arts programs in the schools; New York University Medical Center; and the Young Women's Leadership School in East Harlem.

The list goes on, but you get the point: Just looking around my family taught me, from an early age, that all people are deeply interconnected, and that life is not just about achieving personal success, but also about helping and supporting one another. No matter what line of work I went into, it was probably inevitable that I would approach it not just as a way of making money, but as a way of connecting with people in a positive way.

FROM ITS ORIGINS WITH AL AND SAYDE'S KIDS' CAMPS ALMOST 70 YEARS ago, the Loews Corporation today has grown into a large holding company owning a variety of companies. We think of it as a vehicle for investing in great businesses. I'm one of three members of the next generation of Tisches who make up the Office of the President of Loews Corporation. The other two are my cousins James (he's president and CEO of the corporation) and Andrew (chairman of the executive committee). In addition to my responsibilities with Loews

Corporation, I'm chairman and CEO of Loews Hotels. However, Loews Corporation is a publicly held corporation, which means that anyone who wants to can buy shares and participate in our success—or, occasionally, our struggles.

As of today, our largest single business is CNA Financial Corporation. CNA provides commercial property and casualty insurance. Like most insurance companies, CNA is subject to powerful external influences, including the business and economic cycles and the vagaries of life. In a year when major calamities strike—whether terrorist attacks or natural disasters—CNA takes a hit. In a year when the general investment climate is strong and CNA's financial holdings grow rapidly, the business does well. Fortunately, we've had more good years than bad.

Loews owns 54 percent of Diamond Offshore Drilling, Inc., which is a major supplier of offshore drilling rigs to the energy industry around the world. Diamond owns and operates 45 drilling rigs as well as related facilities for the production and distribution of petroleum products. In May 2003, Loews bought Texas Gas Transmission, a pipeline company that ships natural gas from the Gulf Coast to markets in the Midwest and southern United States.

Loews also owns 97 percent of Bulova Corporation, the well-known watch and clock company. Bulova's brand names include Wittnauer, Accutron, Caravelle, as well as Bulova itself.

Perhaps the corporation's most controversial holding is Lorillard, Inc., which is America's oldest tobacco company. Lorillard makes and markets cigarette brands such as Newport, Maverick, Old Gold, Kent, and True.

Because I often speak about the ethical and philosophical underpinnings of my approach to business, I am sometimes challenged about the Lorillard connection. "How can you claim to be concerned about the well-being of the community when the corporation you are part of sells cigarettes?" I get questions like this especially when I speak on college campuses. It's a good sign, I suppose, that today's young people are just as idealistic and morally engaged as I like to think we were back in the 1960s and 1970s.

There are several answers to this question. First, tobacco is a legal product. It's sold under strict legal limitations, and the marketing and

advertising of cigarettes is regulated by the government so as to discourage young people from starting the habit. It's important that people be made aware of the potential health risks from smoking. So long
as people are making an informed choice about whether or not to use
tobacco, they should have the right to make their own decision in the
matter. Would the world be better off if tobacco were banned? The experience of alcohol prohibition in the 1920s and the long, costly war
on drugs of the past few decades suggests that government attempts to
ban substances that people enjoy are often futile and sometimes counterproductive. It's possible to make a case for tobacco prohibition, but
it's far from obvious that this would be for the best.

Lorillard is a socially responsible tobacco firm. For example, its
Youth Smoking Prevention Program is a nationally acclaimed initiative that runs print and TV advertising urging teens not to smoke, provides incentives to encourage peer leaders to refrain from smoking,
and suggests ways for parents to talk to their kids about smoking.
Provided tobacco is marketed and sold in a socially responsible way—
as Lorillard does—there's no reason why Lorillard shouldn't sell it.

Another very visible business involving the Tisch family is actually
separate from the Loews Corporation. My father Bob is co-owner of
the New York Giants football team, a connection that has given us
tremendous pleasure (as well as occasional heartache) over more than
a decade.

My dad bought 50 percent of the Giants in 1991 in a deal that was
completed before the Giants Super Bowl win of that year but not announced until afterward so as not to distract the team. (Back in 1925,
the entire franchise was reportedly sold for just $500. My father's stake
cost a little more than that.) The other half is owned by the family of
Wellington Mara, one of pro football's most distinguished and admired personalities.

The Giants are managed by a board consisting of two Maras,
Wellington and his son John, and two Tisches, my father Bob and me.
Wellington Mara is our president, and John Mara is executive vice president. Several of John Mara's siblings are involved in the team (there are
11 Mara siblings and some 40 grandchildren), a situation that must

generate unique pressures on him: Imagine the conversations around the family table after a particularly tough Giants loss!

The board usually doesn't get involved with on-the-field decision making: We hire the general manager and the coach and then turn the reins over to them. The general manager seeks approval from the board for major acquisitions, including free agent signings and draft choices, such as our most recent deal, the headline-making trade for touted quarterback Eli Manning in April 2004.

Of all the board members, I'm probably the least involved in the daily operation of the team, although I carry the title of treasurer. On a week-to-week basis, my primary role is to live and die with the team's performance on the field. Lately, that has involved more agony than ecstasy. The recent 2003/2004 season was a major disappointment. Thankfully, I know that the only constant in sports is change; there's every reason to hope that we can return to our winning ways next season. (If you're a disgruntled Giants season ticket holder, please don't write to me. All I can do for you is get you a room in your favorite Loews Hotel—if there's a vacancy.)

For me, the best thing about being involved with the Giants is seeing how much pleasure my dad has derived from his role. For any fan, co-owning an NFL franchise would be a dream come true; for Bob Tisch, a sports fanatic since his boyhood days in Brooklyn, it has been a kind of magic elixir, a wonderful extension of his business expertise into a field he loves. He relishes attending the games and rooting for his guys; he also enjoys his service on the league's finance committee, wrestling with such thorny issues as television contracts, competitive balance, player pensions, and intellectual property rights.

Through Dad's eyes, I've come to see football as a metaphor for life: the importance of teamwork, the need for discipline, and above all the way in which a great organization overcomes injuries and bad luck to make its own breaks. It's another of the valuable life lessons I've absorbed simply by being around the remarkable men and women who created our family business.

How does Loews Hotels fit into the overall picture of the business?

The hotel operation is actually a small part of the whole, representing only about 2 percent of Loews Corporation in terms of revenues. But it's an important part of the business because it was the company's founding business, going back to that 1946 purchase of Laurel-in-the-Pines. All of us at Loews have a special fondness for our hotel business because of that family history.

When the time came for me to choose my own career, I could have gone to work in any subsidiary of Loews. But the hotel business is the one I naturally gravitated toward. Hospitality is the business I love, for many reasons.

First of all, let's distinguish between what I call "the business of hotels" and "the hotel business."

In these early years of the twenty-first century, running a hotel chain has become a very sophisticated and complicated business. In an era of consolidation, mergers, and acquisitions, some companies buy and sell hotel chains almost like properties on a Monopoly game board. This *business of hotels* is a complex and, in its own way, fascinating game that has changed dramatically in recent years, with many corporate buyouts and major investment firms jumping into the fray.

All of this, however, is based on another, much simpler—and ultimately more important—game. I call it the *hotel business*. It's a fundamentally simple business, one whose essence hasn't changed in the thousands of years since weary caravan drivers first sought refuge at a wayside inn. It's a business that is rooted in the tradition of hospitality—one of the most profound and meaningful of human virtues. I like the fact that, as hoteliers, our sole responsibility is to bring comfort, security, and pleasure to travelers. It's a mission we pursue with pride and satisfaction. If you treat your customers as partners, providing them with the kind of experience they most desire, they will return.

The hotel business has great economic prospects for the coming years. It's a key part of the travel and tourism industry, which is poised to be a major force for worldwide economic growth in the twenty-first century.

Travel and tourism currently generates more than $4.2 trillion worldwide, accounting for 10.4 percent of the global economy. It's the world's largest single industry, bigger even than agriculture, car making, or any other manufacturing business.

In the United States, travel and tourism is responsible for more than $500 billion in spending. In many states, travel and tourism is the first or second largest employer, providing nearly 17 million jobs nationwide and generating nearly a $100 billion in federal, state, and local tax revenues. Furthermore, travel and tourism produced (in 2001) an $8.6 billion positive balance of trade, making it our country's second largest services export—an especially important statistic in this time of ballooning trade deficits.

The economic slowdown that began in 2000, the terrorist attacks of September 11, 2001, the resulting increase in security screenings and the "hassle factor" of traveling, the SARS epidemic in the Far East, and the ongoing global unrest (including the wars in Afghanistan and Iraq), have all harmed worldwide travel and tourism. Thankfully, there are signs that a recovery is underway. Travel and tourism is no longer a minor factor in global economic growth. Instead, it's a crucial element in the health of countless cities, states, and nations the world over—including our own. I like being part of this burgeoning industry in part because it's fun to be where the action is—and because it is rewarding to play an important role in helping communities and individuals grow and thrive.

The show business element of hospitality is another big attraction for me. When people visit a hotel, they are suspending their daily reality and entering a new environment in which to conduct business or enjoy a little excitement, fun, and adventure. It's not unlike the experience of going to a movie or a play. So when I walk through one of our properties, I evaluate it like a Broadway show. The lobby, the guest rooms, the restaurants, the pool and spa, even the hallways and elevators make up the stage set; the bell staff, the front desk personnel, the housekeepers, the waiters, and the chefs are all members of the cast. I ask myself: Is this a show I'd want to attend? Does it create a pleasurable atmosphere that would make me want to return?

A new hotel opening is comparable to the opening of a Broadway show. It features a cast of hundreds, many different stages and sets, costumes, music, complicated choreography—everything you associate with show business—all combined in a hugely complex operation with thousands of interrelated pieces. We need to imagine the worst-case scenario in every department of the hotel and then have two or three back-up plans prepared just in case it happens. And we have to make sure that everyone knows all those plans, because two or three of our worst-case scenarios *will* happen.

The biggest difference between a Broadway opening and a hotel opening is that, in the hotel business, we *never* close. We're always on stage, even at 3 A.M. on Christmas Day. So when changes need to be made—the launching of a new amenity, the renovation of a block of rooms, or improvements in service procedures—they have to be done without disrupting the hotel's daily operations. It's like rebuilding a 747—in flight.

You may think that working in this kind of pressure cooker sounds awful. If so, the hospitality business is not for you. I'm one of the crazy ones—I like it.

Furthermore, I love hospitality because it's a people business that relies on both teamwork and individual creativity. And yes, that means partnerships.

TISCH'S TIPS

If you could live your life over again, would you choose the same industry or profession? If so, why? If not, why not? What do you love about the work you do? What do you dislike? Examining the answers to these questions can help you measure the degree to which your personality fits your career. If the fit isn't ideal, that doesn't necessarily mean you need to change occupations. It may mean that you need to seek out partnerships that will complement your strengths and compensate for your weaknesses, enabling you to succeed in a field for which your personality may not be perfectly suited.

Every property in the Loews Hotel chain is run as a separate business. There are commonalities, such as an overall strategic vision for the chain, a set of training and procedural guidelines that every hotel follows, and our branded marketing programs that define the personality of the chain. But beyond these, each hotel has an unusual degree of independence. Each has its distinctive design, its unique setting, its special clientele. Each is a business with revenues of $25 to a $100 million, run by a general manager who is, in effect, its CEO. Each general manager develops his own business plan and maintains his own profit and loss statement; each is rewarded on the basis of results achieved. By delegating power to this extent, we elevate local managers into true partners of the company: Their success is our success, and vice versa.

Another way that partnerships are important in hospitality is in the area of subcontracting. A hotel has dozens of areas requiring hundreds of different kinds of skills to run smoothly. Very few companies can be experts in all these disciplines; no one can be all things to all people. That's why more and more hotels rely on outside contractors to help run portions of their businesses: the restaurants, the retail shops, the spas and salons, the landscaping, the ocean and pool sports, the parking, the audiovisual services for meetings. In many hotels, Kinko's is now running the business centers, while other hotels feature coffee shops run by Starbucks. The decisions about whether and how to partner with outside companies are made on a property-by-property basis, considering individual profit potential, the market, the physical facilities, the expertise available, and many other factors.

One of my favorite examples of partnership in the hospitality business is Feinstein's, the night club that is one of the star attractions of the Loews Regency Hotel in New York City. The story of Feinstein's began with an opportunity—disguised, as opportunities often are, as a problem.

In the mid-1990s, our food and beverage business at the Loews Regency was hurting. We filled our restaurant for breakfast and lunch, but the dinner crowds were sparse. That's understandable; New York has so many great restaurants that no guest is likely to want to patronize a hotel dining room three times a day. As a result, we were losing money every year on food and beverage service. Shutting the kitchen, even for a few hours a day, wasn't an option; round-the-clock room service is one of the essential amenities of a luxury hotel. But we couldn't afford that amount of red ink every year. And our wait staff was suffering from the lack of dinner guests and the work (and tips) they would provide.

We did many studies of the problem, but no one could find an answer. Then fate stepped in. In 1998, the great old Rainbow and Stars room, a famous nightclub on the 65th floor of Rockefeller Center, closed its doors. Fans of classic American popular music were bereft, and many top entertainers were left with no venue in New York City. Here was an opportunity for Loews.

Previously I'd met and befriended Michael Feinstein, one of the country's leading cabaret singers and a noted interpreter of the great American song writers—Gershwin, Porter, Berlin, and so on. We wondered whether there was a way that the Regency and Michael Feinstein could join forces to fill the vacuum left by the departure of Rainbow and Stars.

When we approached Michael Feinstein and his then-agent, Alan Sviridoff, with the idea of opening a nightclub at the Regency, they were intrigued. But there were practical issues that looked insoluble. The restaurant at the Regency was already a well-known New York landmark: It was the home of the "power breakfast," where moguls from politics, media, entertainment, sports, real estate, finance, and other industries would gather on weekday mornings to make deals over bagels and coffee. How could the same space that served as a sunny breakfast spot do double duty as a sophisticated nightclub?

Here's where some creative thinking came into play: We had a clever set designer craft a portable stage that could be broken down into several pieces, so it could be easily set up, removed, and stored every day. We installed spotlights and painted them to match the ceiling and walls, so that most visitors during the day never notice them. We developed a state-of-the-art sound system using hidden speakers, and we hung dark curtains *behind* the brocade-and-silk draperies that cover the windows in the morning. These alterations turned the restaurant into a quick-change artist, capable of gliding gracefully from daytime to nighttime without breaking stride.

Feinstein's at the Regency opened in the fall of 1999. Now our restaurant has a whole new identity. We serve meals all day, then transform at night into a stylish nightclub. Feinstein's has produced a whole new revenue stream for the Regency, reversing the money-losing situation. And that's not considering the additional benefits we get from the club. It generates an enormous amount of media coverage, both on the arts and entertainment pages and in the gossip columns. Suburbanites and out-of-towners alike come to enjoy a show at Feinstein's, then stay for a night or two at the Regency to enjoy other New York attractions.

Feinstein's is one of my favorite examples of the Power of Partnerships. The fame and talents of Michael Feinstein, as well as those of the other performers he attracts, have combined with the elegance of the Regency to create one of the most popular night spots for sophisticated New Yorkers—a very special amenity that helps the Loews Regency stand out among the Big Apple's other fine hotels. As for Michael, he has gained a New York venue for his talents as both performer and impresario, giving him a place to test new material, helping him stay in the media spotlight, and boosting the visibility of his other activities, from CDs to television specials.

The creative use of partnerships is also an important part of Loews' marketing strategy. We do this partly because it is fun, partly out of necessity. As a smallish hotel chain, we don't have the huge dollars it takes to run a nationwide consumer campaign. If we relied on standard marketing techniques, we'd be practically invisible.

Instead, we devote extra energy to devising clever ways of maximizing our marketing clout through creative partnerships. Take something as mundane as trade shows. Like every other company in our business, Loews attends all the main conventions at which travel and tourism providers (including hotel chains, cruise companies, airlines, and others) display their wares to big customers (such as travel agents, corporate travel managers, association executives, and meeting planners). We're relatively small fish at these events—but we always find a way to make a big splash.

One way is by hosting parties concurrent with the conventions to which all our customers are invited. Since there are many parties during convention week, we go out of our way to make our party different and fun. We were planning a party for Chicago around the time of the opening of the movie *Dick Tracy* starring Warren Beatty and Madonna (1990). It so happened that Bloomingdale's was opening a store in Chicago around the same time. "Aha!" we said. "Here's an opportunity for a partnership." We decided to throw a Dick Tracy party at the new Bloomingdale's. I dressed up in Tracy's trademark yellow trenchcoat and fedora (I don't think I made too many of the women forget about Warren Beatty), and our guests got to participate in a staged mystery—the disappearance of a diamond, which we hid in the store.

For another party, we partnered with the Boston Opera House. As dinner was being served, the music from *Phantom of the Opera* began to play, and a spotlight picked out a figure in mask and cape on the balcony overhead. As hundreds of eyes gazed up in my direction, I gave my best dramatic flourish, welcomed our guests, and vanished into the darkness, to applause and many exclamations of, "Was that who I *think* it was?"

We also love to attract attention to our business by partnering with celebrities. Because of my family's NFL connection, as well as the popularity of our hotels with traveling athletes, we enjoy having figures from the sports world lend us their luster. The great basketball coach Pat Riley greeted guests in our booth at a meeting of the American Society of Association Executives (ASAE) one year. (ASAE is an important convention for the travel and tourism industry because every membership association, from astrophysicists to zoologists, has at least one annual meeting that creates big business for hotels, travel agents, tour operators, airlines, and many other companies.)

Another time, Phil Simms, the all-pro quarterback who led the Giants to victory in Super Bowl XXI, was scheduled to appear in our booth at ASAE. The night before, Phil called me, sounding awful. "Jon, I'm sorry. I've got a flu bug. I can't make it tomorrow."

Our marketing team got a little panicky when they heard the news; they'd been promoting our star attraction for days. Jokingly, one of the team leaders turned to me. "Jon," she said, "Why don't you take Phil's place?"

The idea was so ludicrous—and we were so desperate—that I decided to give it a shot. The next morning, decked out in Simms' blue Giants jersey (number 11) complete with shoulder pads and an oversized helmet, I didn't exactly look the part—I'm built more like a coach than a quarterback. But I gamely greeted fans, talked football, and even signed an autograph or two. Phil Simms groupies may have been disappointed, but I think they got a kick out of the fact that the company CEO was willing to get a little goofy in a good cause.

Are you beginning to get some idea why I find the hospitality business so much fun?

FINALLY, I LOVE RUNNING OUR HOTEL BUSINESS BECAUSE OF THE SPECIAL characteristics of the Loews Hotel chain. They play beautifully into our philosophy—our commitment to partnerships as a way of doing business.

With our 20 properties, we have great hotels in many of North America's most vibrant and exciting cities—but we're small enough so that I can get to know most of our employees well and be personally involved as a partner in helping to shape the style and management of each hotel.

We're growing steadily but conservatively, adding properties only when the city, the location, and the specific hotel make a good fit with the Loews' style and culture. This slow-but-steady approach to growth lets us design and manage every property so that it fits attractively into the surrounding community—yet another aspect of partnership.

Best of all, our strategy of building a chain of unique hotels, each different but all featuring four-star or five-star service and amenities in an environment that is relaxed but stylish means that every Loews Hotel is interesting and fun to visit—the kind of place where I like to stay, bring my two kids, and invite my friends.

One of the prime builders of today's Loews Hotel chain is our president and chief operating officer, Jack Adler. He's the guy who runs our business on a day-to-day basis, freeing me to focus on broader strategic issues, industry initiatives, and not-for-profit activities (as well as the occasional opportunity to dress up in costume).

Jack grew up on Long Island and earned his undergraduate degree in business at the University of Pennsylvania's Wharton School. After a stint in banking in Philadelphia, Jack got his MBA at the Kellogg

School at Northwestern University in Chicago, spent several years as assistant treasurer of Bally Manufacturing and Lane Industries, then joined Loews Hotels. He quickly recognized something unusual about our company's leadership style.

"I'll never forget the first time I had to make a presentation to the top management of Loews Corp.," Jack recalls. "I described the prospects for the hotel business in some detail, and we talked about our plans a bit. Then Larry Tisch got up from his seat at the head of the table. 'Okay,' he said. 'Do the best you can.' And he left the room. That was the end of the meeting.

"I was puzzled," Jack recalls. "I was expecting a little more detailed input than that! So I went to Bob Hausman, who was my boss at the time, and said, 'Larry Tisch told me to do the best I can. What does that *mean*?'

"Bob laughed and said, 'It means he trusts you, and you should use your best judgment.'

"That's the way we run the hotels. We trust people and ask them to use their best judgment. Usually, they do—and the results prove it works."

Jack has helped to implement our management philosophy at Loews Hotels over the past decade. It's an approach that emphasizes decentralization and pushing both authority and responsibility as far down the food chain as possible. It's another form of the Power of Partnerships: Rather than treat the managers and employees who run individual hotels as cogs in a machine to be guided by levers in the hands of the executives at headquarters, we consider them partners in the leadership of Loews Hotels.

Managing this decentralized decision-making structure can be difficult. Jack spends half his time keeping the system working. One of the things that makes it tough is that fact that our home office staff is so talented and smart. They've got plenty of creative ideas about how to operate and market the hotels, yet they're not making the line decisions—those are in the hands of the general managers and their own executive teams. So our home office experts must serve as consultants, providing tools, ideas, information, and expertise, but leaving the final say-so to the individual general managers. It's a kind of inversion

---

TISCH'S TIPS

How does the management structure of your organization fit with the size and scope of the organization? Has your business outgrown the systems that should support it? Or is your modest-sized business overburdened by a structure that is unnecessarily large and complex? Making sure that your management structure fits the scale of your organization is an important challenge for any leader. Without a proper fit between the two, your partnership with employees is likely to struggle.

---

of the usual top-down command-and-control model that most businesses use, but an approach that's ideally suited to a partnership-oriented enterprise.

The overall size of our business is an important factor in the effectiveness of our management structure. At 20 hotels, our decentralized approach works beautifully. Most decisions get made at the local level. Some are handled one step higher, by our regional vice presidents who manage groups of hotels. Other decisions, which involve large investments or significant policy choices, must be approved at headquarters. Generally speaking, this structure allows us to move far more nimbly than most of our competitors.

Will we be able to maintain the same structure as our business grows? Up to a point. When we reach 25 or 30 hotels, our management team at headquarters will begin to feel stretched. (Even now, we don't get to visit every property as often as we'd like.) It will probably be necessary to give greater responsibility to the regional vice presidents at that point. If we expand to 50 hotels or more, we may need to rethink our management system.

IN THIS CHAPTER, YOU HAVE SEEN SOME OF THE REASONS WHY I LOVE working in the hospitality business. I'm also convinced that the lessons I've learned in the travel and tourism industries apply to many other leadership challenges, including for-profit and not-for-profit organizations, government agencies and private-sector firms.

Travel and tourism are part of today's service sector explosion—but so are thousands of other organizations in a wide range of industries. As more and more of the world economy shifts from a product orientation to a service orientation, more and more companies must learn the secrets of consistent, reliable service that have long been keys to success in the travel and tourism industry.

Travel and tourism have a large element of show business—but so do more and more businesses in every industry. From retailing to e-commerce to financial services, companies that bring a bit of creative flair to their operations are winning new customers and grabbing market share from their more traditional rivals.

Above all, travel and tourism are built on partnerships. Almost every satisfying consumer experience in travel and tourism, whether for business or leisure, depends on the successful combination of efforts by many organizations: travel agents, airlines, car rental firms, hotels, restaurants, theatres, museums, taxi companies, theme park operators . . . the list goes on. Government agencies play a crucial role as well, from convention and visitors' bureaus to the local and state authorities that build and manage the travel infrastructure (highways, airports, railroads, harbors, you name it).

In most every business today, effective partnerships are highly desirable. In travel and tourism, they're absolutely essential. That's another reason why the lessons we've learned in our business are relevant to you, no matter what field you happen to work in.

The numbers and kinds of partnerships we can employ to multiply our resources and extend our reach are almost limitless. In the chapters that follow, I focus on six kinds of partnerships:

1. Your partnership with your *employees*
2. Your partnership with your *customers*
3. Your partnership with the *communities where you operate*
4. Your partnership with *other businesses*
5. Your partnership with *government*
6. Your partnership with your *owners*

As you'll see, each of these partnerships involves difficult, and fascinating, challenges to your talents and style as a leader and manager. Each also offers enormous potential to make your organization—and yourself—more successful. We'll begin our exploration of the world of partnerships in the next chapter with a look at the single most important partnership of all: your partnership with your employees.

PORTRAIT IN PARTNERSHIP

Marc Morial

In 1994, at age 35, Marc Morial became one of the youngest mayors in the history of New Orleans. Over the next eight years, he led a dramatic turnaround for the city, improving public safety, revitalizing neighborhoods, stimulating economic growth, and bolstering opportunities for youth. Morial's reform of the New Orleans Police Department became a model for municipalities around the world, helping to produce a 60 percent drop in the city's crime rate over six years. He left office in 2002 with a 70 percent approval rating.

In 2003, Morial was elected president and CEO of the National Urban League, which has been a major force in the civil rights movement since its founding in 1920. Today, the National Urban League champions economic development through its Campaign for African American Achievement, its forceful advocacy of affirmative action and the principle of inclusion, and its efforts on behalf of citizen empowerment in education, the economy, and civic engagement.

"For me," Morial told us during a January 8, 2004, interview, "partnership—building bridges—is the way of the twenty-first century. Why? Because the diversity of our world today—not only racial diversity but ethnic, religious, geographic, demographic, and philosophical diversity—makes it hard for people to get anything done by themselves. You've *got* to bring people together if

(Continued)

you want to accomplish anything worthwhile. Otherwise, it just won't happen."

Marc recalled working with me as a representative of the hospitality industry during his years as mayor of New Orleans, a city that depends on tourism for much of its income. We asked whether travel and tourism remain high on his agenda now that he is with the Urban League.

"Absolutely," he replied. "In fact, the Urban League is working on ways to help people in entry-level hospitality jobs move up the ladder. It's okay to start as a housekeeper or a doorman, but you don't want to do that forever. So we're hoping to develop hospitality training centers in a number of cities. It requires partnerships. Industry can't do it alone, nonprofits can't do it alone. We'll work with hotel companies, open centers in a few cities at first, then expand nationwide if we're successful."

Hospitality isn't the only industry the Urban League is focusing on. "We used to help train people for industrial jobs—welders, pipefitters. We still do some of that, but the world is changing. Now a major emphasis is helping people gain computer skills. We have partnerships with Dell Computer, Microsoft, and a company called DigiPen that is working with us on a program to teach young people how to design video games. It's a huge and growing industry."

Morial explained that the Urban League also partners with government agencies.

"For example, we offer home ownership counseling in twenty cities with the help of HUD [the Department of Housing and Urban Development]. We prepare people to become first-time homebuyers by showing them how to get financing and how to work with a real estate agent. When we work with government agencies, they provide more than just funding. They also add intellectual capital and program design. There's a lot of give and take: What age group should we focus on? What industries should we emphasis? What priorities should we set? Everybody benefits from the brainstorming we do together."

During his mayoralty, Morial had become famous for creating the so-called "Gumbo Coalition." When we asked him for the origins of this colorful phrase, Morial laughed.

"During my first campaign, I just grabbed a bowl of gumbo that was being served at a dinner stop and held it up. 'See this?' I said. 'My campaign is a blend of everything, just like this gumbo.' The name stuck. And the more I used it, the more I liked it. You see, the great thing about gumbo is that there's no one way to prepare it. Everybody has their favorite recipe, and they're all good. And you can always add another ingredient. Got some oysters? Toss 'em in. A dozen shrimp? That's good. Some left-over chicken? Go ahead. It just keeps getting better. That's the way I tried to run the city government—by getting everybody involved.

"I used the Gumbo Coalition idea as my model when I was trying to change the city. Some business leaders got a little nervous when I talked about bringing people into the process who had never been involved. I explained to them, 'Hey, I'm not trying to take anyone away from the table. I just want to add a few more chairs.' Many of them got it."

Morial's good-natured style almost makes coalition-building sound easy. We asked about that. "Easy? No way. On issues like housing, we had to bring together the banks, the city council, the state and federal governments, business groups, community groups, unions. There was a lot of distrust in the room—some of these groups really hated each other and blamed each other for their problems. I let them air it out, then asked, 'If we try to do something together for the good of New Orleans, what is your bottom line?' In the end, we found some common ground and made solutions happen. But it took a lot of time and energy to break down those barriers."

Morial also discovered that bringing all the stakeholders together in one room is sometimes *not* the best strategy for creating a partnership. "You've got to know when to bring 'em together and

(Continued)

when to keep 'em apart. Sometimes we had to use shuttle diplomacy, especially on controversial issues like bringing a pro basketball team to New Orleans. All the groups involved had different agendas. We had to talk with one group, find out what they wanted, then travel across town and talk to a second group and a third group, constantly prodding and looking for areas of flexibility and compromise. It's very time-consuming and calls for a lot of patience. It took us three attempts over eight years, but we finally pulled together a deal that brought the NBA to town.

"My model as a politician was Lyndon Johnson. When he was master of the Senate, he perfected the art of using five different arguments to win his point with five different people. He knew when to appeal to vanity, pride, ego, honor, duty, or fear. He knew when to knock heads together, when to sweet-talk, and when to bluff. He knew when to deliver a message personally and when to send a go-between. Above all, he knew how to get things done."

Morial's bottom line? "Building partnerships is time-consuming brain work. It's really tough. And it's the best job in the world."

CHAPTER 4

The Employee Comes First

From the Front Line to the Bottom Line

You can employ men and hire hands to work for you, but you must win their hearts to have them work with you.

—William J. H. Boetcker (1873–1962)
Presbyterian minister

AS CHAIRMAN OF LOEWS HOTELS, ONE OF MY PRIMARY RESPONSIBILITIES is to travel around the country, visiting our properties and meeting the thousands of people who make our company great. It's also one of my favorite jobs.

It's tremendous fun to tour our hotels in all their diversity—the gorgeous Loews Coronado Bay Resort, perched on a sun-drenched peninsula south of San Diego; the elegant Regency Hotel on New York's Upper East Side; the classic art deco-style Loews Miami Beach Hotel; the funky House of Blues Hotel in Chicago; our three amazing hotels at Universal Orlando in Florida, and all the other Loews Hotels properties. I generally spend a day or two at each hotel at least once a year. I stroll the lobby, sizing up the latest decorative embellishments. I sample the newest creations offered by our chefs. I check out the spa, health club, pool, and other amenities, and I give the guest rooms a thorough scrutiny. I try to make sure that everything from the window treatments and the carpeting to the magazines on the bedside table and the pictures hanging on the walls convey the warm and unpretentious style that marks each Loews Hotel and a bit of the unique ambience of the surrounding city, whether it's historic Philadelphia, French Montreal, or jazzy New Orleans.

But the most important part of these tours is the time I spend with employees. Our partnership with employees is the most important partnership of all. And there can be no true partnership unless the partners really know and care about one another. That's why spending time with the Loews Hotels' employees is always near the top of my priority list.

As our chain grows, it's getting harder for me to know every employee. But I do my best. When I visit the kitchen, I enjoy chatting not just with the executive chef but also with the busboys and room service waiters. I like hearing from the housekeepers about their latest adventures, like cleaning up in the wake of a visiting rock star's raucous post-concert party. I enjoy talking with the sales staff about their recent challenges and triumphs, like the corporate meeting they've booked, beating out one of our bigger competitors. I get a kick out of hearing the newest funny story making the rounds among the engineers and security staff ("The guest had *what* stuck in the bathtub faucet?"). And some of our best ideas for improving service and enhancing the guest experience come from the employee roundtables I attend—small-group sessions with hourly employees (no supervisors allowed) at which everyone is encouraged to speak openly about what we are doing right and what we could do better.

September 18, 2003, was one of my typical days on the road. I was scheduled to speak with the students from the Hospitality MBA Program at Daniels College of Business at the University of Denver. Educating the next generation of leaders for our industry is an important cause for Loews Hotels and for me, so I try to make myself available for sessions like this as often as I can.

We decided to combine my trip to Colorado with a visit to our property there—the Loews Denver Hotel, a handsome boutique-style hotel in the Cherry Creek District that caters to business travelers. Several members of our home office team joined me. We spent the morning touring the property. We talked about plans to renovate the restaurant, about promotional efforts we'd recently launched to keep business travelers coming to the hotel, and the community relations programs the hotel had sponsored. We said hello to dozens of the team members and got the latest news about their families and the volunteer efforts at the local hospitals, schools, and recreation centers. We even greeted a few guests as they passed through the lobby, including a poodle and a cocker spaniel who were staying with us under our Loews Loves Pets program.

But the highlight of our visit was a celebration for a special accomplishment: Loews Denver Hotel had outperformed our other hotels in a contest for volunteer hours of community service donated by employees.

At the appointed hour, scores of team members emerged from the "back stage" areas—the kitchen, the laundry, the store rooms—and gathered in the hotel ballroom, which had been decorated with a large banner that read, "Making a Difference in Denver." Soon the place was packed. Practically everyone who works at the hotel had come. At a signal, the lights were dimmed, and the festivities began.

Every department had created its own contribution to the show. The team from Conferences and Banquets performed to the music from the old disco hit "She Works Hard for the Money," singing the lyrics they'd written for today, with the refrain, "We work hard for it, Jonny," accompanied by a dozen hands pointing straight at the guest of honor in the front row—me.

The back-of-the-house Food and Beverage (F&B) team introduced the "new rap star" Effenbee who chanted lyrics about their work: "There are so many accents on our banquet staff / But you don't hear the accents when all we do is laugh." The members of the sales department sang "On the Phone Again" to the tune of "On the Road Again." And the front-of-the-house F&B gang—the folks who deliver room service meals and stock the minibars—recited a poem with the embarrassing title of "The Night Before Tischmas." (They later received a framed certificate commemorating their act as "The Most Blatant Suck-Up to Top Management"—deservedly so.)

The enthusiasm that filled the room during the rally was pretty amazing. Housekeepers and sales reps, cooks and waiters gamely sang or danced or acted, and judging from the screams and applause of their peers, you'd have thought we were witnessing the finals of *American Idol.*

The rally was a fun event, one that people at the Loews Denver Hotel and our home office will be talking about for months to come. But was it a worthwhile investment of our employees' time and energy? Does bringing people together to celebrate shared accomplishments help make Loews Hotels a more successful business?

You'd better believe it. Recognizing your employees as more than just hands that do the work is a vital aspect of partnering with them. And your company's partnership with its employees is a make-it-or-break-it deal. If you and the people who work with you don't really care about one another, *no* business plan or competitive strategy you devise will succeed. But if your employees are true partners—with the personal involvement and heartfelt commitment that implies—then nothing can stop you.

That's why I subscribe to the philosophy stated in the title of this chapter—"The employee comes first." On the surface, this contradicts the conventional wisdom that the *customer* comes first. But only on the surface. Experience shows that, if you make treating your people right your highest priority, your customers will be happier, too. And happier customers mean repeat business, positive word of mouth, more revenues, and a stronger bottom line.

Throughout history, there have been far-sighted business leaders who exemplified this creed:

- In the auto industry, there was Henry Ford. In 1913, he and his general partner, James Couzens, shocked the world by announcing that the Ford Motor Company would pay a guaranteed wage of five dollars a day to every worker—this at a time when millions of skilled workers were earning one-third of that amount. Couzens had sold Ford on the idea by predicting that, in the long run, the company would save money as a result. Couzens was right: Turnover at the firm, which had been running as high as 600 percent, fell to almost nothing. As a result of its new partnership with labor, Ford was able to reduce the price on its Model T while it increased profits—and achieved a dominant position in the auto marketplace.

- In retailing, there was Edward A. Filene. Founder of the Boston-based chain of department stores that bears his name, Filene realized in the early years of the twentieth century that a prosperous workforce would create enormous opportunities for economic growth. He used his influence and example to demonstrate the value of treating employees as partners. Filene willingly entered into collective wage negotiations with his workers, instituted one of the first profit-sharing plans, and offered an innovative array of fringe benefits. After World War I, recognizing the need for credit among working Americans, he helped to found the credit union movement, which brought a higher standard of living to millions.

- In electronics, there was Thomas J. Watson Sr. Most people recognize the role played by technology in the success of the company Watson founded, IBM. But equally important were Watson's innovations in the area of employee partnership. During the 1920s and 1930s, when most manufacturing firms were focused on "atomizing" work so as to reduce the amount of thought and initiative required from workers, Watson moved to enlarge assembly-line jobs to make them more challenging, creative, and rewarding. He transformed supervisors from disciplinarians into assistants to the front-line workers, and he elevated the status of many piecework employees to that of salaried employees with full benefits.

Many of the advances introduced by leaders like these are now taken for granted. Today there are new innovators who are pushing the boundaries of employee-employer partnership. An example is Dov Charney, co-founder and CEO of American Apparel, a Los Angeles-based maker of T-shirts, shorts, and other garments. Charney operates in an industry where employment standards are notoriously low; according to the U.S. Department of Labor, more than half of the garment factories in Los Angeles violate minimum wage and overtime laws. American Apparel is very different. Working conditions are excellent, employee benefits are first-rate, and salaries average between $12 and $18 an hour.

How is this possible? According to Charney, the motivation and morale benefits that derive from treating employees as partners outweigh the costs. "What we're saying is it's inefficient to treat workers poorly." Hopefully, the growing success of American Apparel—$75 million in sales in 2003, up from $40 million the year before—will encourage other firms to follow Charney's example.

No two companies can employ exactly the same techniques to build a strong partnership with their employees. The demands and challenges of different industries call for different responses. But *every* organization must take seriously the needs, aspirations, and goals of the men and women it employs. Unless you develop your own effective approach to treating your employees as partners, you'll find it hard to attract and retain the kind of talent you need to succeed in today's competitive environment.

IN HOSPITALITY, WE FACE SOME UNIQUE CHALLENGES THAT REFLECT THE changing nature of America and of business. As a starting point, consider this random sampling of the employee names that were posted around the ballroom at the Denver rally I described:

Miroslav Zvekic	Halima Amine
Maria Azpeitia	Thiago Sandres
Byamba Dondog	Jennifer Dukstein
Lauren Constable	Lev Tverskoy
Rhonda Banks	Ndeyecodou Sene
Lourdes Areola	Kerrie Darby
Gerald Shibao	Kristen Palmquist

Unless you work at the United Nations, I doubt you've ever seen a more diverse roster of employee names. One of the great strengths of the hospitality industry is that it provides jobs for Americans from many ethnic, racial, and national backgrounds—including many of our country's newest immigrants.

Of course, hiring, training, and managing such a diverse team can be a big challenge. Happily, at Loews Hotels, we've developed leadership techniques that help turn that challenge into a great opportunity, both for our business and for the people who work for us.

As in many service industries, we in hospitality must wrestle with the challenge of employee turnover. Our industry is very competitive, and entry-level workers in particular are understandably willing to consider jumping to a new job if it means a little better income or easier working conditions. Hotels often compete for the same pool of workers as other industries. For example, in the past, we sometimes had trouble staffing our Loews Vanderbilt Hotel in Nashville because of the many hospitals in town; hospital orderlies and hotel housekeepers are drawn from the same populations.

Managing the turnover challenge is hugely important for us, since nothing is more important in hospitality than service. Our front-line employees determine the quality of the guest experience. We take very seriously the need to attract and keep the right people. Furthermore, when you add up the costs of recruiting, screening, interviewing, hiring, and training new employees, you realize that turnover is expensive—yet another reason to seek ways to minimize it.

This challenge is compounded by the fact that some of our employees have had to overcome major obstacles in their personal lives. Many are single parents with only high school diplomas or high school equivalency (GED) certificates. The widely varied ethnic backgrounds of our workers create communication and teamwork challenges, which differ from hotel to hotel. A number of our entry-level employees in Nashville are recent immigrants from Bosnia. In Miami, our many Latino employees include scores of Dominicans, Haitians, and Cubans—three groups that sometimes don't interact well in the community. How do we take such disparate groups and turn them into partners that will stay together and work together effectively?

It isn't easy. But over the years, Loews Hotels has developed some techniques that work well for us. You may find them valuable, too.

Our partnership with employees is based on what we call a *three-legged stool:*

1. Smart selection
2. Effective training
3. Recognition and rewards

The image of the three-legged stool emphasizes the importance of all three parts of our program. If one leg of a stool is weak, broken, or too short, the stool will collapse. In the same way, the Loews human resources program can't succeed unless all three parts of the program are strongly supported. Our three-part human resources program is as effective as any in our industry, helping us foster a true sense of partnership between the company and its people.

Let's start with smart selection—the hiring process. At Loews Hotels, our hiring system includes three separate screens we use for identifying job candidates who will fit well into our company. We devised this system in 1997 when Loews Hotels was about to enter a new high-growth expansion phase, hoping it would help us maintain our corporate culture even as we brought hundreds of new team members on board. It has worked remarkably well.

The job candidate first experiences a prescreening interview. The prescreen focuses on a series of qualifying questions: *What kind of job are you looking for? What do you like and dislike about your current job? How flexible are you? What kind of pay are you looking for?* The answers to these questions may sometimes eliminate a candidate on the spot.

More important, however, is the subtext of the interview, which focuses on *personality.* Technical skills are not the most important thing we are looking for; it may not even matter if a candidate has never held a job before. (That's one reason we've been able to participate in welfare-to-work programs in several cities where we have properties.) Loews Hotels can teach you what it takes to be a good waiter or housekeeper or bell captain. What we need to start with is the kind of person who fits our company culture—someone with a positive outlook, a natural warmth, a willingness to make eye contact and smile, even when meeting a stranger for the first time. Add in a little spontaneity, fun, and a sense of humor, and you have the ideal Loews Hotels' candidate.

Maybe this sounds a bit "touchy-feely." Nonetheless, it works. The trained interviewers who handle our prescreening process do a

---

TISCH'S TIPS

Has your organization developed a personality profile that describes your ideal employee? If not, you should. It's a challenge that calls for brainstorming with people throughout the organization. List the key traits that characterize the kind of people who succeed in your organization—as well as traits you may now lack, but will need in the future. Then look for interview questions or topics that will elicit the traits you want. The result will be an increased number of new hires who bring positive energy to the employer-employee partnership in your organization.

---

remarkable job of identifying people who meet the Loews Hotels' personality profile—generally in 10 minutes or less.

Those who make it through the prescreening interview move on to a more formal structured interview and then through a "fit interview" with their direct supervisor. They're asked to talk about problems they've solved on past jobs (if any), their life ambitions and goals, their personality traits and interests, and so on.

In theory, we expect to eliminate half of the candidates at each of the three screens. Thus, after all three screens are completed, one candidate in eight should be offered a job. In practice, the numbers are uncannily consistent. For example, during the fall of 2003, we conducted a "mass hire" event to staff our new hotel in New Orleans. We started with 900 candidates and ended up with a little over 100 hires—almost exactly the expected ratio.

By the way, a mass hire event, which runs several days, is a traditional part of the process of opening a new hotel. At Loews, however, we've added some unique touches to the system. Some of these grew out of our policy of partnering with each community we do business in. For example, in advance of a mass hire, we reach out to local service organizations and ask them to recommend clients they've worked with—people who are working their way out of poverty, for example, or recovering victims of addiction or abuse. (Our New Orleans mass hire was an especially memorable occasion. When we realized that the available indoor space was inadequate for the crowd we expected, we got a permit from the city to move outside. We decided to take advantage of the opportunity and ended up transforming the mass hire into a virtual street fair, complete with food, drinks, and a mini Mardi Gras-style parade.)

As with any well-designed partnership, everybody benefits from this form of outreach. People desperately in need of a job get the break they've been seeking. The community loses people from its welfare rolls, and gains more contributing taxpayers. And Loews Hotels gets hardworking, dedicated employees—as well as a warmer welcome from the local citizens who appreciate our neighborly approach to business.

EFFECTIVE TRAINING IS THE SECOND LEG OF THE STOOL OF THE LOEWS Hotels system. A crucial aspect of treating employees like partners is investing serious time, effort, and resources into helping new hires develop their skills. Some organizations in labor-intensive, high-turnover industries shy away from this kind of investment: "Why spend money on people who may walk away next week or next month—and maybe take their skills to one of our competitors?"

We don't view it that way. There is simply no substitute for a well-trained employee, especially in a field like hospitality where great customer service is so essential.

Our experience also shows that when you invest in your people they become much less likely to walk away and join your competitors. When you help employees develop their skills, you demonstrate that your organization regards them as human beings with aspirations and career goals that are important and deserve support. The odds are good that they will respond with greater loyalty and dedication, ultimately producing a solid return on your initial investment.

Through our "Star Service" training program, Loews Hotels devotes up to 30 days of every new employee's time to turning them into a professional—whether a housekeeper, banquet server, sales person, or whatever. It's a significant investment, both for us and for the individual involved. But the rewards are enormous.

Some of the skills we teach new employees apply across the board to all staff members. For example, there's the rule we call "10 & 5, First and Last." It says that whenever a guest enters the "hospitality zone" of an employee (that is, within an imaginary 10-foot circle around the employee), the employee should make eye contact, smile, and display "positive body language." Then, once a 5-foot threshold is crossed, a "warm salutation" (like "Good morning") should be offered. Finally, the employee should always address the guest first and last. It doesn't matter exactly what words the employee uses—that's up to his or her personality and taste—but every guest ought to hear a "Good morning, how are you today?" or "Hi there, it's a beautiful evening, isn't it?"

There are many other similar competencies that every Loews employee learns, relating to situations from answering the phone to responding to a guest complaint. There are also Star Service competencies that apply to specific jobs. A restaurant server, for example, masters 57 position-specific competencies, ranging from "Present Specials" and "Taste from the Chef" to "Serve Dessert/After Meal Beverage" and "Place and Process Check."

Having detailed, specific guidelines like these might seem onerous or restrictive. In reality, most Loews employees find the system helpful and even liberating. With a bit of practice, the competencies become second nature and no longer have to be consciously considered—which frees up the mind of the employee to focus on more challenging matters, such as solving guest problems and ensuring that every guest's visit is an enjoyable one.

Every employee gets trained in both a classroom setting and a practice setting. Then they are certified as a Star Employee and presented with a diploma at a formal graduation exercise. Many proudly invite their spouses or children to attend this ceremony; for some, it's the only graduation exercise they've ever experienced. We also require recertification every year, to keep skills up to par.

When we're about to open a new hotel, our training challenge is especially massive. We've developed a system that we last employed in November 2003, prior to the opening of the Loews New Orleans Hotel. We fly in our best managers from around the country as well as Star Performers in each working category—waiters, bell captains, front desk

---

TISCH'S TIPS

Does your organization take advantage of the wisdom and experience your best employees have developed over the years? Think about how you can bring your star performers together with new employees or those who are seeking growth and advancement in the organization. A well-planned program of this kind can speed the dissemination of "best practices" throughout your organization, making every employee into a potential star.

---

personnel, housekeepers, and so on. These experts provide intensive training to their new colleagues for up to two weeks. It's a real honor for those chosen as instructors, and the encouragement they provide the new staff members is tremendously inspirational. Many lifelong mentoring relationships and friendships grow out of these times together.

Loews Hotels doesn't stop with job-related training alone. We also provide our front-line employees with other kinds of education. Several of our hotels maintain online learning centers where employees can enroll in courses. Classes in English as a second language (ESL) are offered at some hotels, taught in native languages that cater to the specific locality. We also provide other courses designed to enhance the quality of life for our employees, from domestic financial management and budgeting to balanced nutrition. Why bother? Because when the lives of our workers are satisfying and happy, they'll be more positive and productive, both on and off the job. Remember, the employee comes first.

THE THIRD LEG OF THE PROGRAM IS RECOGNITION AND REWARDS. WE provide this to our people in a lot of ways—starting with salary, of course. If we didn't pay competitively, people wouldn't stay with us no matter how nice we might be.

At Loews Hotels, salary standards are driven locally. We conduct salary surveys in each city where we operate and strive to keep our pay rates at or above the average in each job category. If a particular general manager wants to set a pay scale higher than this, the variation must be justified based on profitability.

We try to come up with a creative benefits program at each hotel tailored to the needs and concerns of our staffers. In Miami, for example, where local transportation is difficult or costly for many employees, we offer subsidized bus passes. Employees at properties we own such as Miami Beach, Nashville, and Philadelphia also qualify for our pension plan and 401(k) program just like the one that the executives participate in.

We're also great believers in recognizing people in nonfinancial ways. Like many companies, we name an employee of the month at each location. We also offer instant recognition in the form of Star Cards that are given out by managers who "catch" people going the extra mile to help a guest, to resolve a complaint, or to assist a fellow employee. (Too often, businesses devote the bulk of their energy to pointing out what people do wrong; we think it's at least as important to point out what's being done right.) Star Cards can be traded for logo products, meals in our restaurants, even nights in a Loews Hotel.

The highest honor any of our employees can receive is to be named a *Loews Legend*. Every year, each hotel in our chain selects one of its employees of the month as that year's Loews Legend. The selection is based on the quality of their work as well as their contributions to the community. Then we gather the winners from around the country for a very special three-day treat. The Loews Legends are flown with any guest they choose (spouse, mother, daughter, significant other) to the city where we're holding our general managers' meeting that year. We pick them up at the airport, escort them to the local Loews Hotel, and show them all the city sights. Each hotel's winner receives both a cash award and an additional $250 in spending money for their trip. Finally, one company-wide winner is selected.

Each hotel makes a short video about their winner, and all the videos are shown at a special awards banquet. These videos are invariably moving, touching, and funny. Loews Legends night is always one of my favorite events of the year—almost as glamorous as the Golden Globes, and even more fun.

Recognition can't be just a once-a-year or even once-a-month activity. We think that the way we treat people on a daily basis is special. A great example is the daily morning "break-out session" we conduct for our housekeeping staff. Although the details vary from one hotel to another, the overall approach is similar. It starts when the whole team gathers for breakfast in the employee cafeteria. Then they discuss the challenges of the day: Which groups are in the hotel this week? What unusual problems might arise?

Next, a few guest comment cards and letters may be read aloud. Some may reflect areas in need of improvement or trends to be aware of; others may contain compliments, and the individuals who have earned the praise will be singled out for recognition.

Awards and prizes may be distributed: The housekeeper who has gone the longest without an accident might be gifted with a free lunch in a hotel restaurant, while a teammate who has scored especially high on room inspections might receive a sweater from the gift shop.

Then there's the music—it might be anything from disco to salsa—and maybe a cheer or two. Eileen Cronin Davis, director of housekeeping for our three properties at Universal Orlando even likes to play cartoons on a VCR. Finally, the team members high-five one another and head off to work.

Does it sound a little hokey? Maybe so. But as I learned when I did the job, housekeeping is tough work—physically demanding, mentally draining, and lonely. You *need* a few minutes of high-energy

TISCH'S TIPS

Have you taken a critical look at your own organization's methods of recognizing and rewarding employees? If not, you should. Solicit honest feedback from people at every level of the organization, and apply some creativity to the task of devising ways to show employees how highly you value their contributions. Periodically, reexamine your recognition and rewards program and make some changes; over time, the effectiveness of any program will naturally erode, calling for a fresh approach.

encouragement and fellowship to start the day. That's what we try to provide. As a result, the morale, camaraderie, and enthusiasm of Loews' staffers are a lot better than in most hotels.

ALL THREE PORTIONS OF THE LOEWS HOTELS' *PEOPLE PROCESS* ARE designed to convey one vital message to our employees:

> What you do matters. Your job isn't just about cleaning a bathtub, setting a table, or toting a bag—it's about giving guests a positive feeling about Loews. And your dignity, safety, and self-worth are equally important to us. You're our partners, and we'll always treat you accordingly.

Of course, it's easier to *say* this than to convince people you really mean it. We all know companies that describe themselves as "one big happy family," but reveal through their policies and behaviors that this is mere lip service. The only way we can make this message truly meaningful is by applying an upside-down approach to management—empowering our staff members by giving them the tools and resources they need to do their jobs while supporting them from above.

This puts a huge responsibility on our middle managers. They have to build teams that communicate seamlessly and support one another constantly, coordinating all the teams from housekeeping and the front desk to the bell staff and banquet waiters, while providing supplies, information systems, staffing, and other resources whenever and wherever they're needed. On a day when 300 people are checking in and out, the hotel may look like barely controlled chaos; the managers must make it all work as smoothly as a ballet.

The same upside-down philosophy of leadership applies to our executive team in New York. Our goal is to give the local managers the tools to do their jobs while remaining profitable—not simply throwing bodies at problems, but resolving the challenges through creativity and ingenuity.

As you can probably tell, the corporate culture at Loews Hotels is a bit unusual. One of the people with special responsibility for protecting and transmitting that culture is Alan Momeyer, the vice president of human resources for Loews Corporation.

Alan has always recognized that Loews was different from other businesses. Back in November 1980, he was interviewing simultaneously for two jobs, one at Loews Corporation and one at a leading international bank. "The bankers must have liked me. They had me come in for no fewer than *13* interviews. But in the end, they didn't offer me a job. When I asked why, they said, 'When we asked you questions, you gave us too many right answers.' To this day, I have no idea what that means. But I have a feeling it would have been horrible for me if I'd gone to work there. I couldn't have dealt with that degree of bureaucracy."

Instead, after two interviews, Alan was offered a job at Loews. "I instantly found that I really liked the people. They didn't talk like corporate types—the harried men and women I encountered in airport lounges. They were funny, and the level of game-playing and political intrigue at the company was shockingly low. I couldn't quite believe it. I wondered, am I really this lucky, or am I blind? I decided to stay a while to see if I really liked it, and I've been here ever since."

Alan and I have talked a lot about the Power of Partnerships and how we can embody that philosophy in the way we treat our employees at Loews Hotels. One way is by inculcating a sense of respect for the fact that employees—whether hourly staffers or top executives—have lives away from the office. Their involvements in family, community activities, and industry organizations are accepted and encouraged.

We also strive to make Loews Hotels unusually inclusive. For example, we believe we're among the best employers for women in the hospitality business, with two executive vice presidents, a regional vice president, and general managers who are women. It's a higher percentage than you'll find at most other companies in the industry.

Loews is also unusually democratic in terms of career opportunities. You don't need an MBA or an Ivy League background to get ahead at Loews Hotels. Gary Rohanna, the general manager at our Beverly Hills hotel, started out as a bartender and a front desk clerk at our Annapolis Hotel. Lisa Culver, the director of sales and marketing in Beverly Hills, broke in as a Food and Beverage secretary in Annapolis. Kurt

Johnson came to work in our Coronado resort as a doorman; he's now the front office manager.

Another example is Sherrie Laveroni, our executive vice president of operations who reports directly to company president Jack Adler. Sherrie broke into hospitality as a secretary at an airport hotel in California. Although her education was limited to a high school diploma, Sherrie's intelligence and determination made her stand out. She set about climbing the industry ladder, achieving great results everywhere she went. But for years she was frustrated because no company was willing to give her the job she really wanted—general manager of a hotel. At times, she feared that this was an impossible dream for a woman who lacked an MBA or other impressive educational credentials.

But at Loews Hotels, we don't believe in glass ceilings. Years ago, when Loews needed new leadership for our Santa Monica Hotel, I began hearing Sherrie's name. We met in 1989, and within hours Sherrie was our newest general manager.

Since then, Sherrie has worn a number of hats at Loews, taking on ever-increasing responsibilities. For a time, she was a regional vice president, charged with overseeing operations at several of our most important properties in locations ranging from New York City to Montreal and Chicago. (Occasionally, people would wonder how we define a "region," but Sherrie and I didn't let a little thing like geography get in the way of her managerial talent.)

Sherrie's career has benefited from the willingness of Loews to give her just a little more responsibility than other companies might have allowed. That's a key ingredient of our partnership philosophy, and it's one that Sherrie now practices as a mentor to the next generation of Loews' leaders.

"We try to hire people who are willing to take risks, to be gutsy," Sherrie says. "That means they sometimes make mistakes. But if you've hired the right people, the great decisions will outweigh the mistakes.

"Take Kathleen Cochran at our Coronado Bay Resort. Back in March 2001, there was a recession looming. Our first quarter results were looking pretty disappointing, and we realized we'd have to go into cost-cutting mode. I called every general manager and asked them to develop ideas for trimming expenses without hurting service. They came up with dozens of proposals, and we were making great progress on the cost front.

"In the midst of all this, what do you suppose happened? The *Wall Street Journal* ran a cute little item about a hotel manager who had hired an 'intuitive consultant' to analyze and advise her on the flow of energies at her property, as well as to advise group and meeting planners. It was Kathleen at the Loews Coronado Bay! At a time when we were asking all of our hotels to trim expenses to the bone, we felt it sent a really misleading signal to be spending money on a consultant whose expertise might be considered faddish.

"I was fit to be tied. I called Kathleen and we had a long, intense talk about it. But you know what? It worked out all right in the end. The consultant really didn't cost very much, the hotel got a ton of free publicity, and Kathleen's bar and restaurant business actually increased as a result. So in the end, we made money from her plan rather than losing it."

That's the kind of thing that happens when you really treat employees as partners. Will Loews staffers do everything the same way I would? Probably not. But that's all right. As the saying goes, if two people always think exactly alike, then one of them is redundant. We try not to have any redundant people at Loews Hotels—just energetic, creative ones like Sherrie and Kathleen, who are constantly trying new things—and usually making them pay off.

Sometimes it takes a little nerve to trust and truly empower your employees. Six years ago, our executive vice president of marketing Charlotte St. Martin proposed a new pricing process for Loews Hotels. Based on the so-called "yield management" approach used in the airline industry (among other businesses), it was highly complex and technology-driven. It also promised to improve Loews Hotels' profit pattern while at the same time increasing our occupancy rates and bringing more guests into the properties.

When Charlotte presented the plan to our board, we discussed it at length. I'm no technology whiz; I know how to send and receive e-mail, and that's about the extent of my computer savvy. I grasped the outlines of how Charlotte's system would work, though not the details. But I could see that Charlotte knew what she was doing and that she believed in the program. On that basis, we went ahead. It represented a major commitment, both in terms of money and in terms of the change in our operational practices. But it worked. Today, Loews Hotels has improved its bottom line significantly thanks to the new pricing methodology.

LOEWS HOTELS HAS DEVELOPED A DISTINCTIVE APPROACH TO partnering with its employees. It's characterized by an upside-down approach to management; informality and an aversion to bureaucracy; an inclusive, democratic spirit; and a commitment to empowering our people as decision makers. Taken together, these qualities amount to a corporate culture that we think is very special and worthy of preservation.

One of the ways we try to foster this culture for future generations is through the leadership programs Alan Momeyer supervises. In the past couple of years, we've placed increased emphasis on professional training of our managers. We created the new home office position of director of training and career development. Jenny Herman keeps career profiles on each of our managers, detailing their short-term, medium-term, and long-term career objectives and listing the skills they need to develop, training courses they should take, and the job experience they need. (We have a pilot program to create similar profiles for some of the hourly employees in our Nashville hotel. If it works well, we may expand that throughout the company.)

Jenny also monitors our mentoring program, which formalizes the kind of network of mutual support and teaching that always existed at Loews. We link up employees who are in search of career guidance, feedback, and advice ("mentees") with experienced people who are willing to offer their time, energy, and wisdom (mentors). In some cases, the mentee and mentor may work in the same department; in other cases, we connect people from different spheres to broaden the background and knowledge base of the mentee.

The mentee/mentor teams are then provided with a series of valuable tools, from a 360-degree assessment and follow-up surveys to

How does mentoring happen at your organization? Is there a formal process or simply an informal system of friendships and connections that springs up naturally? If you lack a formal process, you may want to consider launching one. An officially sponsored mentoring program sends several beneficial signals. It tells employees that nurturing one another's skills is important work. It encourages younger employees who may be shy or insecure to seek the guidance of more experienced people. And it reinforces the sense that the entire organization is a partnership of people, working together for a common goal—not just a collection of individuals competing against one another for advancement or recognition.

skill-building workshops and meetings. We also encourage the teams through recognition programs, including an annual day at the local ball park for all mentoring pairs and "Coach of the Year" and "MVP" honors—even a mentoring "Hall of Fame."

Perhaps my biggest frustration with Loews Hotels' small size is the fact that we don't always have promotional opportunities to offer our most deserving employees. As a relatively small chain, we may not have an opening for the person who is ready to step up to the next level in the organization.

Consequently, we sometimes lose talented individuals to competing companies, who are eager to add our shining stars to their own rosters. We hate to see it happen, but we never want to stand in the way of someone's opportunity to advance. We make a point of telling departing employees that the door back to Loews is never locked: "Sometime in the future, you may find that you're ready for another career move. When that happens, we hope Loews will be your first phone call." Many Loews Hotels' alumni eventually return when the right position becomes available.

No discussion of employee-employer partnerships would be complete without examining the issue of unionization.

In hospitality, as in some other industries, union labor is an important factor. Here, too, Loews Hotels takes an approach that differs from many of our competitors, some of whom oppose unions strongly. As we do with other labor-management issues, we view the question through the lens of partnership, asking: *How can Loews Hotels work with employees to create a true partnership—whether those employees choose union representation or not?*

The influence of unions in hospitality varies greatly from one city to another. In New York City, about 80 percent of hotel workers are unionized. In many other cities, however, very few hotels are unionized. Of the 20 Loews Hotels, five are unionized: the two in Canada, the Regency in New York, and the two in Washington, DC. Our recently opened New Orleans hotel was financed in part with investments from union pension funds, and we have already recognized the union as the legitimate bargaining agent for employees. A unionization drive is also under way in Santa Monica.

You might assume that unionized hotel workers earn significantly more than nonunionized workers. Actually, that's not the case. Wages and benefits are pretty standard across both union and nonunion hotels. (Loews Hotels in general pay better than average wages.) The major impact of the union is on work rules, which tend to be strictly regulated and rigidly enforced where a union is in existence.

To some extent, these rules are a laudable attempt to protect workers from exploitation. In some cases, however, they impede the flexibility that managers need to run their operations smoothly. For example, in a unionized shop, a number of separate jobs may be defined that may not be interchanged. This can create headaches for management. If the restaurant is slow but room service is busy, management would like to have a restaurant waiter deliver meals to rooms. Similarly, we'd like to be able to move someone from reservations to the front desk. Union rules sometimes make this impossible.

Scheduling rules are particularly strict. A union may typically insist on two weeks' notice for scheduling changes. This causes particular problems for hotel management in today's travel environment, when many guests are booking later and making changes in their plans up to the last minute. In a union environment, if we suddenly find that we are running 75 percent occupancy rather than 90 percent, we must still employ and pay all the workers we thought we would need; and if we find we are running 90 percent rather than 75 percent, we may have to pay time and a half for last-minute call-ins. That's expensive.

Our objective is to treat employees the way we'd like to be treated, thereby making the question of unionization less relevant. As Alan Momeyer, our vice president of human resources, puts it, "We want to manage so that the problems that might drive people to unions—lack of benefits, lack of opportunity, arbitrary treatment by managers—don't exist at Loews Hotels."

However, if employees choose to belong to a union, we respect and honor their choice and negotiate a fair contract in good faith. We pride ourselves on the fact that Loews Hotels maintains good relationships with workers in both union and nonunion environments. Some companies allow a confrontational atmosphere to develop, where every minor annoyance turns into a formal grievance that leads to drawn-out disputes that waste everybody's time and energy. In most cases, labor and management must share the blame for that kind of atmosphere. We never want that to happen at a Loews property—and so far, it never has.

BECAUSE OF RECESSION, TERRORIST ATTACKS, WAR, AND SECURITY FEARS, we've been through the most difficult period in our industry's history. And because hospitality is a people-intensive business, with labor expenses representing around 60 percent of our costs, tough times for us automatically translate into tough times for our employees.

This is when our commitment to a true partnership with our people is tested. With revenues shrinking, would Loews Hotels respond to adversity simply by slashing jobs—or could we find a better way?

Fortunately, we'd already begun to trim our expenses in response to changing economic conditions as early as the spring of 2001. But in the immediate aftermath of September 11, with average hotel occupancies plummeting from around 70 percent to near 25 percent, we went into full crisis mode. Our executive board began meeting daily, focusing on how to streamline our operations without hurting customer service or our employees. The challenge, in short, was to cut costs while protecting our most important partnerships.

In search of answers, we explored many complex variables, from hours of operation for specific amenities (room service, health club, and so on) to levels of staffing. In concert with our general managers, we looked at how we could adjust those without unduly impacting the guests or our employees. Unlike our usual highly decentralized mode of operation, we realized that the home office needed to take the lead under these unusual circumstances, so that the entire chain would understand the gravity of the problem and join in making the necessary sacrifices.

We took certain steps immediately. We asked all administrative personnel to go on a four-day work week for the next 30 days. We also asked all hotels with two food and beverage outlets to close one. We imposed a chainwide salary freeze and hiring freeze as well.

Sherrie Laveroni then met with the managers of each hotel and went through every line item and every aspect of their operations, looking for ways to save based on individual circumstances and market conditions. She brought the resulting plans to the board, and every week Jack Adler sent a memo to all the hotels detailing our decisions. At the same time, our executive vice president of marketing, Charlotte St. Martin was putting together special promotional packages and price reductions to try to shorten the downturn and limit its effects.

As a result of this swift and decisive action, the Loews Hotels suffered a less severe economic impact than our competitors and bounced back stronger when, about a year later, the business began to revive. Meanwhile, we'd learned some valuable lessons from our crisis response program. To give one small example, at our flagship Regency Hotel in New York, we'd always turned down the bed in every room each day. This was just a small amenity that we'd always assumed was an essential part of four-star service. During the crisis, we stopped routine turndowns; instead, we left cards in the rooms offering "turndown

TISCH'S TIPS

Is your organization prepared to cope with a time of crisis? Do you have a plan for minimizing employee hardships during an economic downturn? The behavior of your leadership when times are tough provides a strong indication of your organization's true values. If you espouse values like partnership during good times only to quietly discard them during hard times, you will lay yourself open to charges of hypocrisy. That is worse than having no values at all!

by request." We found that most guests didn't really care whether or not their beds were turned down.

Most important, we were able to sustain Loews Hotels through the crisis with very few employee layoffs. Most of the jobs that were lost came during the initial 45 to 60 days after September 11, and most of those affected had either been rehired by Loews Hotels or gotten other jobs by the end of that time period. Many of our employees did lose a few hours on their time cards each week, but nearly all agreed that this was preferable to layoffs.

IT WOULD BE GREAT TO BE ABLE TO MANAGE A COMPANY WITHOUT EVER having to resort to layoffs. In today's volatile world, that's not possible. But today's smartest leaders are learning that slash-and-burn tactics rarely lead to lasting success or growth. When your organization fosters a real partnership with its employees, and nurtures that partnership through good times and bad, most employees will respond with loyalty, commitment, and dedication.

Partnering with employees also pays off financially. At Loews Hotels, employee turnover runs about half of the industry average (33 percent in 2003, versus an industry norm of 65 percent to 75 percent). Furthermore, our turnover rate has fallen six years in a row. When you consider that the average cost of replacing an employee is around $2,000 (including recruitment, uniforms, background checks, and training), the total we are saving amounts to millions of dollars per year.

Furthermore, the fact that we treat employees as partners has become well known throughout our industry. Loews Hotels now has a great reputation among hospitality employees in all of the cities where we operate. The word is out: Loews Hotels is a place where there are opportunities for people to learn and move up. What's more, it's a cool place to be—a place where work is human and fun as well as a source of a paycheck. That's the kind of reputation that attracts the best employees to our doors. This is yet another reason why the Power of Partnerships works.

PORTRAIT IN PARTNERSHIP

Emeril Lagasse

Chef Emeril Lagasse first learned to cook from his mother, Hilda, as a boy growing up in the small town of Fall River, Massachusetts. Upon graduation from high school, he was offered a full scholarship to the New England Conservatory of Music, but decided to pursue a career as a professional chef. After stints in Paris, Lyon, New York, and other American cities, Emeril was lured to New Orleans by Dick and Ella Brennan, where he became executive chef at their legendary restaurant, Commander's Palace, for seven and a half years.

In 1990, he opened Emeril's Restaurant in the chic Warehouse District in downtown New Orleans. Today, Emeril is chef-proprietor of nine restaurants—including two located in Loews Hotels—as well as a national TV personality and a best-selling cookbook author.

"I take the word partnership very seriously," Emeril told us when we spoke by phone on December 17, 2003. "I've experienced

(Continued)

a lot of partnerships, some good, some bad. What I've learned is that a real partnership isn't just about putting my name on something. It starts with chemistry, then moves on to philosophy and standards, whether it's a hotel restaurant, a television program, a brand of food, or a licensing agreement."

Emeril is quick to attribute the success of his organization to the quality of his employee partners. "I'm the quarterback of the team, but you don't win a Super Bowl with one great player. Where we are is because I have a broad base of talented people. Many have been with me for 14 or 18 years, from the chefs in my restaurants on up to Tony Cruz, my business guy.

"We make a huge investment in service," Emeril continues. "That's something a lot of people don't get. But I find that you attract the quality of people you deserve. When we began planning for our new restaurant at Loews Miami Beach Hotel, I had lots of colleagues in the business phoning me to say, 'You guys are in for a nightmare trying to find 120 people in Miami who are capable of providing great service.' I said, 'We'll see.'

"We scheduled a job fair in Miami to recruit people for the restaurant. I flew in with our human resources staff and most of our directors—our directors of finance, marketing, public relations, and so on. We opened the doors at 8 A.M., and a handful of people showed up. By 9 o'clock, a few more had straggled in, and by 10 o'clock a few more. I was getting a little nervous. But at noon I looked around, and 600 people were in the room. My first lesson about Miami: People don't get up early here!

"We did our interviews, performed background checks and drug testing, and hired our team. Then the interesting part began: a three- to four-week investment in what I call Emerilizing—teaching the team members to think and act like I would if I had their jobs.

"We start with general sessions, where everyone is together, talking about the spirit and philosophy of our organization. I teach the first two days, then HR does a day. After that, we break down into groups: busses with busses, front waiters with front waiters, and so on. Every task is broken down into component steps, which the new team member has to understand, learn, and master. We call this microtraining. Each employee then has to pass a written and oral test to receive a final assignment. If you don't pass muster as a front waiter, for example, you may be assigned a job as a back waiter instead.

"The second week is built around mock meal services, actually cooking and serving dinners to other members of the Emeril's family. In this way, we work out all the bugs in our systems and our training. Finally, for the last three to four days before the restaurant opening, we bring in outside guests and serve meals to them. This makes a great dress rehearsal for our team members. It's also a nice way of thanking people who have helped us. In Miami, we invited folks from Loews Hotels as our guests, then some people from the community, past customers from the Emeril database, and finally a few top media people from the area.

"Not until we are totally comfortable will we open our doors to the public. In Miami, this happened on November 1, 2003—by which time all of our 120 associates were fully prepared to offer high-quality, Emeril-style service."

We asked for an unusual example of Emerilizing—a unique service method that makes Emeril's restaurants special.

"Here's a good one," Emeril told us. "We have both a front waiter and a back waiter serving any particular table. One of our commandments for service is that your cocktail order should be taken within 15 seconds of your being seated. Now, how do we make sure that both waiters know whether the order has been placed? We use the salt and pepper shakers on your table. When you sit down, the two shakers are separated; when one of the waiters takes your drink order, he or she puts them together. That way, you won't be bothered by a second waiter asking you about

(Continued)

drinks. It's a little thing most people would never notice, but that's what great service is all about—little things that add up to a big difference."

Is it hard to maintain service standards when the company leader wears so many hats—as TV personality, author, and business executive as well as chef?

"It's a challenge. But the quality commitment starts with me. I spend one week a month producing TV programs. Most of the rest of my time, I'm in the restaurants.

"We've created a mentoring system that's very important—a formal program where older folks teach the younger folks, not just about job skills but about attitude. And, of course, I try hard to set the right tone personally. I love seeing the cooks in one of our kitchens get excited when I'm in there working on a dish with them."

Emeril summed up his message this way: "I'll never be too proud or too important to get my apron dirty, sweating over an open flame. I learned long ago that when you go to work in a kitchen, you'd better leave your ego outside. Otherwise, you'll end up flat on your ass."

CHAPTER 5

Turning Customers into Partners

Creating Value Together

The thing that people want is genuine understanding. If you can understand the feelings and moods of another person, you have something fine to offer.

—Paul Brock (1932–   )
Distinguished journalist

VIRTUALLY EVERYONE IN BUSINESS ACKNOWLEDGES THE CRUCIAL ROLE of the customer. Without customers and the financial support they provide, we're all out of business. The most successful companies are those that operate as if they never forgot that essential truth. They're the ones that provide thoughtful service and reliable products at a fair price—every time.

In the hospitality business, our relationship to the customer is special, giving us—in comparison to most industries—both a unique advantage and a daunting challenge.

First, the unique advantage. Our customers walk in the door every day and literally live with us—for a few hours, a few days, or even a few weeks at a time. Each guest comes into direct contact with numerous Loews Hotels' employees—the waiter who brings breakfast to the room, the engineer who shows up to fix a balky air conditioner, the concierge who arranges theatre tickets—and into indirect contact with dozens more, from the housekeepers who vacuum the carpets to the pool attendants who put out fresh towels. Each of these encounters gives us the opportunity to make a positive impression and strengthen our bond with the customer.

This unusual degree of intimacy also gives Loews an edge when it comes to interpreting and understanding the needs of our customers. In the auto industry, in movie making, in software, even in banking or finance, the customer can sometimes feel like a distant abstraction; managers in those industries have to make special efforts to meet and learn from their typical clients. Not in hospitality. Our customers are in our faces every day, and most of them are not shy about telling us what they like and don't like about the services we provide.

We tend to get instant feedback about every strategy we try. When we rework our restaurant menu, we find out quickly whether our guests like the changes by whether the tables are full or empty at dinnertime. When we add a new service at one of our spas, we know in a week or two whether guests love it or disdain it. The time lag between action and reaction that most business people experience is much less in our business.

But the challenge posed by our intimate relationship with customers is equally important. Because hotel guests demand and deserve our service 24 hours a day, 365 days a year, there are no off days for us—no weekends or holiday breaks or production down times when we can retool, reenergize, and rethink. We have to be "on" at all times. And there's no way to hide from our mistakes. If the director of a movie has a bad day on the set, he can trash the footage and reshoot the scene tomorrow. If we make an error with a banquet or a business meeting, there's no way to turn back the clock and fix it. We may lose an important customer forever.

The hospitality industry is both unforgiving and deeply rewarding. Get it right, and the appreciation, even delight, of your guests will be immediate and obvious. Get it wrong, and the disappointment will be just as apparent. For those with a thin skin or a low energy level, it's a brutal business. For those who relish a constant challenge and have egos that don't bruise easily, it's tremendous fun.

We think of our first interaction with the customer as a priceless opportunity. It takes the combined effect of all our advertising, marketing, public relations, sales, and word-of-mouth efforts to persuade a new customer to book a room in one of our hotels. When that guest walks into our lobby and up to our registration desk for the first time, he represents a major investment in time, energy, and resources.

Now the challenge shifts to getting that guest to return. At the end of the stay, the guest mentally reviews his experience while paying the final bill, whether consciously or unconsciously. He asks himself: Did I get the kind of experience I expected? Was the value I received worth the money I paid for it? Better still, did I get *more value* for my money than I had any right to expect? If the answer is yes, the guest is likely to return to a Loews Hotel.

The first visit to a Loews Hotel is a priceless opportunity; converting it into lasting success means getting the customer to visit us for the *second* time, and the third. Once we've won him over and transformed him into a partner—someone who thinks of Loews Hotels as "his" place in every city where we operate—then he becomes an ongoing source of revenue for us, often for years to come. He also becomes a channel for new customers, through referrals and recommendations to friends, coworkers, and family members. Maintaining him as a partner is relatively inexpensive and very profitable.

The crucial challenge is making that first stay—that first guest experience—really memorable and pleasant. If we can combine all the disparate elements of the hospitality experience in a wonderful stay, we've achieved a breakthrough that will mean everything to our business.

DURING MY YEARS IN THE BUSINESS, THE CUSTOMER CHALLENGE HAS intensified. Over the past couple of decades, hospitality has become increasingly competitive and demanding. To a degree that most hotel guests scarcely realize, consolidation has swept our industry, bringing many smaller chains under the umbrella of larger companies. Today, for example, Starwood Hotels & Resorts owns Sheraton, Westin, St. Regis, Four Points, and the W chain of boutique hotels. Marriott owns Ritz-Carlton, Ramada, and several variations on its own Marriott brand, from JW Hotels & Resorts to Residence Inn and Courtyard by

Marriott. Cendant owns Howard Johnson, Super 8, Days Inn, Ameri-Host Inn, and several other brands.

This consolidation gives the big companies enormous competitive clout through their combined purchasing power, their global distribution systems, and their interlinked customer rewards programs, which encourage travelers to use the same family of chains repeatedly rather than spread their dollars among various companies. It's hard for a small player like Loews Hotels to compete with the hospitality Goliaths.

Furthermore, today's traveler is knowledgeable, demanding, and spoiled. The Internet is helping to revolutionize people's expectations. When a person planning a business trip or a pleasure jaunt can visit hundreds of properties with a few clicks on the computer, you'd better make darn sure that your hotel competes effectively, not just with the hotels down the street and around the corner but also with those at the other end of the state and even across the country.

As a result, standards keep rising. Amenities few people dreamed of 10 years ago, such as high-speed Internet access, are quickly morphing from high-end luxuries to desirable benefits to basic necessities. At the same time, more and more customers are demanding competitive prices, discounts, and deals. Throw in the recession of 2001 to 2003 and the dampening impact of war and terror threats, and you have a pretty challenging environment for today's hospitality companies.

A final wrinkle is the complexity of our customer base. On one level, this relates to the personal profile, interests, and objectives of the individual hotel guest. There are almost as many different reasons for staying at a Loews Hotel as there are guests. The people in room 701 are in town for a friend's wedding; the woman in 702 is attending an industry meeting; the family with two small children in 703 is on vacation; the older couple in 704 is here to take in the local museums and shows; the man in 705 is a business person who has to make eight sales calls in two days; and the husband and wife in 706 are scouting locations for a movie. Our hotel has to offer a mix of services, styles, and amenities that will satisfy all of them.

But the varying needs of guests aren't the only form of customer complexity we must deal with. Our customers also include a variety of travel professionals whose widely differing—sometimes conflicting—

interests we seek to serve: travel agents, tour companies, association executives in charge of conventions, meeting planners for businesses, Internet-based travel retailers, and many others.

In this tough, complicated, and competitive universe, Loews Hotels must somehow differentiate itself from other luxury hotel chains in ways that are meaningful both to our guests and to the many others in our customer base. This challenge is far from trivial. Every luxury hotel has a nice lobby, marble vanities in the guest bathrooms, a health club or gym, Internet access, and free bottles of shampoo in the shower. What makes a Loews Hotel different?

If you're read this far in the book, you won't be surprised that my response centers on the concept of *partnership*. At Loews Hotels, we've built our success by treating customers as partners—another in the network of partnerships that is the basis of our management philosophy. But what does it mean to "treat customers as partners"? As I see it, the idea has three key components:

1. *Communicating from the bottom up:* Businesses must recognize that today's customer isn't content to be merely a passive target of advertising or marketing campaigns. Instead, she actively participates in shaping the popular perception of companies, products, and services through "buzz" and word-of-mouth (positive or negative) perceptions. Companies that want to partner with customers have to change their thinking about marketing from top-down to bottom-up. Rather than trusting in the power of big media to push ideas onto a passive mass audience, they must find ways to generate buzz about their products and services among consumers themselves.

2. *Focusing on the customer experience:* Companies have traditionally had a product-centric or service-centric view of the marketplace: They concentrated on making excellent products or services, assuming that this would capture the allegiance of customers. Today, this view of competition is simplistic. Most customers don't care about products or services as such; what they care about is the *quality of the experience* we can help them to enjoy. Partnering with customers demands that companies see the experiences they create

through the eyes of customers and find ways to make those experiences as rewarding as possible.

3. *Linking with customer communities:* Traditional marketing and advertising were oriented to the mass market: The monolithic organization broadcast a message to thousands or millions of individual consumers. Today, more and more companies are recognizing the existence of customer communities—groups of customers who identify with one another, have shared ideas and feelings, and want to help shape their relationship with your business. Partnering with customers includes facilitating the creation of customer communities and making those communities part of your marketing system.

At Loews Hotels, we use all three of these approaches to help turn our customers into partners—people who recognize, trust, and seek out the Loews name whenever they travel. In fact, partnership is the heart of our marketing strategy, defining everything from the branded programs we develop to the design of our hotel lobbies.

Every successful company is customer-centric. That's fundamental to our free-market economy. Most of the specific techniques Loews uses to market its services are not unique to us; many other good companies have developed their own variations on these methods. However, we think the partnership concept gives a special twist to our approach to marketing—one you may find helpful as you contemplate the customer challenges in your own industry.

LET'S BEGIN WITH THE FIRST KEY ELEMENT OF CUSTOMER PARTNERING—bottom-up communication, using the power of buzz to augment or replace the traditional power of top-down marketing.

In recent years, there's been a lot of interest in the phenomenon of buzz, fueled in part by journalist Malcolm Gladwell's book *The Tipping Point,* which analyzes the subtle process by which buzz spreads from a small, select group of insiders to a broader universe. Gladwell offers some fascinating case histories about buzz "epidemics," along with pointers as to how business people, community leaders, politicians, and others can create some buzz of their own.

Smart business leaders have long known the power of buzz. Decades ago, manufacturers used product endorsements from movie stars and baseball players to get people talking about their products; even first lady Eleanor Roosevelt appeared in magazine ads for Good Luck margarine.

More recently, savvy marketers have developed multipronged strategies for generating buzz. For example, whenever Starbucks opens its first coffee shop in a new city, the company creates lists of local people who might serve as "ambassadors," including friends and families of Starbucks employees, local shareholders, mail-order customers, and supporters of charities that Starbucks promotes. In the days leading up to the grand opening, a series of events is held, including product tastings with local reporters, critics, and chefs, and preopening parties to benefit local nonprofit groups. With each event, the circle of contacts generating buzz about Starbucks grows wider.

Loews Hotels uses a similar strategy. A hotel opening is a grand opportunity to generate buzz and make the new property into an integral part of the community, as we did, for example, in March 2004, when we brought together civic leaders, nonprofit groups, and hundreds of local artists, musicians, writers, food lovers, and ordinary citizens for a series of celebratory events around the opening of Loews New Orleans Hotel.

But our belief in buzz isn't restricted to opening events. As I've mentioned, Loews Hotels puts a special emphasis on public relations in its marketing strategy. In part, this is simple necessity: As a small chain, we don't have the marketing or advertising budgets of our larger competitors. To compensate, we're forced to find ways to spread our message through "free" media—coverage in newspapers, magazines, the broadcast media, and the Internet.

Nearly every marketing success we've achieved at Loews Hotels is a result of this strategy: Craft a public relations-friendly message that will resonate with the media and the public, and thereby produce positive buzz for our hotels. This approach *forces* a bottoms-up communication strategy. Companies that rely on advertising often end up wasting millions on ads that stroke their own egos without connecting to customers. We cannot afford to allow this to happen to us. Unlike paid media, free media is not under our control. Loews Hotels can pitch a story idea, but the editors and producers decide what kind of pickup we get and how favorable the stories will be. And ultimately, it's readers, viewers, and web surfers who decide whether or not our story will resonate with audiences. If they flip the pages, change the channel, or click the mouse, our message will disappear; if they pause to read, look, or listen, it will get through.

As a result, we're forced to be a little more creative, a little more dramatic, a little more surprising, a little more colorful in every message we create. Otherwise, the editors and producers will never pick it up, the story will never appear, and the buzz we seek will never happen.

For an example of how we use this approach, consider Home Sweet Loews, a program we unveiled in 2002. It's a branded service under which we offer a host of extras to make any stay at a Loews Hotel more comfortable, enjoyable, and fun. We've provided bits and pieces of this service at our hotels for many years, but the idea of gathering all these elements under a single umbrella grew out of a fresh insight into the changing needs of our customer/partners—one that we quickly sensed could translate into both media coverage and positive buzz for Loews Hotels.

In December 2001, Charlotte St. Martin, our executive vice president of marketing, attended a meeting run by a home-building company on whose board she serves. The meeting was held in the wake of September 11, and as you can imagine, the mood was somber. The attendees were wondering, how will the new realities of terrorism and a world at war affect our customers and our businesses in the years ahead?

One speaker caught Charlotte's attention: an expert from a polling and trend-watching firm who described a new feeling among Americans. Travelers, he said, wanted above all to feel comfortable and secure. They wanted to remain close to their families even when they traveled and to feel as though the comforts of home were available to them wherever they went.

Does your organization make a conscious effort to stay abreast of cultural, economic, and social trends that may affect your customers? If not, you should. Seek out opportunities to hear from experts in shifting attitudes, and develop your own sensitivity to such changes. Then spend time brainstorming ways to draw meaningful connections between your organization and the emerging trends you identify, thereby strengthening the partnership between you and your customers.

When Charlotte heard this discussion, she literally slapped her forehead. "This describes Loews," she exclaimed. "All we have to do is communicate it."

Under the umbrella of Home Sweet Loews, we collected a number of branded programs that are centered on family-style comfort and convenience. They include:

- *Loews Loves Pets,* which makes it easier for travelers to bring their dog, cat, or other animal companion on a stay at a Loews Hotel. On arrival, the pet is greeted with a "Dear Fido" or "Dear Fluffy" letter (signed, of course, with a paw print), and we provide feeding bowls, litter boxes, pet toys and treats, and even room service menu items especially for pets. (Hosting animals creates surprisingly few maintenance problems for us. Sometimes I joke that our four-legged friends are better behaved that our two-legged friends.)
- *Loews Loves Kids,* designed to make family travel fun and relaxing. Children under eighteen always stay free in the same room with their parents; adjoining rooms, appropriate for older kids, qualify for special discounts. We provide kid-friendly amenities, including a free gift bag for children under 10, children's restaurant and room-service menus, and the Kids Kloset, which lets families borrow electronic games, VCRs, car seats, strollers, baby tubs, even night lights and outlet protectors.

- *Generation G,* which caters to grandparents and grandchildren traveling together. We welcome them with treats like a photo memory album, a free movie and popcorn, a phonecard for calling home, and the various amenities kids enjoy under the *Loews Loves Kids* program.

As soon as Home Sweet Loews and its various components were in place, we set about promoting them—not through traditional advertising, but mainly through the news media. The coverage has been phenomenal, with scores of articles, reviews, and reports on national and local TV and radio stations, in the travel and business sections of newspapers and magazines, and on countless web pages.

Media-generated buzz like this is more valuable than millions of dollars' worth of advertising. Why? There are several reasons. First of all, unlike advertising, news coverage is considered unbiased and therefore has greater credibility among consumers. A news story about Loews Hotels gives us a kind of stamp of approval, certifying our efforts as worthy of attention.

As a result, news coverage is far more likely to generate buzz and word-of-mouth than advertising. Think about it: How often do you talk about the contents of advertisements with your friends or family? On the other hand, most people talk about interesting, colorful, or funny news items on a daily basis.

Finally, media coverage validates the experiences of Loews Hotels' customers and encourages them to spread the word about us. Again, reflect on your own experiences. If you've ever seen a favorable news story about a company you've personally patronized, the chances are good that the coverage made you feel a little "special" or "in the know," prompting you to talk about the company with other people. That happens for us—a lot.

Media coverage is like a pebble tossed into a pond: It generates ever-spreading concentric circles of buzz, fed by the reactions of thousands or millions of individuals. In time, the message reaches even the furthest corners of the marketplace.

In search of new opportunities to create buzz about Loews, Charlotte St. Martin and the Loews Hotels' marketing team conduct weekly brainstorming sessions. These meetings may run an hour or two, or even longer; once every four months, she holds an all-day planning session. Charlotte uses these meetings to study each of our service programs and special offers, asking questions like, *How could we do this better? Is this program still relevant? If so, how can we improve it? What's the next phase?* The brainstorming meetings provide a forum for constantly reexamining what Loews Hotels stands for and what new trends in travel, hospitality, and customer needs may be emerging. These are exciting, high-energy gatherings that I try to attend whenever I can—I have a lot of fun and learn a lot.

By tapping into current happenings on the cultural scene, we stay at the cutting edge of what our guests are interested in and keep the buzz about Loews Hotels lively. For example, during the fall of 2003, a new word entered the English language: *metrosexual.* Actually invented as early as 1994 by British writer Mark Simpson, the term refers to a straight urban male who is deeply interested in fashion, fitness, pop culture, personal appearance, upscale dining, home decorating, and other topics traditionally disdained by "macho men."

We quickly latched onto the phenomenon. Within weeks, Loews Hotels had launched a special *Metro Man* promotion. The basic package is a luxurious 24-hour "transformation" that includes a two-hour tasting meal, lessons on etiquette and wine, a manicure or pedicure, a haircut and shave, and a consultation with a personal shopper. The deluxe two-night version throws in a waxing, a facial, a dental bleaching, and more. We market the package as a gift item for women to buy for the less-than-stylish man in their life, using the headline, "You love him just the way he is . . . and just the way he'll be after a Loews Metro Man package."

The Metro Man promotion is typical Loews Hotels: unique, contemporary, and fun. And the publicity has been priceless. Loews Hotels and the Metro Man story have been covered by the *Today Show,* ABC Local News, BBC International, and newspapers ranging from *USA Today* to the *London Telegraph.* By getting people everywhere talking about Loews Hotels, we've given our customers/partners yet another reason to visit our properties. (Now in the works are two new promotions: Healthy Kids, which will offer an array of tasty foods and fun activities to help kids stay fit when they travel, and a partnership that will allow us to feature meals tailored for the South Beach Diet on our restaurant and room service menus.)

THE SECOND ASPECT OF PARTNERING WITH CUSTOMERS IS LEARNING TO focus on the total customer experience, viewed not from the company's perspective but from that of the customer.

For me, the customer experience should be central to the definition of our company's brand identity. The key questions are: *When a guest chooses Loews Hotels, what kind of experience should she expect? What's the meaning of the Loews Hotels' name?* If the answers to these questions are unclear or confusing, it means that the nature of the customer experience is also inconsistent. That's not a formula for a satisfying customer partnership.

Of course, companies in every industry face the same challenge. The winners are those that define a positive customer experience and make that experience a consistent part of their brand identity.

As an example, consider the investment firm of Charles Schwab. The services Schwab offers to its discount brokerage customers are fundamentally similar to those offered by the competition: execution of trades, periodic account statements, telephone and online service, and the like. What sets Schwab apart is the consistency with which it works on enhancing and improving the overall customer experience, looking for the "wow!" zone in which customer expectations are not only met but exceeded.

The effort includes some seemingly small things, for example, reducing the average time it takes for a customer's phone call to be answered from 45 seconds to under 20 seconds. It also includes major initiatives, such as Schwab's ongoing effort to streamline the task of comparing, choosing, and investing in mutual funds by providing ever-clearer, more-comprehensive, and more-sophisticated forms of online research data to customers.

The combined impact of these efforts makes the overall experience of investing with Schwab easier, less irritating, and more profitable than with many of Schwab's competitors. As a result, the Schwab brand name has taken on a special meaning for millions of investors: Many think of it as the brokerage firm that treats its customers as partners.

When I became CEO of the Loews Hotels' chain in 1989, one of the first issues we needed to address was our own brand identity and the nature of the customer experience it stood for. At the time, this identity and that experience were both ambiguous and inconsistent. The properties we owned and managed were so diverse that it was difficult even for me to articulate what they had in common. We had five-star hotels, two-star hotels, and everything in between. In New York City alone, we owned the busy three-star Summit Hotel on Lexington Avenue and the elegant Regency on Park Avenue, while across town we were operating a Howard Johnson and a Days Inn. What did it all add up to? It was hard to say.

To address the problem, we had to start by defining the niche we wanted to occupy. Given our size, it made little sense for us to try to compete at the mass-market end of the hospitality business. Chains like Days Inn and Courtyard by Marriott capture customers by operating reliable, standardized properties in hundreds of locations; they're the McDonald's of the hotel business. I couldn't see transforming Loews into a chain of that kind.

Instead, we focused on the more selective, more lucrative, and faster growing upper end of the business—specifically, the four-star luxury niche. The difference between a four-star hotel and a five-star hotel is rather subtle. Both attract the top 3 percent of travelers, and at a glance, it might be hard to distinguish one of our four-star properties from a five-star resort by Ritz-Carlton or Four Seasons. The distinction is based on dozens of small differences in service and amenities, many of which few customers care about. But there's a big financial difference. Five-star service requires up to a third more employees, which forces room rates to be significantly higher. As a result, while both four-star and five-star hotels earn strong profits in flush economic times, five-star chains tend to suffer more severely when recessions hit. Given the traditional fiscal conservatism of Loews Corporation, we decided that the four-star niche was right for us, and that decision has paid off over the years.

The transition from a loosely linked assortment of properties to a true brand of four-star hotels took several years. Of course, it required that we divest ourselves of properties that didn't fit our desired profile; in New York, for example, Howard Johnson, the Days Inn, and the Summit are now all owned by other companies, while the four-star Regency retains its status as our flagship New York hotel.

It wasn't enough to simply own a number of four-star hotels. To turn Loews Hotels into a truly national brand, we also had to expand into new locations. During the 1980s and 1990s, we added hotels in Chicago, Philadelphia, Miami, Orlando, Tucson, Santa Monica, and several other locations in the West. Today we have hotels in most of the major cities and regions of the United States. We still have some geographic holes we'd love to fill—I'd especially like to have Loews Hotels in San Francisco and Hawaii—but we are a national chain.

So far, so good. But defining a consistent experience for our customers/partners also requires articulating a common personality for all our properties. This isn't an easy task.

All Loews Hotels offer a similar level of service and a shared array of branded programs (like Home Sweet Loews). They also adhere to a common set of graphics standards, which define a consistent style and appearance for certain printed materials—room service menus, guest service directories, and the like. But unlike some other hotel chains, our properties haven't been built to fit a common architectural design. Our chain includes luxurious beach resorts (like our places in Santa Monica and Miami Beach), elegant urban *pieds à terre* (like New York's Regency, the Loews Hotel Vogue in Montreal, and the Jefferson in Washington, DC), and themed hotels (like the three hotels we operate on the grounds of Universal Orlando and our House of Blues Hotel in Chicago). How do we define and explain what all these properties have in common?

Our approach has been a slightly paradoxical one: What ties all the Loews Hotels together is their very *uniqueness.* Rather than being uniform in design, every Loews Hotel is deliberately planned as a reflection of its locale. We plant our properties in the heart of their cities or areas, as close as possible to the leading attractions that lure travelers in the first place, or in locations that are highly desirable in their own right (like the Coronado Peninsula near San Diego). Then we design the guest experience to bring a little of the excitement of the locale into the hotel itself, through everything from the decor in the guest rooms to the items on the room service menu.

Our modest advertising program is designed to support this approach. For the past five years, we've worked with Ziccardi Partners Frierson Mee, a highly respected advertising agency with special expertise in fashion, media, and entertainment, as well as travel and tourism. For the corporate meeting market, Ziccardi helped us create the message, "Meet *with* a city, not just in it." The theme is carried through in ads for each property. Thus, we urge meeting planners to "Meet Philadelphia at Loews Philadelphia Hotel," and our ad stresses both the proximity of our hotel to all the greatest sights in the city and the status of the property itself as a beloved city landmark. Our promotions for the Coronado Bay Resort emphasize its location within 15 minutes of downtown San Diego as well as its placement on a private peninsula surrounded by the Pacific Ocean, while the Loews Miami Beach is presented as being both three blocks from the city's great convention center and a stylish centerpiece of the historic Art Deco district.

This unusual branding strategy—commonality through uniqueness—makes design particularly important to us. I personally enjoy focusing on this challenge. The esthetic element is a powerful aspect of

---

TISCH'S TIPS

What role does esthetics play in the life of your organization? Do the various design elements in your organization, from your logo and your advertising to the architecture of your offices, send a message that is consistent with your brand identity? If you haven't done a *design audit* of your organization, you should. Spend time examining all the esthetic components of your organization and evaluating how they help or hinder your quest for a strong, appealing, and consistent identity. If customers become confused about what you stand for, creating and maintaining your partnership with them will be needlessly complicated.

the guest experience, and one that helps Loews Hotels stand apart from the competition.

As I've already mentioned, one of my first jobs was in television. I learned to be a cameraman and editor while working at WBZ television in Boston. I started there in 1975 during my senior year at Tufts University, then stayed on after graduation in June 1976. It was there that I developed an eye for image making and stage setting that I've relied on ever since.

Producer Barry Rosenthal was my mentor at WBZ, and he taught me a great deal. Over three to four months, Barry taught me to shoot and edit film (in those days before videotape, we used 16-millimeter film), how to light a scene, how to edit and incorporate audio, and all the other elements of creating a television experience. I was given an opprtunity to do nearly everything. By April 1976, I was producing my own segments for *Action4*, a public affairs program that aired on WBZ every Sunday evening and was a kind of local version of *60 Minutes*. Eventually, I did kids' programs, public affairs programs, and sports shows, including the pregame show for the New England Patriots football broadcasts. I was nominated for two local Emmys for videotape editing and co-production during my three years at WBZ.

My last big show in August 1979 was a program about a new craze that was sweeping the country—jogging. Joel Douglas was the producer of the show, and his brother, an actor, served as the host. You may have heard of him: Michael Douglas. At the time, he was best known as one of the stars of the TV detective show *The Streets of San Francisco*. Only later did he become a motion picture star. We're still friends (and yes, Catherine Zeta-Jones is every bit as gorgeous in real life).

In retrospect, my years at WBZ were invaluable training for the future hotelier. In essence, the job of the TV producer is to take thousands of images, choose and select from among them, and bring them together into a story that will vividly convey an experience, an emotion, or an idea. In pursuit of this goal, we sometimes had to spend hours (often working until two or three in the morning) on a single edit—a simple cut from one image to the next that might seem unimportant in itself but could have a profound impact on the flow, emphasis, and logic of the story.

Today, I think of what I do at Loews Hotels as "editing" the guest experience. That experience is affected by architecture, interior design, staff uniforms, signs and other displays inside and outside the guest rooms, the attitude and efficiency of employees, restaurant menus, amenities offered, the relationship of the property to the surrounding neighborhood, and dozens of other factors. If Loews Hotels provides a rewarding and enjoyable experience, the guest will come back—and eventually, we hope, become a true partner, who seeks out the nearest Loews' property whenever she travels.

Of course, transplanting this sensibility from TV to hospitality took some experience and self-training. I've taught myself how to read blueprints (I sometimes describe myself as a frustrated architect), to understand how mechanical systems work, and to recognize quality in fabrics and furniture. To put the esthetics of innkeeping into a business context, I learned the intricacies of hotel finance and management both from my dad and my Uncle Larry, as well as from one of my hotel industry mentors, the late Bob Hausman. My predecessor as president of Loews Hotels, Bob taught me the financial basics of running a hotel company and how to read a balance sheet.

With the help of a number of great designers, architects, and builders, we've been able to make a unique esthetic sensibility into a distinguishing feature of the Loews Hotels chain.

Loews Hotels isn't the only business that has made a special esthetic sensibility into a special selling point. We're not even the only hotel chain to do so. The boutique hotel movement, founded by Bill Kimpton, has inspired a number of hoteliers to make esthetics a key element of their appeal. I especially admire the work of Ian Schrager, whose hotels constitute a textbook of edgy, provocative design. The same goes for André Balazs, who designed the elegant Mercer Hotel (New York) and the Standard Hotels (New York and Los Angeles). All of these creative leaders developed stylistic concepts that were unique and were at the core of their hotels' success.

Then there's Barry Sternlicht, Chairman and CEO of Starwood Hotels & Resorts. In creating the W Hotels, Sternlicht in effect took the boutique formula and made it the basis for a chain of properties. In January 2004, he extended the brand further by buying the Bliss spa chain from LVMH Moet Hennessy Louis Vuitton; within a year, the company expects to begin opening Bliss spas designed specifically to complement W Hotels. Barry is another highly successful business person whose creative concepts I greatly admire.

In other industries, the brilliant fashion designer Tom Ford almost single-handedly put Gucci back on the map from 1994 to 2003 with his sexy, sensual creations, while Apple (in technology) and Target (in retailing) also use advanced design to separate themselves from a host of competitors.

No one would compare me to a Tom Ford in terms of artistic talent. But I do have strong tastes and preferences that I rely on in shaping the overall look of Loews Hotels. My taste is reflected in the classic modernist credo (usually attributed to architect Mies van der Rohe) of "less is more." I don't like surfaces to be too shiny or too new-looking; for example, I will sometimes ask to have brand-new gilt picture frames "roughened" up a bit, giving them an older patina that enhances the effect of a room.

Beyond these kinds of basic preferences, I don't have a thoroughly worked-out esthetic philosophy. I try to keep on top of trends in popular culture, track the latest innovations from our competitors in the hospitality business, and look for great design ideas wherever they may surface. When it's necessary, I bend my own sensibilities in deference to practicality or to demonstrable client preferences. But because my tastes are fairly mainstream, the designs I favor usually seem to work for our guests as well.

The Regency Hotel, our flagship New York property, is a prime example of our approach to the customer partnership. The concepts of building a business around customer needs and of bringing the unique character of the city into the heart of the guest experience are epitomized in the *Power Breakfasts* for which the Regency is renowned.

The Power Breakfast idea got its start in the 1970s, when New York was facing a serious financial crisis. My dad coined the phrase when he gathered with many of the city's movers and shakers—leaders of industry, finance, government, labor, and media—in the dining room at the Regency for early morning meetings at which solutions to the crisis were hammered out. The expression stuck, and soon the Regency became New York's favorite spot to see and be seen at breakfast time.

As a result, our maitre d' became a local celebrity and one of the most powerful people in New York—at least between the hours of 7 and 10 A.M. We refined the art of seating CEOs, politicos, and movie moguls to a science, keeping rivals and enemies at opposite ends of the room. Later, we played with the idea by hosting early morning Monopoly tournaments for the benefit of charity, at which the competitors were many of New York's most famous power brokers (some of whom could easily have played the game with genuine cash and real property deeds).

We'd love for every Loews Hotel to be as vibrant a part of the local community as the Regency is in New York—and we're working to accomplish just that.

Today, whenever I visit one of our properties, I study its esthetics in search of ways we can enhance the guest experience. Last fall, I traveled with several of our executives to visit a property we'd been managing for some time that was about to become part of the Loews Hotels' chain. After the visit, I sent an e-mail memo with my comments to the members of our executive team. My co-author on this book, Karl Weber, suggested I share it with you. Here it is (in slightly edited form):

Dear Colleagues,

Please note some of my observations from our trip to the hotel this week.

1. In general, I really like the hotel. But I think we agree the property is a bit stiff and formal. That shows up in many areas . . . interior design, graphics, menu items, and food. We have to find ways to make it a bit more fun and give it a little bit of soul. ["Soul" is an important word in my vocabulary. As Billy Joel sings in one of my favorite songs of his, "It's all about soul."]

2. The lobby seems too matchy/matchy, with every seating area being very formal and symmetrical. It might be fun to mix things up a little bit and see how it looks. Also, the lights could be dimmed at night, and a lot could be done with candles and accessories to warm

it up. It is very formal. Additionally, I think it is a little strange how the piano just sits on the marble floor in the center by itself. It looks so lonely. Maybe we should add a great rug underneath the piano and put some casual seating around it. Finally, the lobby and lobby bar area need some music.

3. As I mentioned, I think the graphics in the rooms, like the turn-down breakfast menu and the signs around the hotel promoting the outlets, need attention. Also, there are no elevator signs promoting the outlets or saying where anything is.

4. The room I stayed in needs a portable phone so you can move around the room as you talk. There is a desk phone, but then you cannot watch TV while using it. So I bet that portable phones in the suites would be welcome. Also, there should be some kind of night light in the bathroom, as there is only one switch that controls every light in the area. It is very dark in there.

5. The big suites are a little noisy with the elevators adjacent. During the upcoming renovation process, we have to make sure that they are made quieter.

6. Obviously, we have to do some serious space planning as it relates to the addition of a spa/fitness area. Also, the bar space on the mez-zanine level seems to be a wasted area. Is there more that we could do there?

7. The food at dinner last night was excellent. At lunch, maybe we could also offer some bread sticks or flat bread in the basket.

8. My welcome gift consisted of a nice bottle of Evian, some fancy chocolates, and a small fruit plate. While walking through the sweet shop off the lobby, I noticed they were selling all these Florida-style cool candies and toys. Maybe some could be incorporated into the amenities to make them more fun and creative.

If you have any questions, please let me know.

As you can see, I am constantly observing and analyzing my own reactions as a hotel guest, as well as dreaming up ideas about how the experience might be improved. If you think this seems like fun, you're right. I spend a night or two living like all our other guests and get to speak on their behalf, knowing that my suggestions have a pretty good chance of getting implemented. The opportunity to contribute ideas

---

TISCH'S TIPS

How often do you experience your organization the same way a customer does? This should be part of every leader's routine. Visit your organization's web site, call the help desk, visit a retail store where your products are sold, or ask for service at a typical outlet. You may be amazed to learn what a typical customer experiences (in ways both good and bad), and you'll certainly discover ways your organization can improve its operations in the future.

---

like this is one of the great perks of my job—as well as one of my crucial responsibilities.

It may seem idiosyncratic for the CEO of a company to focus so heavily on esthetics. But as we've seen, a hospitality firm that seeks a true partnership with its customers must hone the guest experience until it is as powerfully appealing as possible. And at Loews Hotels, we view our warm and unpretentious style as one of our biggest differentiating factors—our unique way of enhancing the guest experience to make it unforgettable and rewarding.

THE THIRD ELEMENT OF OUR PARTNERSHIP STRATEGY IS LINKING WITH customer communities. It's a strategy that some of today's most successful companies have used to powerful effect.

Consider, for example, how Ben & Jerry's business was built through an expanding partnership between the company and a close-knit community of ice cream lovers who shared a range of interests, values, and concerns, ranging from environmentalism to a love for the music of the Grateful Dead. These people buy the company's products; they also contribute in ways most company's customers don't. For example, the idea of naming an ice cream flavor "Cherry Garcia" in honor of the Dead's lead guitarist came directly, via postcard, from a member of the Ben & Jerry's customer community: "You know it will sell because Dead paraphernalia *always* sells. We are talking good business sense here, plus it will be a real hoot for the fans." It's the kind of quirky, fun, and highly profitable idea that companies get when they are really close to the people they serve.

Similarly, the remarkable business renaissance of the Harley Davidson motorcycle company has been driven largely by the firm's active partnership with its loyal—some would say fanatical—customer community, centered around the worldwide Harley Owners Group (HOG). Over 800,000 HOG members lavish thousands on personalizing their machines, buy loads of accessories, and gather for rallies and conventions at which they celebrate the Harley lifestyle.

Another recent example is the emergence of NASCAR auto racing fans as a powerful force in marketing, lifestyles, and even politics. Seventy-five million people call themselves NASCAR fans; 36 million attended races last year. Contrary to stereotypes, the average NASCAR follower is more affluent than the typical American and does *not* live in the Southeast; over 40 percent of fans are female. "NASCAR is a way of life. It's a lifestyle," says NASCAR president Mike Helton. "It becomes a lifestyle because the fans are very loyal to whoever their favorite driver and team are. They're very loyal to the sponsors of the cars. They live it week in and week out. They can't get enough." As a result, companies from Disney to Anheuser-Busch are sponsoring auto racing events, hoping some of the "NASCAR after-glow" will rub off on them, and politicians from George W. Bush to Howard Dean have targeted "NASCAR dads" as a crucial voting bloc.

Loews Hotels can't boast an equally devoted clan of followers—at least, not yet. But we spend lot of time studying, communicating with, and working to serve our own customer communities as well as defined subgroups within them. Treating them as partners helps nurture their loyalty and enhances the success of the firm immeasurably.

In recent years, information technology (IT) has become hugely important in our industry. It plays a big role in helping us analyze and understand the customer communities we serve. After all, any true partnership requires that you know a lot about your partners and what they need and want.

Our methods of tracking and analyzing customers include our guest loyalty program (*Loews First*), our database of other guests, and our group customer management systems. Our goal is to develop and maintain detailed histories of our guests' interactions with us, their spending patterns, and the kinds of services and amenities they value. What makes people stay at a Loews Hotel? Which properties do they visit, and why? Will the same people who visit the Vogue in Montreal be likely to visit the Jefferson in Washington—or are they more likely to show up at the Vanderbilt in Nashville? Which special offers that are popular at the Regency might be appropriate for the Ventana Canyon property?

Some of the things we've learned about our guests from these studies are counterintuitive. For example, in terms of customer base, the hotel in our chain that most closely resembles the Regency is the Santa Monica Beach Hotel. The two properties may seem like an odd couple, since the former stands on New York's regal Park Avenue, while the latter overlooks the Pacific Ocean. Yet, both hotels attract many of the same kind of customers—writers, artists, movie makers, musicians, athletes, and politicians. We work to tailor our offerings to accommodate their needs in similar ways in both properties.

To a lesser degree, we've found a similar convergence among all the Loews Hotels' properties. As I've stressed, every hotel in our chain has its own personality. Yet, they all share a common spirit. A traveler who enjoys the service, amenities, comfort, value, and style provided at one Loews Hotel is likely to enjoy the same offerings at another Loews Hotel. It's another reason why converting one-time guests at a particular property into partners who think of the entire Loews chain as "their" home away from home is crucial to our marketing efforts. One of the key numbers we look at is the measurement of "guest intention to return." Our factor is in the 90s, which is very high for the industry.

In every true partnership, communication must be a two-way street. Like all smart marketers, we work hard at listening to the real-life concerns of our customer communities as expressed through letters and e-mails, surveys, ratings cards, and focus groups. In fact, focus group discussions were central to our development of Loews Loves Kids, Generation G, and other parts of the Home Sweet Loews package.

During 2003, we worked with *Seventeen* magazine to survey the attitudes, interests, and needs of young people, and used their insights to shape our T Loews program for teenagers. We are in the midst of similar forums for business travelers in key Loews Hotels' cities, which will help us create still other programs designed to respond to the needs of that subset of customers/partners.

In hospitality, individual guests (often called *transient guests*) aren't the only important customer community. Another is travel agents, who have been a beleaguered group in recent years thanks to competitive pressure from online travel companies like Expedia. Recognizing their special needs, Loews Hotels has taken steps to strengthen our partnership with travel agents, not only increasing their commissions on Loews Hotels' bookings but also processing payments more quickly, improving the competitive rates we offer through agents, and offering other incentives to bolster their business and encourage them to think of Loews Hotels first.

Still another important customer group is meeting planners—professionals who work for corporations, associations, government agencies, and other groups that conduct meetings and conventions that attract hundreds or even thousands of travelers. Meeting planners generate an enormous amount of business for our industry and for Loews Hotels in particular, and they constitute a customer community we work hard to partner with.

Meeting planners today face special problems. At most associations, meetings account for 40 to 60 percent of annual revenues. Thus, encouraging high attendance at meetings is very important for the success and even the survival of the association.

But for years, attendance rates have been falling. There are many reasons. People are feeling increasingly busy and stressed at their jobs. More and more families have two working parents, making it harder for either or both to travel. And since September 11, the litany of woes that has affected all travel has influenced meeting attendance similarly. As a result, over the past few years, the life of the meeting planner has become especially difficult.

In response, Loews Hotels partnered with the planners, asking them how we could help. Together we developed our *Family Matters*

program. It's a special incentive-laden program designed to encourage
families to travel to meetings. Family Matters offers credits for airline
tickets, room upgrades, special discounts for a second room, and fun
amenities like a bottle of wine (to welcome a spouse) or cookies and
milk (for the kids). Thanks to this program, many association members
are bringing their spouses and kids along to the meeting, then tacking
on an extra day, or two, or three, for a mini-vacation at reduced cost,
transforming a time of separation into a time of togetherness.

The shared benefits are apparent. The association members get
more family time while maintaining an active interest in their organization; the meeting planners look good in the eyes of their bosses,
since meeting attendance is increased; and, of course, Loews Hotels
gets extra business—all signs of an effective partnership at work.

IN A PREVIOUS CHAPTER, I CONTRASTED "THE BUSINESS OF HOTELS"
with "the hotel business." The rule for success in the hotel business is a
simple one: If you treat your customers as partners, providing them
with the kind of experience they most desire, they will return.

We like to think that the difference between Loews and some of
our competitors is that we have not forgotten what the hotel business

is really about. Like other businesses, we care about financial results. But we achieve those results through single-minded focus on the basics. The numbers are merely tools. The heart of our business remains the partnership with customers, a connection we strive to nurture every day.

David Neeleman

JetBlue Airways is CEO David Neeleman's third successful aviation business. In 1984, he co-founded Morris Air, a low-fare airline that implemented the industry's first electronic ticketing system. After selling Morris Air and spending a brief period with Southwest Airlines, Neeleman established Open Skies, "the world's simplest airline reservation system," which he sold to Hewlett-Packard in 1999.

That same year, JetBlue Airlines was established. Its mission: to bring high-quality, low-fare service to one of the nation's largest aviation markets—New York City. The upstart carrier now serves 20 cities across the country with a fleet of 57 brand-new Airbus A320 aircraft. Neeleman has been named one of the Top Ten Entrepreneurs of 2000 by *BusinessWeek* magazine, a travel industry innovator by *Time*, and one of the most influential business travel executives by *Business Travel News*.

When we caught up with David recently (December 2003), we asked him what sets JetBlue apart from its competitors.

"Unlike most airlines," David said, "We're not selling transportation. Transportation is a commodity business—something you put up with it. We are selling an experience. We want people to look forward to the journey. To make this happen, we take care of people from start to finish. The leather seats in our planes, the enhanced legroom, the personal TVs—these bring air travel a degree of glamour that makes people want to travel more often. The result

(Continued)

of glamour that makes people want to travel more often. The result is an experience people talk about with their friends. The word of mouth factor is huge in our growth—in fact, 60 percent of our customers come through word of mouth."

JetBlue prides itself on the quality of its service. As David explained, this is based on some small things—and some big ones. "One aspect of our partnership with customers is simple, honest communication. We treat people as if they have a right to know what's happening. When they call us for updates on schedules or weather, we don't shunt them onto recordings. We give them a live person to answer their questions. This requires adequate staffing, a constantly updated web site, and above all, a willingness to tell people the truth.

"We also take responsibility when things go wrong, even when they're out of our control. Recently, a JetBlue plane on its way to New Orleans collided with a bird. The flight had to turn around, delaying travelers by an hour or so. The accident was no one's fault—an act of God. But we apologized and gave everyone on the flight a $25 coupon they could apply to their next trip. Last Christmas Eve, in the wake of a snowstorm at JFK [John F. Kennedy International] Airport in New York, runway clearing problems caused delays of several hours. Later, we gave over two million dollars in credits to customers. Again, we didn't have to do this. But it's the right way to treat people. And it benefits us in the long run by turning travelers into repeat customers."

As anyone in a service business knows, building a reputation for quality service isn't easy. It takes a highly dedicated and motivated corps of employees. How does JetBlue nurture its employee partnerships? Neeleman commented, "I try to set a good example. I'm on flights at least once a week, serving customers and helping the flight attendants. I talk to customers a lot. We also do confidential surveys of our employees to make sure they are feeling well treated and respected. The results are important to us. In one recent survey, 94 percent of our employees said they hope to

(Continued)

be with JetBlue five years from now. That kind of loyalty is very gratifying.

"Of course, you don't earn loyalty unless you treat employees well. Here, too, the concept of partnership is crucial. We have excellent profit sharing and stock purchase plans. Statistics show that, in most companies, the top five executives get 75 percent of the employee stock options. At JetBlue, it's reversed: 85 percent of the options go to people below the officer level.

"I also try to set an example by the way I'm personally rewarded. I receive the lowest compensation of any CEO in the industry—a salary of $200,000 plus a $100,000 bonus. And I donate $200,000 of the total to the Jet Blue Crisis Fund, which helps crew members who have suffered a catastrophic life event—a family illness, a fire that destroys their home."

Even for an unconventional CEO like David Neeleman, that level of compensation seems startlingly low, and we said as much. "Oh, don't worry about me," he laughed. "I own 8 percent of the company. That's why I don't need stock options or a sky-high salary."

JetBlue's partnership with employees involves more than just a generous compensation package. "We've never resorted to employee layoffs or furloughs," Neeleman noted. "Of course, it helps that we are a growing company, continually adding flights and planes. We grew right through the September 11 crisis and the war in Iraq. As long as we keep growing, we should be able to avoid layoffs. 'Bigger and better' is our battle cry."

We wondered how JetBlue manages to combine three things that might seem, at a glance, contradictory: excellent customer service, highly competitive compensation, and low fares. Neeleman explained, "We keep costs low by being unusually productive. For example, the FAA [Federal Aviation Administration] allows pilots to fly a maximum of 1,000 hours a year. But at most airlines, they fly only 500 or 600 hours. That's partly because of union restrictions, partly because those airlines fly many kinds of planes, which means that their pilots need constant retraining. We fly just one type of plane, although we have a second, smaller craft coming on-line soon. As a result, our pilots can safely fly 850 to 900 hours per year. The savings are huge."

So far, Neeleman's comments had focused on JetBlue's partnerships with customers and employees. What about the community? Neeleman told us, "We work hard at being good citizens of New York City. Our success at JFK Airport has had a huge impact on the community.

"New York is the largest travel market in the world, but it hadn't grown since 1985, mostly because airfares were too high. So we applied for slots at JFK, and after extensive lobbying we got a foothold at the airport with the help of people like Senator Charles Schumer. He was interested in bringing us to JFK partly because of his personal experiences with flying. Whenever he had to travel upstate—to Buffalo, for example—it cost him something like $800. He knew that was outrageous. Once we started operating out of JFK, we began offering flights to Buffalo for $79. Other airlines have been forced to match us. And those low fares create traffic. Instead of 500 people a day flying from New York City to Buffalo, traffic on the route is up to 2,000 a day. It's great for New York, and it's great for the city of Buffalo.

"Affordable air travel is essential to the growth of communities. JetBlue and the low fares we offer have already created six million new flyers per year. In time, we hope to raise that figure to twenty million. That means we're creating new business rather than just taking it from competitors. And in the process, we've made JFK into the largest airport in the New York City area.

"Our partnership with New York City is thriving. We're now planning to refurbish the old TWA terminal at JFK, rebuilding it around the famous Eero Saarinan 'wingspan' design. With some financial support from the city, we'll give new life to a landmark

(Continued)

building, create 7,000 jobs on top of the 3,000 we've already created, and ultimately have a two-billion-dollar impact on the local economy."

JetBlue's formula for success—controlling costs, providing excellent service, and developing strong partnerships with customers, employees, and communities—isn't rocket science. We asked David Neeleman for his theory as to why more airlines haven't followed in JetBlue's footsteps.

"It's not that difficult to raise the bar on service," Neeleman agreed, "but it takes creativity, hard work, and attention to detail. In other words, you need total dedication, and not many people are prepared to give that." That dedication is the simple difference that makes JetBlue—and David Neeleman—something special.

CHAPTER 6

Being a Good Neighbor

Hanging Up Your Tux and Rolling Up Your Sleeves

When he took time to help the man up the mountain, lo, he scaled it himself.

—Tibetan proverb

MANY BUSINESS PEOPLE TALK ABOUT "GIVING SOMETHING BACK TO THE community." Their motives are good, but I don't particularly like their choice of phrase. The implication, it seems to me, is that their businesses have drained money and resources from the community . . . and that later, out of the goodness of their hearts, they will return a fraction of that largesse to the people who provided it.

My idea of a partnership between a business and the community that supports it is very different. It's not about putting on a tuxedo a couple of times a year and writing a check for a worthy cause. It's about understanding and shouldering our responsibility to the community we belong to. Like every true partnership, it must bring clear benefits to both parties from day one. It must be built on shared interests, goals, and obligations, and reflect the pooling of money, time, effort, and other resources in pursuit of common objectives. When a business partners with the community, it means a shared commitment to the long-term social and economic health of the area and its people . . . which, in turn, provides the only kind of environment in which business can really expect to thrive.

In this regard, I disagree with some champions of laissez-faire capitalism who contend that making profits is the *only* responsibility of a business. This is a point of view that was eloquently summarized by the great theorist of free markets, Nobel-prize-winning economist Milton Friedman in his classic book *Capitalism and Freedom:*

> The view has been gaining widespread acceptance that corporate officials and labor leaders have a "social responsibility" that goes beyond serving the interest of their stockholders or their members. This view shows a fundamental misconception of the character and nature of a free economy. In such an economy, there is one and only one social responsibility of business—to use its resources and engage in activities designed to increase its profits so long as it stays within the rules of the game, which is to say, engages in open and free competition, without deception or fraud. . . . Few trends could so thoroughly undermine the very foundations of our free society as the acceptance by corporate officials of a social responsibility other than to make as much money for their stockholders as possible. (p. 133)

Friedman is a brilliant economist, but I can't accept his notion that businesses have no responsibility to the community other than profit making. Under American law, corporations are treated as "persons," with rights and obligations similar to those of flesh-and-blood individuals. They enjoy protections that are guaranteed by the society, such as free speech; in return, they must contribute to the welfare of society just as individuals must do—by paying taxes, for example. It seems to me a natural extension of this principle that companies should accept some responsibility for the economic and social health of their communities, just like individual citizens.

This can be a big commitment. But at Loews Hotels, we've found that doing business in accordance with this philosophy yields enormous benefits, not just for the communities we're part of but also for the people who work at Loews . . . and even for our bottom line.

We're not the only company to have made this discovery. In fact, scholars who study patterns of business success have found that companies that define their mission in broader terms than *merely* earning profits tend to out-perform comparable firms that lack such a vision.

In their best-selling book *Built to Last: Successful Habits of Visionary Companies,* James C. Collins and Jerry I. Porras call this insight "the Genius of the AND," making the point that great businesses pursue both profits *and* ideals, viewing these goals not as contradictory but as complementary.

As one example, Collins and Porras cite the great pharmaceutical company Merck, which (among other noteworthy acts of corporate generosity) donated millions of doses of their drug, Mectizan, to help prevent river blindness in nations of the Third World. (More about this remarkable story.) When asked to explain Merck's decision, the company's then-CEO, Roy Vagelos, made this revealing comment:

> When I first went to Japan fifteen years ago, I was told by Japanese business people that it was Merck that brought streptomycin to Japan after World War II, to eliminate tuberculosis which was eating up their society. We did that. We didn't make any money. But it's no accident that Merck is the largest American pharmaceutical company in Japan today. The long-term consequences of [such actions] are not always clear, but somehow I think they always pay off.

Vagelos is right: Merck's preeminent position in Japan, decades after the firm's act of generosity toward the people of that war-torn country, is no accident. When a company treats a community as a partner, it should come as no surprise when the people of that community respond with gratitude, warmth, appreciation, and support.

Is corporate generosity a guarantee of bottom-line success? No— there are no guarantees in business. But it's clear that making the community your partner is not just good citizenship—it's good business, too.

AT LOEWS HOTELS, WE'VE GATHERED ALL OF OUR COMMUNITY PARTNER-ing efforts under what we call the *Loews Good Neighbor Policy.* When the program was launched in 1991, it set a precedent as the most comprehensive community outreach program in the hospitality industry.

It works by using the resources that are intrinsic to a hotel's daily operations to help the communities where we operate.

There are certain Good Neighbor programs that every Loews
Hotel is required to carry out. These include donating excess food to
local food banks, shelters, and hunger relief programs; providing
meeting rooms at no cost to local not-for-profit organizations; donating used goods, such as linens and furniture, to local organizations and
shelters; and extensive recycling programs.

In addition, every hotel in our chain develops its own array of
unique outreach activities, tailored to the interests of the employees
and the needs of local people. These activities are coordinated by a
self-selected group of Loews Hotel workers who form what's called the
Good Neighbor Council. As with most Loews Hotel activities, we lean
toward decentralization—letting the local people make the key decisions within certain broad guidelines.

To illustrate, let's take a close look at how this philosophy works at
a specific Loews Hotel.

Allison Esquivel and Kurt Johnson are two members of the Good
Neighbor Council at the Loews Coronado Bay Resort in San Diego.
For Allison, a reservations manager, participating in the Good Neighbor Council is one of the things that makes working at Loews Hotels
special.

"I grew up in the hotel world," Allison explains. "My mom worked
in hotels. As a little girl, I would hang out with her, learning to wrap
silverware and set tables. When I grew up, I went to work at one of
Loews' larger competitors. The atmosphere there was very corporate—
you just did your work and went home. It's different at Loews. The
Good Neighbor Council and the support we get from Loews keeps me
excited every day." Allison joined the Council almost immediately after
coming to Loews a little over four years ago. She has been a member
ever since, serving for one year as its president.

Kurt Johnson, a front office manager, joined the Loews Coronado
Bay Resort in January 1992, about three months after the hotel opened.
The hotel's Good Neighbor Council was launched in 1993. Kurt recalls, "We heard that Loews wanted to have a good neighbor program,
and we wondered exactly what that meant. Then we discovered that it

was up to us to figure it out. We started out by asking a very basic question: What can we do around the neighborhood to help make this a better place to live?" Kurt has been involved in helping to shape the Good Neighbor Program in Coronado Bay ever since.

One of the first causes the council chose to focus on was the beach. That's not surprising. The Coronado Bay peninsula where the Loews Hotel is located is one of the most lovely natural spots for miles around; many of the people who live in the community were originally drawn by its beauty. The Good Neighbor Council decided to tackle the job of cleaning up Silver Strand State Beach, an activity that has now evolved into an annual community event.

One Saturday in September, about 40 volunteer employees, many with spouses and kids in tow, spend half a day filling trash bags with refuse gathered from the sands and shoreline. Local folks from the nearby residential community of Coronado Cays also take part, as does a group called I Love a Clean San Diego. Soft drinks and snacks to fuel the volunteers' efforts are provided by the Loews Hotel kitchen.

Loews supports community spruce-up programs more than just once a year. The Coronado Bay Good Neighbor Council also makes donations to the fund-raising auctions held by I Love a Clean San Diego, and many of the hotel's employees volunteer for specific clean-up projects throughout the year.

Momma's Kitchen is a second local cause that gets major support from Loews. It's an outreach program in downtown San Diego that provides meals for homebound AIDS patients. The Good Neighbor Program donates food and volunteers labor, including one day a year (usually during Thanksgiving season) when the entire effort is mounted by Loews' employees. The volunteers show up at the hotel's kitchen around 6:30 A.M. (many, as Kurt puts it, with severe cases of "bed hair") and set to work cooking a holiday-style meal. (Last year it was turkey with all the trimmings.) They transport the goodies to Momma's Kitchen downtown, pack the meals in individual containers, and load them into a van for delivery to homebound clients.

Another food-related activity is the annual Taste of the Nation event. Working with the local committee of Share Our Strength, a national hunger relief organization, Loews hosts a "grazing event" where

Tisch's Tips

What kinds of goods or services does your organization use—and perhaps discard or waste? Loews Hotels donates thousands of pounds of surplus food and other goods to charitable causes each year. Take some time to examine the supply chain within your own organization and identify places where occasional excesses are unavoidable. You may be able to help your community at little or no cost by arranging donations to worthy groups or individuals who may be desperate for items that otherwise would go unused.

guests can sample dishes prepared by many of the area's finest chefs. Hotel employees volunteer to clean up and set up, and the money raised goes to support Share Our Strength's local programs.

Still another Loews partnership involves a holiday event that has become a favorite San Diego tradition. One of the area's most prominent citizens is Audrey Geisel, the widow of Theodore Geisel—better known as the beloved children's book author, Dr. Seuss. In a gesture of civic generosity, Audrey Geisel gave Loews Coronado Bay the exclusive right to use the costumed character of the Cat in the Hat without fee, provided that annual holiday performances are open to the local

Tisch's Tips

Most organizations have a significant physical presence (a factory, an office, a retail store) in the communities where they do business, but not all are welcoming to local residents. Look for an opportunity to invite the community into your organization's local facility—for example, by hosting an open house, a holiday party, or a charitable benefit. You'll create good will, initiate friendships, and promote the sense that your organization is a partner to the community rather than an intrusive presence.

community at no charge. Now every December, the youngsters from the acting program at local Chula Vista High School invade Loews Coronado and perform "The Grinch Who Stole Christmas," with the Cat in the Hat as narrator, every night of the week before Christmas. Audrey Geisel often attends the first night's performance.

The show fills the hotel's lobby and its grand staircase, with dozens of Chula Vista students (and a few kids of Loews' employees) enacting the roles before an audience that includes hotel guests and many local families. Kurt Johnson's daughter still talks about the time she played the role of Cindy Who (from Whoville), a highlight of her young life.

GENE G. LAMKE, PROJECT DIRECTOR OF CAMP ABLE OF CORONADO, speaks fondly of the Loews Coronado Bay and its Good Neighbor Policy. Camp Able is a day camp for kids with all kinds of handicaps: emotional problems, physical problems, histories of abuse. The camp provides 60 to 70 kids with ocean-based activities that include swimming, sailing, and canoeing. Many of the youngsters just love wading or "going to the wild side"—their name for the side of the beach where the big waves roll in. Camp Able even has special beach wheelchairs that let kids who can't walk roll right down into the water and play independently.

A colleague of Gene's at San Diego State University came up with idea for the camp, and the state agreed to let them use Silver Strand State Beach in exchange for an annual fee of one dollar. Providing service costs Camp Able about $160 per week per client. State assistance covers around $100 of that cost. They raise the rest with a lot of help from their friends—especially Loews Hotels.

Art Bartlett, a local resident who founded the Century 21 real estate chain, became Camp Able's special angel. Bartlett went to Loews Coronado Bay with the idea of holding an annual gala to raise funds for the camp. "Loews helped us create the plans for the gala," Lamke says, "and they provide lots of volunteer help, in effect reducing the tab for running the event by half. We've been holding the gala for 10 years now, and it raises between $50 and $80 thousand for our kids annually."

This isn't all that Loews has done for Camp Able. The hotel provides special discounted room rates for kids and their families who come from as far away as Australia and Japan to participate in camp activities. One week, all the employees at the Coronado Bay decided to pool their spare change and donate it to the Camp—$275 in all. And in 2001, when Loews Hotels held its annual executive meeting in San Diego, Camp Able was the local organization chosen to receive the benefits of the volunteer workfest we traditionally hold during the meeting.

"We had about 70 people from Loews at our camp," Lamke recalls, "working from 8 in the morning until 2 P.M. Thanks to their help, we were able to upgrade our infrastructure in ways that wouldn't otherwise have been possible.

"We'd always wanted to install a ramp for easier access to the aquatic center for disabled kids who arrive by bus. The Loews people contacted a community partner to bring in cement and they framed out the ramp for us. Other teams of Loews executives built storage racks for the campers' belongings, installed permanent supports for our huge tent awning, and cleaned and refinished the bottoms of our boats. Still another group built us a new canoe rack. Now moving our four canoes from storage down to the water takes two people rather than eight."

"Camp Able serves kids from Southern California—and also from around the world. But the local community has really embraced us as their own. Nobody exemplifies that more fully than Loews Hotels."

TISCH'S TIPS

Does the ethos of community partnership extend to every level in your organization? It's important to encourage and support your front-line employees in their volunteer efforts and community outreach; it's equally important for your executive leadership to demonstrate its own commitment to the same kind of activities. Cash donations are fine, but hands-on work is even more meaningful, especially when it's provided by the people at the top of the company pyramid.

Perhaps the biggest single beneficiary of the good works emanating from Loews Coronado Bay is the San Diego chapter of the Multiple Sclerosis Society, which supports research to find a cure as well as helping current patients and their families. Alan Shaw is president and CEO of the local chapter, which has about 18 employees and a thousand volunteers.

"When I first got involved," Shaw recalls, "the chapter was holding 10 different fund-raising events every year. It was very inefficient. No one had ever analyzed the true costs of holding so many events in terms of staffers' time and salaries. We did that, and we realized we had just two events with real potential: our annual MS Walk and our MS Auction."

Shaw visited Loews Coronado Bay with his wife Linda and quickly realized that it would be a great place for the auction dinner. He also found that the hotel's leadership was very sympathetic to his organization. "Shannon Mulligan was a catering manager for the hotel then, and her mom had MS. Loews understood what our mission was. John Thacker, the hotel's general manager, decided that Loews should do more than just host the dinner—instead, it should become a real partner for the event." (Thacker has since become a regional vice president for Loews Hotels.)

"Over the years, our relationship with Loews has grown and expanded," Shaw says. "We get terrific assistance from the hotel, from great rates on the meals and accommodations to lots of volunteer help."

Today the annual MS Auction (usually held the Saturday before Thanksgiving) is San Diego's preeminent charity event. In 2002, it attracted about 750 attendees and raised over $450,000 for the society. It features both a live auction and six one-hour silent auction segments, with a total of about a thousand items for sale. There are great items to purchase in every price range, from an apple pie from the Julian Bakery to last year's top-end item—a Wimbledon tennis package including luxury accommodations, center court seats for the championship match, and passage on the QE2, which fetched around $30,000. Some guests arrive up to two hours before the official starting time, so they can position themselves to bid on the items of their dreams.

"There are some larger hotels in town," Shaw notes. "We could probably draw a few more people if we moved to a different venue. In each of the last three years, we filled every available space. But our relationship with Loews Coronado Bay means a lot more to us than a business deal."

THE LOEWS CORONADO BAY GOOD NEIGHBOR COUNCIL HAS A CORE membership of six employees (including Allison and Kurt) who plan the activities for the year, while many others become involved on specific projects as volunteer organizers and coordinators.

In practical terms, it's impossible for any one hotel to provide formal support to every worthy local charity. The Good Neighbor Council at Coronado Bay is working to remedy that problem through a new pilot program called the *Good Neighbors.* When a local charity requests a donation, they're invited to fill out a form explaining what they do and the kind of help they need. Then we invite our local managers to donate up to 40 hours of paid volunteer time to the charities of their choice. Multiply 40 hours by over 60 managers, and you can see that Loews provides up to 2,500 hours of volunteer labor to the community.

In a wonderful way, our Good Neighbor Policy—which was created to focus on our partnership with the community—has also become an integral part of our partnership with employees. For Allison Esquivel, it's one of the special perks she enjoys as a Loews' employee. "Whenever I interview prospective employees, I tell them about the Good Neighbor Council. I love it when I see their faces light up. As I tell them, for those who choose to participate, it makes Loews much more than a job—it's also a family."

Kurt Johnson offers a slightly different perspective. "One of the things that's fun about the Good Neighbor Council is the way it breaks down barriers between people in different departments. It's fun to work hand-in-hand on a project with someone from food and beverage, housekeeping, or some other department." He adds, "I love taking part in our Good Neighbor programs because they get me out of my little bubble. Some days, after handling 240 check-ins and 40 check-outs, I feel pretty frazzled. Thinking about one of our Good Neighbor activities helps remind me why are we here and what makes our company special."

One of the ways the Good Neighbor Policy benefits Loews Hotels is by helping us to attract and retain people like Allison and Kurt: generous, caring, energetic people who want to help others and have fun doing it—exactly the kinds of people we enjoy working with.

Being a good neighbor benefits Loews Hotels in other ways. We've found that being a responsible part of the communities in which we operate generates enormous goodwill. There's no doubt that individuals, businesses, and community groups that feel positively about Loews Hotels are more likely to bring us their business and to support us in other ways when we need their help.

A couple of years ago, Loews Coronado Bay faced an uphill climb when we developed a plan to expand our spa operations at the property. Like many communities, San Diego has strict zoning regulations that can make it difficult to build new facilities. We followed all the local rules, submitting detailed plans and paperwork to show that our spa wouldn't harm the environment or damage the quality of life of local residents. Still, there are always concerns that the necessary approvals might be delayed or even withheld altogether.

Our friendships in the area made an enormous difference when we appeared before the Coastal Commission, a local planning board. Alan Shaw of the Multiple Sclerosis Society explains his position this way: "We advocated for Loews Hotels on the spa issue because we knew the company was a quality organization, and the spa would be good for the community." In the end, a budding controversy practically evaporated because local opinion proved to be overwhelmingly favorable to Loews Hotels.

Don't get me wrong. I would never urge the leader of a business or any other organization to adopt a Good Neighbor Policy like ours in order to reap public relations benefits. People are smart; they can recognize when generous behavior is heartfelt and when it's an empty gesture designed to make you look good. You should treat the communities in which you operate as partners, not because it'll benefit your bottom line but simply because it's the appropriate way for a business leader to behave.

Nonetheless, it's comforting to know that being a good member of your community isn't a waste of time, energy, or resources. In the long run, operating in a spirit of true partnership is smart business.

Some companies have even made community partnering into an integral part of their business strategy. Take Tom's of Maine, the successful maker of natural toothpaste, deodorant, mouthwash, and other personal care products sold in health food stores, groceries, and pharmacies around the country. Since its founding by Tom and Kate Chappell in 1970, Tom's of Maine has built its reputation—and its bond with consumers—in large part through partnerships with not-for-profit organizations, finding ways to contribute to the broader community while also building their business.

Tom Chappell describes one striking example in his book *The Soul of a Business: Managing for Profit and the Common Good.* When WGBH, the Boston-based public TV station, approached Tom's of Maine in 1992 seeking a $400,000 grant to cosponsor *Earthkeeping,* an important series on the environment, the company was hesitant. Their budget for annual giving had already been allocated, and the amount sought would be a major commitment for a relatively small private company. Still, the project was compelling and an excellent fit for the values of Tom's of Maine's and its customers. The company leaders realized they could justify the cost of the project by making it the cornerstone of an innovative marketing program.

The plan they developed involved several components, including:

- A contest for which ordinary citizens submitted videos depicting local environmental projects, promoted through inserts in toothpaste cartons and outreach by grassroots environmental groups.
- A joint promotion for the TV series between Tom's of Maine and the CVS drugstore chain, including instore displays and a 200,000-piece mailing to CVS customers announcing the program and enclosing coupons for Tom's products, redeemable only at CVS.

In the end, these and other publicity tie-ins piggybacking on the TV series created the biggest sales explosion in the company's history up to that time. Chappell summarizes the lesson this way: "Tom's of Maine had achieved a landmark marketing coup with an idea that had not grown out of our advertising and promotion budget. It was simply a gift that dropped out of the sky because we were trying to serve the common good."

EVERY RESPONSIBLE BUSINESS SHOULD STRIVE FOR GOOD CORPORATE citizenship. But a hotel is special. Open 24 hours a day, seven days a week, a hotel is a very visible, integral part of the neighborhood—a landmark that attracts attention and gathers visitors from around the city and often around the world. A hotel is often the economic and emotional anchor of a community. And if the hotel isn't performing well financially, the owners can't just pull up stakes and move.

For all these reasons, it's incumbent on us to be especially responsive to the needs and challenges of the communities where we operate. Our futures are deeply intertwined with those of our neighborhoods. Our employees generally live and raise their families in those neighborhoods. We must do our part to make the communities great places to live, work, and visit. That's why every Loews Hotel has its list of unique Good Neighbor initiatives, created by local staff members and targeted to the needs of the particular community. Here's just a sampling:

- For over 15 years, Loews Vanderbilt Hotel in Nashville has sponsored an annual gingerbread house competition that has raised more than $300,000 for Dede Ward Mental Health Center and the Children's Ward of Metropolitan General Hospital. The hotel also feeds five thousand people each month through food donations to local hunger programs.
- Employees at Loews L'Enfant Plaza Hotel in Washington, DC, participate in the city's Komen National Race for the Cure to support breast cancer research. The hotel also hosts the "Bark Ball," a fundraiser for an animal rescue service.

- Loews Denver Hotel donates food each week to the Catholic Workers Soup Kitchen, co-sponsors a local benefit walk for people with AIDS, and hosts an annual Thanksgiving dinner for the Mount Saint Vincent Home for troubled youngsters.
- The three Loews Hotels at Universal Orlando host more than a hundred families from the Howard Phillips Center for Children and Families, including families from the local "Hug Me" program assisting kids with HIV and AIDS, for a day of fun at Universal's theme parks.
- Employees at the House of Blues Hotel, a Loews Hotel in Chicago, have refurbished nearby Jefferson Park, painting benches, creating murals, and landscaping the grounds. The hotel also sponsored a Halloween gala that raised almost $10,000 for the Children's Memorial Hospital Pediatric AIDS Unit.
- During a catastrophic ice storm, Loews Le Concorde in Quebec City, Canada, provided food and shelter for 275 stranded people for three days. As part of its ongoing efforts to support children's causes, the hotels offers free rooms to parents with sick children in cooperation with the organization Désires d'Enfants.
- Volunteers from Loews Philadelphia Hotel work with Head Start, helping kids one-on-one improve their readings skills and organizing donations of books and other supplies.

There's so much happening under the Good Neighbor umbrella around the Loews Hotels chain that we have trouble keeping track of it all. We're now working on developing a standard process that all our properties can use for tracking, quantifying, and coordinating Good Neighbor activities. Once this is in place, we'll know more about the overall impact of our programs.

Why is it important for us to record and measure our Good Neighbor activities? For the same reason we track revenues, occupancy rates, and profits. In business, you get what you measure and reward. We consider the Good Neighbor Policy one of the crucial mandates every manager in our chain must fulfill—in fact, the bonuses earned by members of each hotel's executive committee are based in part on the Good Neighbor activities at the hotel. The more thoroughly we track the Good Neighbor numbers, the better we'll be able to recognize and reward the hotels that perform the most community service. And we like the fact that the leaders and employees at our hotels enjoy competing with one another to produce the most impressive Good Neighbor results. It's a form of rivalry that benefits everyone.

The Good Neighbor Policy has been so effective that it was honored in 1996 with the President's Service Award from the Points of Light Foundation—the highest honor the president can give for corporate responsibility. The Good Neighbor Policy has also received a host of other awards from our colleagues in the travel industry, including the Odyssey Award for Hunger Relief from the Travel Industry Association of America, the *Travel & Leisure* Mark of Innovation Award, *Successful Meetings* magazine's Hospitality Industry Humanitarian Award, and the New York State Hospitality and Tourism Association's Gold Key Award for Community Service.

Loews Hotels isn't the only organization in travel and tourism that focuses on community service. Many other companies see the needs and respond admirably. The San Francisco Marriott, which opened on the very day of the October 17, 1989, earthquake, won kudos for providing food, shelter, and comfort to those from the neighborhood who needed it. The Hilton Waikoloa Village on Hawaii's Big Island boasts a thousand volunteer team members who raised over $100,000 last year for a range of community outreach organizations. Employees at the Sheraton New York Hotel and Towers participate in walkathons supporting research into women's cancer, juvenile diabetes, and AIDS.

TISCH'S TIPS

Does your organization have a program for tracking and measuring its community partnership efforts? If not, consider creating one. Monitoring and recording your activities sends an unmistakable message to your people: The organization is serious about its commitment to the community, and your work in this area will be noticed and recognized.

At Loews Hotels, we're proud to have helped create a climate that encourages such initiatives throughout our industry. The more widely the philosophy of corporate responsibility spreads, the stronger the partnerships between our communities and the world of business will become. The long-term result: A better world, both for us in business and for the people, the neighborhoods, the cities, and the nations we serve.

PORTRAIT IN PARTNERSHIP

President Jimmy Carter

In 1976, Jimmy Carter, a former governor of Georgia, startled the political world by winning the presidency of the United States, the first citizen from the "Deep South" to achieve this office since before the Civil War. Carter's term in office was marked by a number of accomplishments, including the Panama Canal Treaties, the SALT II treaty with the Soviet Union, the establishment of diplomatic relations with the People's Republic of China, and the Camp David Accords.

However, former President Carter is perhaps most admired for his work on behalf of peace, health, and human rights in his years since leaving office. As co-directors of The Carter Center in Atlanta, Georgia, Jimmy Carter and his wife, Rosalynn, have created a worldwide network of partnerships that have helped to relieve human suffering and advance the cause of freedom in countries from Africa and Asia to Latin America. In recognition of his work, Jimmy Carter was awarded the Nobel Prize for Peace in 2002.

For over 20 years, The Carter Center has brought together businesses, not-for-profit organizations, and government agencies in support of humanitarian efforts, divided into two broad categories: Health Programs and Peace Programs. One of the most remarkable examples of how the Center forges partnerships in pursuit of its goals is its much-admired health program focusing on the dread disease of onchocerciasis, commonly known as river blindness.

River blindness affects over 18 million people around the world, especially in Africa and Latin America. Tragically, 500,000 of those infected are blinded or visually impaired. The Carter Center is one of several organizations that have joined in an ambitious global effort to control the disease in Africa and to eliminate it completely in Latin America by 2007.

River blindness is spread through the bite of a small black fly that breeds on the banks of rapidly flowing rivers and streams. When the fly bites, it releases millions of microscopic worms, causing incessant itching and, when the worms enter the eyes, blindness.

Remarkably, a powerful medication called Ivermectin can treat river blindness through a single annual dose, which kills the microscopic infant worms, thereby halting the spread of the disease and the threat of blindness. Known by its trade name, Mectizan, the medication was developed by the pharmaceutical firm of Merck & Company to prevent heartworm in dogs and other animals. It was only by chance that a Merck research scientist discovered that Mectizan could save humans from the scourge of river blindness. Merck's then-CEO, Dr. Roy Vagelos, visited The Carter Center with this news and with a generous offer: If The Carter Center could develop a system for delivering the medication, Merck would provide the drugs to every affected village in the world—free of charge.

The Carter Center launched its River Blindness Program in 1996, working with a coalition of organizations that include the World Health Organization, the Lions Clubs International Foundation, and the World Bank. Through the program's field offices in countries from Guatemala to Uganda, over 50 million doses of Mectizan have so far been delivered. In 2003 alone, The Carter Center treated 9.3 million people. It has already been proven that

(Continued)

the disease can be completely eradicated in Latin America, and further efforts are underway to extend this blessing to all endemic nations.

Merck is only one example of many businesses that partner with The Carter Center. The Center's health programs draw support from companies that include Bristol-Myers Squibb, DuPont, Glaxo Smith Kline, Johnson & Johnson, Eli Lilly, Novartis, and Pfizer, while the peace programs have a list of partners that includes Coca-Cola, Reebok International, Rothschild North America, and Chick-Fil-A, Inc. In a recent example, when The Carter Center's China Village Elections Project needed high-tech equipment to help improve electoral practices and thereby support the spread of democracy in China, Dell Computers stepped up to the plate with a donation of 240 desktop computers.

Clearly, corporate partnerships have been a significant element in the continued success of The Carter Center. We asked former President Carter in February 2004 what he does to create and nurture such partnerships. In response, he emphasized the value of face-to-face communication. "Personal contact with top officials is crucial," he told us, "and the presentation must be clear and specific. I try to go to the international headquarters whenever possible to thank them and to give them full information about our personal work in the villages and huts where the medicines and other supplies are delivered."

Spreading the good word about the generosity of corporate partners also creates important incentives. "Donor companies must be recognized as much as possible," President Carter noted, "both for their own public relations and for the uplifting and inspiration of their own personnel, who need to understand the humanitarian benefits of their corporate contribution."

Meanwhile, the role of government provokes controversy. We sometimes hear complaints from American citizens about taxpayer moneys being spent on international aid rather than on problems here at home. The implication is that the federal government is devoting significant funds to humanitarian efforts overseas. When we asked President Carter about this perception, he was quick to challenge it. "The United States government does less than any other industrialized nation in providing humanitarian assistance," he pointed out. "This is true whether the sums are measured on a per capita basis or as a percentage of our gross national product. We donate about one-fourth as much as the average European country and one-fifteenth as much as the most generous Scandinavian governments."

The failure or inability of government to respond to global humanitarian crises makes public/private partnerships all the more important. Fortunately, many private organizations are responding generously. "The stinginess of government," President Carter noted, "is overcome to some degree by private contributions from U.S. foundations like Gates [the Bill and Melinda Gates Foundation] and from corporations like Merck, DuPont, and others."

Finally, we asked President Carter what private citizens can do to support initiatives like those The Carter Center has launched. "Citizens can contribute directly to active non-governmental organizations," he advised, "and perhaps encourage their political leaders to be more generous in funding efforts to support peace, freedom, democracy, the environment, and the alleviation of human suffering."

The efforts of Jimmy and Rosalynn Carter and the work of The Carter Center have helped to improve the lot of millions around the world. But there's much more work to be done. Partnerships like those fostered by the Center are only as strong as the commitment of the organizations and individual citizens that support them. As long as the human needs persist, people, companies, and nonprofit organizations around the world must continue to do their part.

CHAPTER 7

E Pluribus Plenty

When Competition Gives Way to Cooperation

A true measure of your worth includes all the benefits others have gained from your success.

—Cullen Hightower
American sales executive, trainer, and author (1923–   )

LOEWS HOTELS OCCUPIES AN INTERESTING NICHE IN THE ECOLOGY OF business. We're part of Loews Corporation, a holding company with almost $80 billion in assets, which provides us with a number of distinct advantages: access to a pool of investment capital; legal and other services beyond what we could afford on our own; the stellar reputation of our parent corporation in financial markets. Yet compared to some other hotel companies, we're on the small side, with just 20 properties in our chain. Thus, Loews Hotels is like a small, entrepreneurial firm inside the body of a giant corporation. Like other small companies, we *must* work through partnerships with other for-profit entities if we hope to compete with bigger organizations.

Businesses can partner with one another for mutual benefit in dozens of different ways, limited only by your imagination and by antitrust regulations that forbid companies to form combinations that constrain rather than strengthen free markets. At Loews Hotels, we've made extensive use of three kinds of business-to-business partnerships:

1. *Co-branding partnerships,* in which companies with different types of expertise join forces to create a more marketable product or service.
2. *Association partnerships,* in which competing companies unite to promote initiatives that will benefit the entire industry.
3. *Civic partnerships,* in which disparate companies from a particular city or region work together to promote the economic health of their community.

Let's begin with co-branding partnerships, which have proven to be a very effective tool for us in strengthening the appeal of Loews Hotels. Co-branding is a partnership technique that richly rewards your business creativity; in many cases, when two attractive and compatible brand names are linked, the customer offering that results is far more appealing than either company could have created alone. An example I've discussed in an earlier chapter is the creation of Feinstein's at the Regency, a New York supper club whose appeal is built on the fame of well-known singer Michael Feinstein.

Another example is our expanding partnership with the restaurateur and celebrity chef, Emeril Lagasse. Emeril has come a long way from his early days baking bread in a Portuguese shop in the little town of Fall River, Massachusetts. Today, he hosts two popular cooking shows on the Food Network, has authored eight books with a total of over 3.5 million copies in print, sells his own line of food products and cooking accessories, and is the chef-proprietor of nine restaurants. All of these businesses are operated out of Emeril's Homebase that includes a test kitchen and a store where Emeril products are for sale, the corporate headquarters in Emeril's adopted hometown of New Orleans.

Emeril's warm and exuberant personal style matches beautifully with the fun, casual image we've sought to build for Loews Hotels. So does his business philosophy. Emeril considers his restaurants part of the entertainment business, just as we do our hotels, and he's as deeply committed to training and empowering employees as we are. So a partnership between us seemed natural. It started with the opening of Emeril's Tchoup Chop at the Royal Pacific Resort at Universal Orlando. Emeril already ran Emeril's Orlando, located at Universal Orlando's City Walk. So we knew that a fresh concept was needed, one that would mesh with the South China Seas theme that is at the heart of the guest experience at the Royal Pacific Resort.

Luckily, Emeril had the perfect idea up his sleeve. "I'd wanted to do to a restaurant called Tchoup Chop for 10 years," he explains. "I'd registered the concept and even bought a building in New Orleans to house it, but I never found the right time to open the place. So when Loews came to me, I said, I have a concept that's ready to go." The idea was for a restaurant offering an exotic blend of Asian and Polynesian dishes complemented by Emeril's characteristically bold flavors. The name? Pronounced simply "chop chop," it combines a hint of New Orleans' famous Tchoupitoulas Street, where Emeril's flagship restaurant is located, with the culinary term "chop."

Of course, a name and a concept aren't enough to define a restaurant. How do decisions on things like architecture and design get made when powerful brands like Emeril's, Universal Orlando and Loews are collaborating? It starts with pulling together a great team. We met with Emeril and Eric Lindquist, the design and construction expert who has worked with Emeril for years and is chief operating officer of his company. Together we batted around a host of ideas for a restaurant that would evoke the romance and charm of the South China Seas without resembling a stage set from a high school production of *South Pacific*.

Armed with this guidance, Emeril and his team took charge. Eric and he enlisted the help of the gifted architect David Rockwell, known for creating spaces that are imaginative, stylish, warmly tactile, and deeply surprising. (As it happens, one of Rockwell's first projects was the creation of the Library bar at the Loews Regency Hotel.) After describing his outlandishly vibrant design for the Mohegan Sun Casino in Connecticut, an *Esquire* writer summed Rockwell up this way: "He wants to make the world a stage set where magical things can happen."

With the right people on board, it was time to talk, explore, dream, debate, and talk some more. Teams from all three organizations brainstormed with Rockwell for two solid days, after which Rockwell went off to create sketches, plans, and drawings for a formal presentation to Emeril. The concepts included having much of the furniture constructed in Bali. The plans were worked and reworked based on Emeril's feedback, and a set of color palettes was developed for everything from window treatments and floor coverings to table linens and waiters' uniforms. Then the Loews' team rejoined the process. We scrutinized it all, liked nearly everything, and offered a number of suggestions, honing the concept even further. These were incorporated into the final plans, and the project was up and running.

Eric Lindquist spearheaded construction, working with Rockwell and the various contractors and subcontractors. The final result is magnificent. It features a facade with wooden carvings that appear to glow from within, a bar with hard-carved wooden tikis, wooden pilasters covered with woven bamboo matting, pierced-metal light fixtures, cast-glass chandeliers, and a host of other vivid, colorful details. The restaurant has an open kitchen, so you can watch Emeril's chefs as they prepare your Kiawe smoked pork ribs with hoisin barbecue sauce, macadamia nut-crusted Atlantic salmon served with ginger soy butter sauce, or one of the other marvelous Asian-inspired dishes.

The latest addition to the Emeril/Loews partnership is the Emeril's restaurant in our Miami Beach hotel. It opened in November 2003 to rave reviews; as the *Miami Herald* wrote, the "Menu is as big and loud as the boss, and portions range from bountiful to behemoth," and the "food is full of innovative, intriguing touches." Emeril explains, "Our relationship with Loews works because the philosophies are the same and the standards are the same. We both focus on being part of the community and being the best you can be."

TISCH'S TIPS

How well do your co-branding partnerships work? Which individuals, businesses, or other organizations do you currently partner with? If there is friction, inefficiency, or a lack of creativity, it may be because the goals and values of the two partners are not fully compatible. Perhaps it's time to consider changing the nature of the partnership, or to shift to a different partner whose philosophy is closer to your own.

At Loews Hotels, we've worked with a number of great brand names. In each case, it's important to partner with a company whose values, style, and objectives mesh with ours.

We've worked with more than one airline company—a natural fit for any company in travel and tourism, of course. Back in the 1990s, financier Kirk Kerkorian launched MGM Grand Air, an ambitious attempt to create a premium single-class airline traveling between New York and Los Angeles—two Loews Hotels' cities. The first time I flew on MGM Grand Air, I was entranced by the smell of fresh chocolate chip cookies baking on the plane. I immediately decided, "Loews Hotels ought to sponsor these cookies."

We struck a deal. Thereafter, when the snack of cookies and milk arrived at each passenger's seat 60 minutes prior to landing, it was accompanied by a napkin and a note bearing the Loews Hotels' logo and a welcoming message from us. I'm sure that some MGM Grand passengers ended up choosing the Regency for their stays in New York as a result of our association with that delicious special feature of the airline. Since the dissolution of MGM Grand Air in 1994, we've linked up for marketing purposes with several other carriers, including most recently JetBlue, one of today's most innovative and successful airlines.

Some of our most important partnerships underlie the branding of several of our hotels. Our three hotels at Universal Orlando are a prime example. All three owe much of their appeal to the brand connection with Universal and its successful Orlando theme parks. Among other benefits, guests at the Hard Rock Hotel, the Portofino Bay Hotel, and the Royal Pacific Resort can bypass the normal lines for rides at the Universal Orlando attractions just by showing their room keys. This Universal Express amenity alone is enough of a reason for some thrill-ride lovers to seek out our hotels in preference to the scores of others in the Orlando area. (It's also unique in the area. Guests at the various Disney hotel properties don't enjoy the same benefit at the Disney parks, mainly because there are thousands more hotel rooms at Disney World; it wouldn't be practical for Disney to allow that many guests to skip to the head of the lines.)

TISCH'S TIPS

What unique benefits can you offer your customers through partnerships? How can you outflank competitors by teaming up with a partner to provide customers with a product or service no one else can match? Try brainstorming the "dream package" of benefits that would truly delight your customers . . . then figure out which partners can help you make the dream a reality.

The Hard Rock Hotel at Universal Orlando benefits from *triple* branding—Loews, Universal, and the Hard Rock Café, one of the most popular brands in the world. Originating with the first Hard Rock Café in London in 1971, the business has grown to embrace over a hundred restaurants in 41 countries. Each is decorated with selections from the company's amazing, continually expanding collection of over 60,000 pieces of rock 'n roll memorabilia; the guitars, gold records, sheet music, costumes, handwritten lyrics, and other treasures are rotated from restaurant to restaurant. There are also five Hard Rock Hotels, with two more due to open during 2004. (The Hard Rock Hotel in Orlando is operated by Loews Hotels; the others are under different management.) The Hard Rock brand is owned by The Rank Group, a London-based leisure company that also runs casinos and a variety of entertainment services businesses, such as a DVD replication company.

Combining the family fun of the Universal theme parks (Universal Studios and Islands of Adventure) with the rock-oriented excitement of the Hard Rock Café is fairly brilliant two-for-one marketing. Our guests have easy access both to the theme parks and to the world's largest Hard Rock Café and Hard Rock Live concert venue. The style of the Hard Rock Hotel is casually hip, from the Aquarian-Age motto ("Love all, serve all") to the look of our employees, who can sport anything from purple spiked hair to an assortment of piercings in unfamiliar places. The effect is definitely unconventional, and the appeal to varied demographics is enormous, from the tots and parents who naturally gravitate to Orlando, to teenagers and Generation Xers who love rock music, to nostalgic baby boomers (like me) who grew up on the Beatles, Stones, and Jimi Hendrix.

We enjoy a similar marketing double-whammy at our House of Blues Hotel in Chicago. House of Blues Entertainment, Inc., originated when the first House of Blues concert venue opened in an historic house in Cambridge, Massachusetts, in 1992. The privately held firm is now a major promoter of live music, operating five of its own concert halls and booking performers throughout North America. (It's also strongly committed to community outreach; a cherished part of their corporate legend is the story of how the original House of Blues opened on Thanksgiving Day only *after* serving a meal to the local homeless.)

Our House of Blues Hotel is just a few steps away from the Chicago House of Blues Club. The hotel features decorative items from the House of Blues' great collection of American folk art and offers such special amenities as a Gospel Brunch package, which includes deluxe Saturday night accommodations, a great Sunday brunch, and tickets to the Gospel Brunch show at the House of Blues Club.

SUCCESSFUL CO-BRANDING PARTNERSHIPS DON'T JUST HAPPEN. THERE'S much more to building them than having a photo op at which two company presidents sign a contract and shake hands. Over the years, we've learned the secrets behind a powerful, lasting, mutually profitable partnership—as well as the pitfalls that can destroy a poorly conceived alliance. Some of the things we've learned are discussed in this chapter.

One key, as we've already seen, is to make certain that the partnering organizations are deeply compatible in values and personalities. This is partly a matter of smart marketing. An effective partnership must link companies whose target audiences are fundamentally similar in terms of taste, demographics, income, and interests. The archetypal Loews Hotels' guest is upscale, casual, adventurous, hip, sophisticated, and fun loving. It's a similar profile to that of fans of Emeril Lagasse's cuisine and the entertainment provided by the Hard Rock Café or the House of Blues.

Compatibility, however, is more than a matter of marketing. It also helps if the leaders of the partnering companies know, respect, and like one another. If you "speak the same language" and have fundamentally similar values and philosophies, there's less likelihood of encountering conflicts or difficulties that will torpedo the partnership. The fact that Emeril Lagasse and I can sit down for a glass of Chardonnay together and laugh at the same jokes isn't the only requirement for a strong partnership between our firms—but it sure doesn't hurt. And the commitment of House of Blues to community giving—so reminiscent of Loews Hotels' own Good Neighbor Policy—is one of the things that makes us comfortable partnering with one another.

Here are some other crucial requirements that will give a partnership between organizations the best chance of working:

- Assign the care and feeding of the partnership to the right people—managers who are open-minded, creative, and good listeners, who understand the importance of finding solutions to problems that work for *everyone* involved.
- Make sure the managers in charge of the partnership have enough clout within their own organizations to be effective sponsors of the partnership, able to defend the needs and interests *of the partner* even when these create unexpected costs or challenges.
- Draw up the partnership agreement so that the obligations, responsibilities, and benefits are shared in a way that is truly equitable. A take-no-prisoners negotiating style is destructive when your goal is to build a long-lasting partnership; leave something on the table for the other guy.
- Finally, build flexibility into the partnership agreement. Your goal is to create a relationship that will remain beneficial to both parties rather than turning into a financial or management millstone as business circumstances and corporate objectives evolve.

A business partnership is like a marriage: Sometimes it can last forever, sometimes it runs its course and comes to a natural end. When the latter occurs, it's important to handle the breakup with maturity and good grace rather than rancor, bitterness, or accusations.

It's not just because behaving with generosity and courtesy will help you to feel better about yourself (although that's true). It's also true for highly practical business reasons. The world is a small place. I've found that the company or person I part company with today may prove to be crucial to another project one year or five years down the road. That's why it pays *not* to burn bridges, but always to end relationships on a positive, friendly note. What goes around, comes around, and the way you treat someone today will be reflected in the way people treat you tomorrow.

ASSOCIATION PARTNERSHIPS ARE PERHAPS THE BEST EXAMPLE OF HOW partners—including companies that normally compete—can put aside their differences to work together in favor of a common good.

Some partnerships of this kind are limited coalitions of a few companies created for specific purposes, such as marketing. There are many examples from the travel and tourism industry, including:

- In New York City, the Hilton and Sheraton Hotels are just a block apart in the West 50s. Neither is large enough by itself to serve as the host for the largest industry gatherings. So the two hotels have joined forces for marketing purposes, offering themselves as joint hosts for major business meetings.
- Most travelers today belong to one or more frequent flyer programs. The value of these programs is enhanced when the number and variety of destinations available is increased (an example of what economists call the *network effect*). To extend the reach of their frequent flyer programs, many airlines have formed partnerships with noncompeting carriers—for example, the oneworld alliance formed by American Airlines, which includes Aer Lingus, British Airways, Cathay Pacific, Finnair, Iberia, LanChile, Qantas, and Swiss International Airlines.

- Seeking a way to compete more profitably with burgeoning online travel agents like Expedia and Travelocity, five of the largest airlines—Continental, Northwest, United, Delta, and American—joined forces in 2001 to create a new travel web site called Orbitz. Because commissions and outside booking fees are excluded, Orbitz can offer lower fares than other travel sites.

These kinds of marketing coalitions must pass rigorous legal scrutiny, of course; companies aren't permitted to join forces so as to fix prices or squelch competition.

Most association partnerships are open to all companies in an industry. They play a variety of roles, including advocacy in the political arena and the provision of educational, training, and information services that help spread understanding about the industry in the community at large.

When I joined the hotel business after my stint in television, I worked closely with Charlotte St. Martin, who is now the executive vice president of marketing for Loews Hotels. One of the first things I learned from my work with Charlotte was the importance of the association market for the hospitality business and for Loews Hotels in particular. This was a market Charlotte was particularly adept at serving.

In 1977, Charlotte was the very first employee at the Anatole Hotel, a grand property built in Dallas, Texas, by the developer Trammell Crow. When Loews Hotels entered an agreement to manage the hotel for Trammell Crow, Charlotte was "adopted" as a Loews' employee. Her primary job was to promote the Anatole—then the largest hotel in the entire Southwest—as a great all-in-one venue for business meetings and conventions. "There is truly an association for everything," Charlotte comments. "I remember going into the office of the director of marketing one time and expressing amazement that I had just been negotiating with something called the American Association of Wiping Cloth Manufacturers!" Every such organization—no matter how seemingly obscure—holds an annual meeting or convention, and Loews Hotels wanted to bring more than its share of these gatherings to the Anatole.

One of Charlotte's strategies was to become active in the industry associations that brought together managers who were responsible for hosting meetings—associations of associations, if you will. Over time, she reasoned, participating in these organizations would make her, the Anatole, and Loews Hotels very familiar to important meeting planners. Charlotte volunteered to serve on committees for organizations ranging from the American Society of Association Executives (ASAE) and Meeting Planners International (MPI) to the Professional Convention Management Association (PCMA) and the American Hotel and Lodging Association (AH&LA).

The strategy worked even better than Charlotte had expected. "Because there were relatively few women in the business at the time," she explains, "I found that I was in demand, as a representative of the woman's point of view. So I was selected for active roles on committees and boards much faster than if I'd been a man. And once I got the chance, I proved that I had a lot to contribute. I became a chapter president of MPI, then a member of their international board. Much the same happened with PCMA and ASAE. All of this brought enormous attention to the Loews Anatole." Soon the Anatole had become one of the country's most successful—and profitable—meetings hotels.

Charlotte couldn't have pursued her strategy without the support and encouragement of my dad, Bob Tisch. "That was important," she says, "because when you have an association role it takes time away from the office and from your personal life. Just working at Loews is enough to fill most people's days! Without the green light from the top, it would be hard to take on these outside responsibilities."

Charlotte's example helped me understand the value of participating in industry organizations, and I've devoted significant time and energy to this form of partnership over the past 12 years.

One of my first highly visible industry roles was chairing a capital campaign for the ASAE Foundation back in 1992. The ASAE Foundation is a leader in research and education for association managers, and at the time it was struggling financially; as I recall, the organization's coffers held only about $450,000, a small fraction of the money they needed. I threw myself into the effort, attending meetings, contributing ideas, and making phone call after phone call in an effort to drum up checks for the Foundation.

Some of my colleagues expressed surprise over my hands-on involvement; I gather that some executives who chair fund-raising drives are merely figureheads rather than active participants. But that's not my style. I wouldn't feel comfortable asking others to tackle jobs I won't do myself, so when I take on a project, I like to get into the trenches with my partners.

We set a goal for the drive of raising five million dollars, which was considered pretty aggressive. But in the end, we raised six million dollars. Our success was personally gratifying to me, and it helped solidify the reputation of Loews Hotels as an industry leader.

Soon I found that many organizations in the travel and tourism industry were asking for my help. I worked my way up through the membership ranks at AH&LA, eventually achieving the post of chairman. Again, I surprised people by the depth and seriousness of my involvement. My natural curiosity, which has served me well in business, came to the fore in my association involvements. I was forever asking "naive" questions: Why do we do things this way? Why is this activity important? Is there a better way? Sometimes the answers convinced me that the traditional methods were the best; in other cases, I discovered that a change could make our efforts more powerful. Either way, I was learning and growing.

One of the major challenges I tackled as an industry leader was excessive taxation of hotel rooms. Local governments are always hurting for money, and hotel occupancy taxes are a tempting solution: Since most of the guests who pay the taxes are out-of-towners, they'll never have a chance to express their displeasure by voting against the politicians who impose the taxes. I sympathize with government's need to fund vital social programs and services. But when hotel taxes become extreme, they discourage travel and hurt the economy—not just hoteliers, but restaurateurs, tour operators, airlines, and all the other businesses that are part of the travel and tourism network.

By the early 1990s, it was clearly time to reverse the trend. In New York City, the hotel tax had reached a high of 21.25 percent, and other cities around the country weren't far behind. A special concern was the fact that, in many cities (including New York), hotel taxes were not used to support the travel and tourism industry but instead went straight into the general fund, exacerbating the dependence of civic leaders on these moneys whenever schools, uniformed services, street repairs, or other causes were hurting.

My visibility as an industry spokesman helped me take on this problem, working closely with business and labor leaders from every facet of the travel and tourism world to mount a lobbying effort aimed at state and local officials. Our goal was to persuade them to lower the hotel tax or to devote at least a portion of the money raised for travel promotion—or both.

The effort paid off. In New York City, our coalition of business leaders, union officials, and enlightened politicians succeeded in lowering the hotel tax by more than 6 percent. In many other cities, the tax rate was reduced, and some cities began earmarking a portion of the hotel tax for travel marketing purposes; in Dallas, for example, a portion of the money is used to support the convention center, to promote the city, and to provide resources for meeting planners. When this happens, the hotel tax changes its nature from an economic drag to an economic stimulus.

Today, Loews Hotels has made my father's informal encouragement of organization activity into an explicit part of our corporate culture. We urge our executives to get involved in local and national organizations, supporting not just industry groups but civic, charitable, and social groups. Maintaining the right balance can be tricky. Some industry assignments can eat up as much as 20 to 30 percent of your time. So, if two or three executive committee members at a given hotel are deeply involved in local organizations, we encourage the others to focus on

TISCH'S TIPS

Do the culture and policies of your organization encourage individual employees to participate in industry, civic, or charitable organizations? Do the leaders of the organization set an example through their own enthusiastic efforts in this area? If not, consider making a change. Look for the right organizations to support, and lead the way by personally getting involved. Playing an active role in such partnerships enhances the reputation of your organization and increases your attractiveness as an employer of quality people.

day-to-day operations, so there's always an experienced eye watching the shop.

ANOTHER PARTNERSHIP THAT'S CLOSE TO MY HEART IS NYC & COMPANY, a nonprofit organization whose roughly 15-million-dollar budget is funded partly by the city government and partly, as I'll explain, by private partners. As the official tourism agency and the convention and visitors bureau for my hometown of New York City, it's a prime example of what I call a civic partnership, in which companies work together to promote the economic vitality of their community. I'm currently the chairman of NYC & Company, and working to bring travelers from around the world to enjoy the vitality, sophistication, and sheer fun of the Big Apple is truly a labor of love for me.

Part of the organization's mandate is attracting major events to New York City. This is a cause I've helped to champion for many years. In 1987, when I was still relatively new to the travel and tourism industry, then-mayor Ed Koch called to ask me to spearhead an effort to bring the Grammy Awards (the biggest annual event in the music industry) back to New York. "I'll be happy to help," I replied, "Where do we start? What do we do for funding?"

Ed chuckled. "That's your problem," he answered.

Fortunately, I don't mind being thrown into the deep end of the pool—sometimes that's the best way to learn how to swim. We created a committee to work with the people at the National Academy of Recording Arts and Sciences (organizers of the Grammys), selling them on all the powerful cultural and economic reasons why the awards belonged in New York. Within two years, we succeeded in bringing the 1988 Grammy ceremony—along with over $20 million in business revenues—to the city.

In the years since then, the Grammys have been the subject of an annual tug-of-war between Los Angeles and New York. We'll continue to battle to bring our region its fair share of the Grammys, along with other similar national events which I've helped to host over the years, like the NBA All-Star Game. As I write, we're hard at work on plans for the 2004 Republican National Convention in New York. (Putting aside my own partisan leanings, I'm serving as vice-chair of the host committee for that gathering, which should generate some $250 million in economic activity for the city.) We've also set our sights on capturing the 2009 NFL Super Bowl and the 2012 Olympic Games for New York.

One of the key people who makes NYC & Company effective is the organization's president and CEO, Cristyne L. Nicholas, formerly the director of communications in Rudolph W. Giuliani's mayoral administration. Cristyne and I have different political leanings, but our shared belief in the future of New York has made us an effective team. (I like to joke that we're "the James Carville and Mary Matalin of NYC tourism," referring to another odd-couple pairing that also seems to work.)

Since 1999, Cristyne has been leading the organization through a number of transitions, including a change of name, from the New York Convention & Visitors Bureau to NYC & Company, a name designed to emphasize the importance of travel and tourism to the city's economy. The organization is also moving to shift the nature and balance of the partnerships we rely on. Formerly, the city government had been our main supporter. Under Cristyne's leadership, NYC & Company has been aggressively pursuing corporate sponsorships to lessen its reliance on government funds. As a result, the ratio of government to private moneys in NYC & Company's budget has changed from 70:30 to 40:60.

NYC & Company is now a case study in the power of strategic partnerships. Corporations like Delta Airlines, American Express, Coca-Cola, and Time Warner have become major partners, providing a significant share of the organization's budget.

The new funding structure creates both opportunities and challenges. Relying on partnerships is personally demanding and time-intensive. NYC & Company has two to three people on its staff who serve as liaisons with the corporate partners, making sure they receive the attention and services they expect. Some exciting programs have been developed through these partnerships. For example, NYC & Company worked with Time Warner and the League of American Theatres and Producers to create Broadway Under the Stars, a free concert held every June in Bryant Park (not far from the headquarters of Time Warner). And the program continues to expand, involving new partners: CBS is planning to broadcast this year's concert on their network-owned affiliates, while Time Warner has used the event to showcase stars from some of their popular cable TV programs, like *The Sopranos.*

At the same time, it's important to service the broader membership of NYC & Company. About 1,600 companies are dues-paying members. They include restaurants, hotels, retail stores, tour operators, and many other kinds of companies. It's hard to know 1,600 members and the many contacts we may have at each member firm. So Cristyne and her team have created a number of programs to keep us in touch with our members and help them benefit from their membership.

Every two months, NYC & Company hosts a Membership 101 class, where new members can visit the organization's offices, meet the staff, and learn how to get the most out of their membership. There are periodic Meet-the-Member breakfasts at which new members are showcased, as well as networking opportunities ranging from breakfasts and discussions to issue-oriented forums. Many of our members end up doing business together as a result.

A key benefit of membership is a listing in the *Official NYC Guide,* a seasonal publication that's distributed to about a million people each year, from potential tourists and business travelers to travel agents and meeting planners. Members are also listed on our web site, which receives about three million hits every month.

Our members can also participate in special programs like Restaurant Week, one of NYC & Company's most popular and successful

TISCH'S TIPS

Do you participate in partnerships that involve both large organizations and smaller ones? If so, how do you balance the competing needs of these very different groups? You may need to spend time deliberately strategizing ways to service your major partners without neglecting the valid interests of the minor players. And remember, today's smaller partner may grow to be a major partner in the future.

promotions. It dates back to 1992 when New York hosted the Democratic National Convention and was conceived by me, Tim Zagat, publisher of the popular restaurant guides that bear his name, and several others.

Restaurants that sign up for the annual Restaurant Week agree to offer a special prix fixe luncheon at a price that matches the year—for example, during our first Restaurant Week, you could get a great lunch for $19.92. (People familiar with prices in New York recognize that this is a very attractive deal, especially since many of the city's finest and most expensive restaurants participate.) Originally, some restaurants were reluctant to join us; they worried that the price was too low to cover their costs. But the results were so phenomenal that more and more restaurateurs are eager to take part. "We had 200 participants last year," Cristyne notes, "which is almost too many. We run their names in a two-page ad in the *New York Times,* and if the numbers grew any larger, the listings would verge on the illegible!"

We now have two Restaurant Weeks each year, one in the summer and one in the winter. They've become citywide celebrations of great New York eating, an opportunity for food-lovers to sample the menus at pricey establishments they might not have tried before. Even restaurants that are not official participants of the week try to benefit by posting hand-drawn signs in their windows and offering lunch at the special price.

Other cities are now conducting their own restaurant weeks in imitation of New York. "Boston was the first to borrow our idea," Cristyne says. "I called the president of Boston's visitor's bureau and teased him about it. But we really don't mind—it helps spread the idea of Restaurant Week, which we consider our brand."

Of course, inflation (even at the low rates of the last decade) gradually wreaked havoc with our pricing strategy. Restaurants could only raise their prix fixe by a penny a year. Our new idea is to set the price at $20.12, to symbolize our bid to win the 2012 Summer Olympic Games for New York. That price should hold the inflation monster at bay for a few more years.

A major sponsor of Restaurant Week is Coca-Cola. A soft drink marketer may not be an obvious partner for a travel and tourism organization—after all, people don't drink Coke only when they travel.

But experience shows that when tourism is down, sales of Coke in restaurants, theme parks, and hotels suffer. So Coke is an enthusiastic partner of NYC & Company. By sponsoring Restaurant Week, they get to promote their brand even in restaurants that serve Pepsi products.

Our latest idea for promoting New York's status as the dining capital of the world is *The New York Restaurant Cookbook,* sponsored by NYC & Company and published in 2003 by Rizzoli. It's filled with wonderful recipes from many of the city's greatest eateries, from legendary palaces of haute cuisine like Le Cirque to exciting ethnic restaurants like Tamarind (Indian), Nobu (Japanese), Noche (Cuban-Argentine), and Fresco by Scotto (Italian). All the recipes have been edited and tested by the well-respected food writer Florence Fabricant. Yes, you can prepare the recipes and enjoy a taste of New York in your own kitchen. But we think the book will help bring food lovers from Florida, Texas, California, and parts east and west to the Big Apple to sample the original dishes. It's a marketing tool that costs us nothing.

Amid the daily press of activities, we try to maintain our focus on major initiatives to benefit the city. For example, we're working with political leaders, community organizations, labor groups, and others in support of expanding the Jacob K. Javits Convention Center. Believe it or not, New York's convention center ranks *eighteenth* in North America in exhibit space, *fifteenth* in meeting space. No wonder we routinely lose major conventions to cities like Orlando, Chicago, and New Orleans. Don't get me wrong, these are all wonderful cities (and we invite you to stay in the local Loews Hotels when you visit them). But in New York, convention-goers can tour the Metropolitan Museum of Art, shop on Fifth Avenue, catch a Broadway play, admire the Statue of Liberty, and ride to the top of the Empire State Building between speeches. Doesn't the world's greatest city deserve a bigger share of those meetings?

You can see that I'm passionate about NYC & Company. It gathers resources of time, talent, and treasure from government and private industry, and from companies of every size and scope, and uses those resources to craft programs that benefit millions of people. The efforts of NYC & Company attract visitors to the city from around the world, enhance their travel experiences, boost the local economy, generate enormous tax revenues, and help create thousands of jobs.

Not a bad return on a relatively modest investment. NYC & Company represents many of the best qualities of the Power of Partnership in action. It's a great example of how businesses can join in a common cause, thereby benefiting both the citizens of their communities and their own industries, producing a virtual cycle of ever-increasing prosperity.

PORTRAIT IN PARTNERSHIP

Paul Tagliabue

Paul Tagliabue became commissioner of the National Football League (NFL) in 1989. He succeeded the legendary Pete Rozelle, the executive who helped make professional football into America's most successful sports enterprise.

Under Tagliabue's leadership, the NFL has addressed several key priorities: The NFL has grown from 28 to 32 teams, revised its divisional alignment and scheduling formula, negotiated successive long-term labor agreements with the NFL Players Association, and secured the largest television contracts in entertainment history.

In the Tagliabue era, the NFL has also expanded League and team commitments to community service and refocused the NFL's efforts in developing public/private partnerships for new stadiums. In addition, the NFL has been the new media leader in sports, creating the first leaguewide Internet network for fans and unprecedented Internet "portal" distribution.

In recognition of these accomplishments, Tagliabue was named the 2000 Sports Industrialist of the Year by the *Sports Business Daily*, the 2001 Sports Executive of the Year by the *Sports Business Journal*, and the 2001 Most Powerful Person in Sports by *Sporting News*.

(Continued)

When we spoke with Tagliabue by phone on April 19, 2004, he emphasized the unusual way in which the NFL combines the spirit of competition with the spirit of partnership.

"A sports league is unique," he told us. "All 32 teams work together to produce a common product, at the same time that they are fierce competitors. My job is to keep the partnership working in the interests of everybody concerned—the teams, the players, the TV networks, the communities where we operate, and especially the fans."

Tagliabue recognizes that most complex organizations involve forces that pull in different directions. "I've been with the NFL for 35 years now, but I started out as a policy analyst in the Pentagon. That was my first experience working in a highly complex organization with a multiplicity of interests from which a consensus must be developed. It was a great start to my education in partnership.

"One of the crucial lessons I've learned about building or maintaining a partnership is the importance of focusing on structural issues. When the organizational structure is right, good decisions usually get made. When the structure is defective, no amount of personal leadership can overcome it."

A small example that provided Tagliabue with some unexpected headaches in 2004 arose in connection with the halftime show at the Super Bowl, where Janet Jackson's notorious "wardrobe malfunction" caused a worldwide uproar and significant embarrassment to the league. Can we expect the commissioner to personally approve the script for next year's halftime show? "Definitely not," he told us. "If the CEO has to get involved in what should be lower level decisions, that's a telltale sign that you probably have the wrong structure in place. In examining our process after the fact, we came to realize that we were using flawed timelines for checking our decisions about the entertainment, and in some cases had the wrong people making those decisions. We've cleaned up our structure, and as a result I can promise that next year's show will be both tasteful and entertaining."

Tagliabue was fortunate in that he inherited some key structural elements that had helped make the NFL successful. Since 1961, the League has maintained control of all TV rights, mandating equal sharing of TV revenues among all the teams. As a result, pro football has been spared the difficult struggles over competitive balance that afflict Major League Baseball, where a few teams command huge TV revenues that give them an enormous competitive advantage over their rivals.

In addition, the NFL's governance system includes a requirement that three quarters of the League's members must approve all major decisions. This puts a premium on consensus, which Tagliabue sharply differentiates from "expedient compromise." He explains the distinction this way: "Consensus finds a way to accommodate all the interests involved as well as the needs of the fans and the essential priorities of the League. By contrast, an expedient compromise is a solution achieved through force that brushes aside the legitimate concerns of some partners. As a result, trust is destroyed and the essential structure of the partnership is undermined."

It's one thing to recognize the importance of consensus; it's another to have techniques for achieving it. We asked Tagliabue about how he forges consensus among a large group of strong-willed leaders like the NFL owners. "One way is by building outward, in concentric circles. I start by working out a tentative solution with a small group of owners. Once we've reached consensus, they fan out to talk with their fellow owners, gradually drawing them into the process. In a way, it's more like managing a legislative body than the usual executive process. Multiple points of leadership are required, not just a single head.

"Another key is timing. You need to hold off on ratifying any decision until a true consensus has been reached, not push toward a vote prematurely. Any solution you devise too hastily is likely to fall apart quickly. True consensus produces long-term solutions."

(Continued)

The success of the NFL also relies on strong partnerships with other groups, such as the TV networks and the players' and referees' unions. How does Tagliabue manage tough negotiations in such a way as to build alliances rather than dissension? "Any successful negotiation has to provide what's essential for each side. This means learning to listen to the other side—to be willing to walk in the shoes of your adversary.

"The NFL has a great track record of labor peace when it comes to our players. But in 2001, our negotiations with the NFL referees became very contentious. We ended up having to use replacement officials before ultimately reaching an agreement. The problem, I think, is that our negotiating partners violated the golden rule of listening. We'd been trying to tell them for months that certain demands they were making were simply impossible for us to meet. Unfortunately, they assumed we were posturing. The result was a breakdown in communications. Thankfully, the relationship is on a much stronger footing today, and I don't think the same mistakes will happen again."

One of the secrets of the League's positive relationship with the Players' Association is Tagliabue's deliberate search for areas of shared interest. "We look for opportunities to partner with the players. For example, we have shared programs dealing with youth football, our European league, and other topics. When it comes to our core economic issues, these are ancillary matters. But they enable us to work together and help both sides recognize that neither is a demon. The difference in tone this creates makes a real difference when contract negotiations get underway."

"I try to approach negotiations with a long-term perspective. The best partnerships are those that continue for decades. The biggest mistake is to be penny-wise and pound-foolish—preoccupied with short-term financial benefit as opposed to creating a long-term partnership. And when you enter partnerships that fall apart quickly, you hurt yourself. After a few such divorces, the number of potential new partners begins to dwindle. So your track record for dealing fairly becomes critical to your success."

CHAPTER 8

Beyond the Ballot Box

Good Corporate Citizenship Takes More Than Your Vote

*If men could combine thus earnestly, and patiently, and
harmonious to some really worthy end, what might they not
accomplish? . . . If they could put their hands and heads and
hearts all together, such a cooperation and harmony would be the
very end and success for which government now exists in vain.*

—Henry David Thoreau (1817–1862)
American essayist, naturalist, and philosopher

SOME OF MY COLLEAGUES IN BUSINESS EXPRESS SURPRISE WHEN I SPEAK
about the importance of partnering with government. The instinct
of many business people is to want to distance themselves from government: "I'll leave them alone. All I ask is that they leave me alone in
return."

In the real world, this isn't a practical policy. The world has become so complex that government has a continuing impact on business. Of course, we all must pay taxes. But beyond that, government
regulations regarding safety, security, wages, contracts, the environment, and hundreds of other activities impinge on business constantly. Many of these "intrusions" have been beneficial both for the
average citizen and for our economy. Does the existence of the Food
and Drug Administration make it more complicated for a meat

packer or a grocer to do business today than, say, a hundred years ago? It probably does. But the confidence of Americans in the safety of their food supply is a crucial underpinning for the growth of the grocery and restaurant industries—as we rediscover whenever a momentary problem shakes that confidence, as with the recent "mad cow" scare.

Government involvement in business activities is here to stay. Therefore, as corporate citizens, we must be involved in helping to shape government policies, both for the good of our industries and for the benefit of our communities.

We also need to approach this challenge in a responsible fashion. Lobbying by business leaders should never become a mad scramble for handouts. The public has become understandably wary of the power exercised by special interests over government policy, whether those interests are political extremists, labor or environmental groups, or business organizations. It is up to our elected officials to balance the needs of many groups and individuals and make decisions that will benefit the nation as a whole. But we in business must play our part, formulating policy recommendations that are designed to promote strong communities and a healthy economic climate to benefit all our citizens—not just a few.

The broader your horizons, the better. That's why, as a leader in the travel and tourism community, I'm involved in supporting our industry as a whole, both locally and nationally.

As we've seen, the period since the terrorist attacks of September 11, 2001, has been a troubled time for travel and tourism. International travel has been especially hard hit. That's a cause for enormous concern, since international travelers tend to stay longer and spend more money than domestic visitors. Take New York City as an example. In 2002, international visitors made up just 14 percent of all visitors to New York, but were responsible for 42 percent of all visitor spending. Clearly it's crucial for the long-term economic health of New York to bring overseas visitors back to our streets. The same is true of other cities, states, and regions throughout the United States.

Here is one place where the federal government should be partnering with business. The governments of other countries spend hundreds of millions of dollars to promote themselves as international destinations. And when travel declines, other countries redouble their efforts. During the fall of 2003, the prime minister of France announced a 40 percent increase in the country's global tourism promotion budget in an effort to "put tourism at the heart of France's growth strategy." And Australia has just announced a new $181 million ad campaign to attract international tourists.

Meanwhile, the United States has spent nothing. No wonder the United States, despite its unparalleled natural, cultural, and historic attractions, is now the world's third most popular destination, after France and Spain.

Getting the U.S. government to respond to this challenge has been a long, uphill battle. In 1995, a number of leaders in our industry encouraged the Clinton administration to host a White House Conference on Travel and Tourism, which brought together representatives from every corner of our industry to share ideas about how we could promote America as a travel destination around the world. In the aftermath of that conference, I helped to found the Travel Business Roundtable (TBR), an organization that brings together some 87 company and association CEOs to speak with a powerful, unified voice for our industry and the millions of workers we employ.

TBR's mission is to make our elected officials in Washington and in state and local capitals more aware of the importance of travel and tourism and the significant economic and social contributions of the industry. Members of TBR include executives from all of the businesses you'd expect—hotels, airlines, car rental agencies, theme parks—as well as some you might not expect, such as the National Football League, *USA Today*, Gucci, the International Council of Shopping Centers, and the U.S. Conference of Mayors.

As chairman of TBR, I've spent a fair amount of time in Washington, meeting with members of Congress from both sides of the aisle, cabinet members of both the Clinton and Bush administrations, and key members of the White House staff. We've sought both to clear away legal and administrative roadblocks that discourage travel and tourism, and to obtain governmental support and encouragement for travel promotion efforts that no single company or association can handle. These causes have been especially important in the difficult years since the terrorist attacks of September 11.

Colleagues of every political persuasion have worked alongside me in TBR's lobbying efforts. I've made visits to Capitol Hill as part of a team that included hotel executive Bill Marriott (as stalwart a Republican as I am a Democrat) and labor leader John Wilhelm, the president of the Hotel Employees and Restaurant Employees International Union. Bringing together such diverse interests in a common cause is precisely what makes TBR such an effective partnership.

In the fall of 2003, our lobbying efforts began to pay off. Thanks in large part to the leadership of Republican Senator Ted Stevens of Alaska, an omnibus appropriations bill, passed by Congress and signed into law by President Bush, included an allocation of $50 million to create a new program to promote and market the United States as a travel destination. Our initial blueprint called for a focus on the five countries that represent America's largest sources of international tourism—Germany, France, the United Kingdom, Canada, and Japan.

Unfortunately, budgetary pressures and the vagaries of Congressional politics have sidetracked the program, at least for the moment. The $50 million appropriation was subsequently cut to just $6 million. Our current plan is to focus on the United Kingdom, hoping that, in time, a broader marketing program can be restarted. In many other countries, the minister of tourism has a huge marketing budget to spend, a seat in the cabinet, and a regular voice in the deliberations of the government. We're not asking for all of that, but we do think it's time that the United States began to spend at least a little money promoting our nation and its wonderful people as the worldwide magnet they deserve to be.

We're also calling for the creation of a presidential advisory council on travel and tourism. More than 130 foreign countries have official government-sponsored tourism office. Establishing a presidential advisory council to play a similar role in crafting long-term growth strategies for our industry is the least we can do.

We're still negotiating with the Bush administration on the creation of this council. But the same bill that authorized the $50 million program also created the U.S. Travel and Tourism Promotion Advisory

Board to work with Commerce Secretary Don Evans on the creation and implementation of a marketing campaign. It's a big step in the right direction. I was honored to be one of the 15 industry leaders named to this board, along with such notables as Bill Marriott of Marriott International, Jon Linen of American Express, Glenn Tilton of United Airlines, Jay Rasulo of Walt Disney Parks and Resorts, Jeremy Jacobs of Delaware North Companies, and others.

Promoting travel to the United States from other countries is likely to produce enormous benefits for our country. The potential economic impact in terms of job creation is huge. But almost equally important are the less tangible benefits. We live in a time when citizens in some countries are questioning American leadership, when cultural clashes between East and West are exploding in deadly fashion, and when the struggle between liberal democracy and the forces of repression is more crucial than ever. In such an era, inviting millions of people from around the world to experience the vibrancy and freedom of America firsthand can do much to enhance our status and strengthen our ties to other countries. The opportunity tourism creates for foreign visitors to meet average Americans is a more powerful force for international friendship than any amount of propaganda.

Unfortunately, the trauma of September 11 has led our government to propose some policies that would discourage rather than facilitate travel. For example, the U.S. State Department had long planned a transition to requiring machine-readable passports and other security measures from individuals traveling to America from so-called "visa waiver program" countries—a total of 27 countries including many of our closest allies. This policy change had been scheduled to go into effect in 2007, but the U.S. Patriot Act, passed after the terror attacks, moved the deadline up by four years, to October 2003.

The changes, including personal interviews for visas and machine-readable passports with biometric screening devices, are designed to make our citizens and our visitors more safe. And clearly security must be a top priority. But we must develop balanced policies that protect travelers while minimizing the disruption of people's lives. When the new restrictions were announced, the outcry from citizens and governments around the world made it clear that many countries would be unable to comply; some even contemplated introducing similar restrictions on U.S. citizens in retaliation.

It's difficult to overstate the negative effects these new policies could have. When the volume of travel between the United States and other countries diminishes, thousands of businesses and not-for-profit institutions, from airlines, hotels, and restaurants to museums, theatres, and historic sites are impacted, and millions of jobs may be affected, both here and abroad.

The leaders of the travel and tourism industry mounted a successful effort to modify the new policy. Secretary of State Colin Powell agreed to delay implementation of the machine-readable passport regulation by more than a year, to October 26, 2004. The change in timing will give countries around the world a much better chance of complying with the new requirements.

The growth of travel and tourism also needs to be nurtured internationally. Loews Hotels supports the World Travel and Tourism Council (WTTC), a forum for global business leaders comprising the presidents, chairs, and CEOs of 100 of the world's foremost companies. The mission of WTTC is to raise awareness among governments around the world of the full economic impact of travel and tourism, and to promote a vision of what we call "New Tourism," built on a partnership between private and public organizations.

The global significance of travel and tourism is truly staggering. In 2004, the industry will post economic activity estimated at $4.2 *trillion*, a

---

TISCH'S TIPS

How are national or world trends affecting your industry or the organizations you support? Could government policies at the local, state, or federal level have a positive impact on these trends? If so, look for ways to combine forces with colleagues or other organizations to advocate effectively for the changes you seek. And in your communications, emphasize not just the needs of your industry but also the potential benefits for the community as a whole.

figure that is forecast to grow to $8.9 trillion by 2013. The broadly defined "Travel and Tourism Economy" contributes over 10 percent to world GDP and generates one in every 13.2 jobs worldwide.

If this massive economic engine is to continue to grow, governments around the world need to do their part. This involves several elements:

- An intelligent program of taxation, which treats travel and tourism on a level footing with other industries and which reinvests some of the revenues generated by the sector into the infrastructure that will produce still more growth in the future.
- Liberalizing trade, transport, and communications regulations to encourage rather than inhibit travel.
- Providing educational, employment, and training opportunities that will help ensure a strong labor force.
- Establishing clear guidelines for sustainable tourism development in line with national culture and character.
- Continuing to build the confidence of travelers in areas ranging from the fight against terrorism to health safety.

Businesspeople need to be strong, effective advocates for these kinds of government policies in our own countries. But we also have other responsibilities. We need to think strategically and for the long term, working to develop a broad range of tourism products so that many markets are served, with maximum economic and social value. And we need to be leaders in the development and spread of best practices in every area of social responsibility, from environmental protection to fair labor practices.

Above all, we need to show that partnership between business and government is not about handouts to support profits. It must be a real partnership—one that benefits everyone involved, especially the citizens of the communities in which we live and operate.

THE AMERICAN TRAVEL AND TOURISM INDUSTRY IS ONE OF OUR NATION'S most important employers. In particular, travel and tourism has a special role as the first employer for millions of immigrants, those trying to escape from poverty, and those with minimal job skills. The welfare-to-work movement is one place where our economic role intersects beautifully with our responsibility as corporate citizens.

As we saw in Chapter 2, landmark legislation passed by Congress and signed by President Bill Clinton in 1996 took a major step toward solving this problem. The Personal Responsibility and Work Opportunity Reconciliation Act (often called simply "welfare reform") made a series of crucial changes in the welfare system. It imposed a five-year limit on cash assistance for low-income families and created a new funding system whereby states received fixed block grants each year along with significant discretion over how to use those grants. At the same time, the law expanded eligibility for Medicaid, strengthened child-support enforcement, and adopted "participation-rate" requirements, which penalized states unless a specified percentage of families receiving assistance were working or training for work every month. Welfare reform was a complex combination of sticks and carrots designed to create an incentive for work and discourage long-term dependence on government help.

It was clear, however, that government action alone couldn't resolve the welfare dilemma. After all, government couldn't provide jobs for the millions of dependent citizens who needed work. In May 1997, President Clinton helped spearhead the next phase of the effort. He hosted a meeting at the White House with representatives of five companies that were committed to hiring welfare recipients. These companies—Burger King, Monsanto, Sprint, United Airlines, and UPS—were the first members of a new organization called the Welfare to Work Partnership. Loews Hotels promptly joined the partnership.

Soon thereafter, the opening of the Loews Miami Beach Hotel gave us a wonderful opportunity to put our role in the Partnership into action. As mentioned in a previous chapter, the consortium of 45 hotels in the Miami area that we helped to form has found jobs for over a thousand former welfare recipients.

We've incorporated the welfare-to-work approach at other Loews' properties. When we opened the new Loews Philadelphia Hotel in 2000, about 10 percent of the employees were former welfare recipients. And we are working with nearly 30 community-based agencies, some of them linked to the Welfare to Work Partnership, to recruit new employees from among their formerly dependent clients.

Once we hire these new employees, we try to give them not only training and resources that relate to their specific jobs, but also classes to help them succeed in all aspects of returning to the workforce. For example, many of our new employees in Philadelphia had never had a bank account. We brought in representatives from a local bank to help more than 60 employees open their first checking account. We now have classes that address other areas of personal finance, such as how to balance your checkbook and even how to invest the money you are earning in your first real job.

We also keep looking for new opportunities to strengthen the welfare-to-work movement. One example is a program called Women on the Path to Success. Loews Hotels helped to launch this program in November 2000, partnering with the Women's Alliance, a national organization of independent community-based members who provide training and services to low-income women seeking employment. At Loews Hotels around the country, we hosted a day dedicated to providing women making the transition from welfare to work with basic business and communication skills. The women heard from Loews Hotels' employees at various job levels about their personal experiences in the hospitality industry; some had the opportunity to do "job shadowing," following Loews employees around for a day to watch and learn.

The women also received tips on how to present themselves when looking for a job and how to handle interviews. At our Regency Hotel in New York, Malaak Compton-Rock, founder of StyleWORKS (and the wife of comedian Chris Rock), gave a number of women complete makeovers, including new hair, makeup, and clothing styles designed to instill self-confidence and make them look and feel great when applying for a job.

Women on the Path to Success has now become an annual event, with Lifetime Television for Women and the Estée Lauder Companies having joined the sponsoring partnership.

Other firms in our industry have played a huge role in the welfare-to-work movement. For example, Marriott International, with whom we compete for lodging customers even as we cooperate in many industry-related and social programs, has long been a leader in helping welfare recipients to transition to work. Marriott's "Pathways to Independence" program has helped transition over 3,000 former welfare recipients into the hospitality business through a six-week training program administered by Marriott with the assistance of government funding.

Welfare to work is a classic example of how public/private partnerships can achieve results that would otherwise be impossible. Helping people escape dependence on welfare is an initiative that the business community would naturally tend to support: It increases the tax rolls, transforms people with few or no resources into potential consumers, strengthens communities, and reduces the tax burden on businesses. Yet it is not something that government alone can do in response to business lobbying. Instead, government and business must work together to solve the problem.

In the process, we've been able to help dispel a host of destructive myths, for example:

MYTH: People on welfare are lazy, undisciplined, and unwilling to work.

REALITY: The majority of welfare recipients are eager to work and will demonstrate tremendous resolve and determination when given a chance.

MYTH: Companies that hire former welfare recipients should expect to lose money due to high levels of absenteeism and turnover.

REALITY: Former welfare recipients show rates of attendance and retention that compare favorably with any other group of entry-level employees.

MYTH: When companies devote time, energy, and money to meeting their social responsibilities, the shareholders inevitably suffer.

REALITY: It's possible to do good and to do well at the same time.

> ### TISCH'S TIPS
>
> What social problems in your community seem to be the most intractable? Look for ways that you or your organization can have a positive impact on one of those problems, either working alone or in partnership with other groups. Not only will your community benefit, but so will your organization.

For a time, I served as the vice chairman of the Welfare to Work Partnership. Starting from that original group of five founding firms, some 20,000 companies have become involved, seeking information on hiring welfare recipients. The Partnership's Business Resource Group (BRG) puts businesses in touch with community-based organizations and training partners who can link them to well-trained, work-ready employees. The BRG's offices in Chicago, Miami, New York, and Washington also help companies develop employee retention and advancement strategies, provide information on tax incentives and credits, and offer other supportive services to businesses that want to join the movement.

Many employers are finding that hiring former welfare recipients pays off in several ways. For example, a recent study of companies in the San Francisco Bay area found that the Medical Center of the University of California in San Francisco, for instance, attributed $122,720 in cost savings to its participation in Welfare to Work, while Pennzoil 10 Minute Oil Change reported trimming recruitment and turnover costs by 40 percent per hire.

Thanks in large part to the efforts of the Welfare to Work Partnership, many of the broader objectives of the 1996 welfare reform law have also been met. Even critics (largely from the liberal side of the political spectrum) who feared that the law went too far in placing the onus on welfare recipients have acknowledged that the economic pain it caused was far less than they feared. Most of those required to find work succeeded in doing so, even those many feared would be unable to get jobs. For example, the proportion of single moms who worked throughout the year jumped from 48 percent in 1995 to 60 percent in 2000, while the official federal poverty rate among the same group fell from 42 percent when the law was passed to just 33 percent in 2000. As journalist Christopher Jencks observed, "These were unprecedented increases: Nothing similar had happened during any earlier boom."

Welfare to work can't take sole credit for these gains. The booming economy of the late 1990s was a major factor. The 1993 expansion of the Earned Income Tax Credit proposed by President Clinton and passed by Congress provided enormous help to working families that needed an extra boost to stay above the poverty line. More aggressive child-support enforcement and extension of Medicaid coverage among the working poor has also helped. Nonetheless, a large portion of the gains in the war on poverty of the late 1990s must be attributed to the movement from welfare to work, which our partnership helped make possible.

Today, there is controversy over the next stage of welfare reform. Reauthorization of the 1996 law is still pending before Congress; as of this writing, it has been temporarily extended. The Bush administration has advocated changes to the law, some of which, critics claim, would put an undue additional burden on families trying to break out of dependence. With both individuals and local governments hurting as a result of two years of recession, and with the job creation engine of the 1990s having slowed, it's a difficult time for those of us who'd like to see further gains in the battle against poverty.

It's important for the federal government to continue to build on the successes of the past few years, taking any steps necessary to nurture the public-private partnership that has made those successes possible—even in a time of massive budget deficits.

THE WELFARE TO WORK PARTNERSHIP ISN'T THE ONLY EXAMPLE OF HOW private-public cooperation can hold the key to economic advancement for individuals and communities. In cities and states around the country, partnerships between businesses and local governments have played an important role in improving the quality of life for millions of people.

A typical example is the story of how, in the late 1990s, Loews Hotels helped create a great new hotel, a revitalized center city, a strengthened economic base, and economic opportunity for thousands of citizens through a working partnership with the city of Philadelphia.

One of the driving forces behind this partnership was the dynamic Ed Rendell, then Philadelphia's mayor (and now governor of Pennsylvania). A firm believer in the significant impact that travel and tourism can have on a city's economic well-being, Ed made a commitment in 1995 to arrange for the construction of 2,000 new hotel rooms in Philadelphia. According to the city's economic experts, this expansion would generate more than 3,200 new full-time jobs. It would also offer tremendous benefits to Philadelphia's economy long-term, drawing larger conventions and trade shows to the newly expanded Pennsylvania Convention Center, starting with the Republican National Convention in 2000.

Ed Rendell was determined to make this new development a reality. But government couldn't do it alone. A public/private partnership would be needed. That's where Loews Hotels came in.

Plans were developed to create the Loews Philadelphia Hotel, a project that we hoped would have enormous historic significance. The hotel would be located in a national landmark—the building that was constructed for the Philadelphia Saving Fund Society from 1929 to 1932 at a then-staggering cost of eight million dollars.

The PSFS Building was no ordinary office tower. Art historians consider it one of the most important skyscrapers in the country. When it opened, one critic declared, "If architecture is frozen music, the Society has gone Gershwin," while a later expert called the structure "a summation of European Modernism."

The building also has a special place in the heart of Philadelphians. Over the decades, thousands of youngsters had participated in school savings programs sponsored by PSFS; for many of them, an exciting rite of passage into the mysterious world of grown-up finance centered on a trip downtown to the PSFS building to make a deposit into their passbook savings account.

When the Great Depression struck, the glowing sign with the PSFS logo atop the building was kept lit as a palpable symbol of hope and

continuity for residents of the beleaguered city. (At the press conference announcing that Loews Hotels would be renovating the building,
the very first question asked by a reporter was, "Will you be keeping
the sign?")

When our hotel project was launched, this elegant, important
structure had been vacant for years, and the local market didn't support the idea of using it either for office space or residential use. Transforming it into a hotel was an ideal solution. Not only would it bring
back to life a treasured building, but it could help change the dynamic
of a neighborhood that had been sadly neglected.

During the 1980s, much of Philadelphia's Center City had been refurbished and revitalized. But the PSFS Building was on the "wrong"
side of City Hall, in a neighborhood that remained somewhat desolate
and underutilized. The area needed an anchor, and the Loews Philadelphia Hotel could help fill that role.

The project had the potential to be a triumph of smart business,
good government, and enlightened citizenship. Yet, it very nearly
failed to get off the ground. Rebuilding the PSFS Building would be a
big job, costing some $125 million—more than our company would
want to take on alone. Finances had to be gathered from a variety of
sources, both public and private. The city created a special Tax Incre-
ment Financing (TIF) district, which allowed us to obtain $16 mil-
lion worth of private financing for the project. Through a so-called
"108 loan" from the Department of Housing and Urban Development, Philadelphia provided an additional $20.75 million. Finally,
the Philadelphia Industrial Development Corporation provided another $3.5 million loan. Together with moneys provided by Loews,
banks, and other investors, the entire project was finally funded—or
so it seemed.

But at the eleventh hour, just days before the ceremony that would
launch the project, some of the participants got cold feet. The deal was
on the verge of falling apart. I called on Ed Rendell and asked if he
could help.

Ed put the Power of Partnerships to work. He called the key participants into his office. "This project is too important for the city and its
people," he announced. "We're not leaving here until it's back on

track." When Ed Rendell puts his foot down, people pay attention. Within a day, we'd worked out a formula for bridging the financial gap. The project moved forward.

The decisive role played by Ed Rendell was typical of him. During his eight years as mayor, Ed became famous as a consensus-builder and coalition-forger. He even arm-wrestled Philadelphia's notoriously feisty and independent city council into supporting his programs. Today, as governor, Ed is tackling even bigger challenges, including a state budget devastated by economic slowdown, global uncertainty, and shrinking tax revenues. If anyone can solve the problem, Ed Rendell can.

We wanted to convert the old office building into a luxury 583-room hotel filled with up-to-date amenities while also preserving its historic character. The design we developed succeeded admirably. The massive steel bank-vault doors were incorporated into the walls of the lobby and the ballroom; the original Cartier clocks by the elevators on each floor were preserved; new features like the lobby restaurant were designed in keeping with the building's Art Deco style. In partnership with the local NBC-TV affiliate, we designed and built a glass-walled, street level news studio that has become a favorite city attraction.

We opened the Loews Philadelphia Hotel in April 2000. Today, the original PSFS sign once again shines brightly across the Philadelphia skyline. We're honored to have stewardship over a property that's so much a part of the community. We still get visitors to the hotel who say, "May I take a look at the eleventh floor? That's where my dad's office was back in the 1950s."

As Ed Rendell hoped, the hotel has brought new economic growth for the city—including some parts of the community that don't always benefit from development projects. Ten percent of the 500 employees we hired in advance of the hotel's opening came from the ranks of Philadelphians on public assistance. These former welfare recipients are now contributing members of the community. Are they capable workers? Absolutely. Loews Philadelphia has become one of the area's most popular hotels and has been voted the best banquet facility in the city.

The Loews Philadelphia story illustrates in a nutshell what the Power of Partnerships can achieve when businesses and local governments work together. I'm proud that, the day after the hotel's opening, the *Philadelphia Inquirer* ran an unusual editorial about it, commenting, "this project gives area residents reason to cheer," praising the artistic qualities of our design and detailing the economic benefits that the project was bringing to the community. The editorial concluded, simply: "Welcome to Philadelphia, Loews."

OF COURSE, THE POTENTIAL FOR GOVERNMENT/BUSINESS PARTNERSHIPS extends far beyond the confines of the travel and tourism economy. Many of today's most hopeful social and economic movements involve public/private partnerships. One example is the growth of venture capital funds that specialize in supporting small companies that employ low-income workers or operate in poor neighborhoods.

The first of these so-called community development venture capital funds was the Kentucky Highlands Investment Corporation, founded in 1968 as a not-for-profit outgrowth of President Johnson's Great Society initiatives. In time, Kentucky Highlands morphed into a for-profit venture capital fund, investing in and lending to start-ups in eastern Kentucky, then one of the most economically depressed parts of the country. The result was both satisfactory returns for investors and economic revival for down-and-out communities.

In recent years, funds modeled on Kentucky Highlands have multiplied and grown. Community venture funds now have over half a billion dollars in money under management. At first glance, this may not sound like much. But the beauty of community venture funds is that most of the companies they support require only modest investments— usually a few hundred thousand rather than the millions provided by conventional venture funds. Thus, a little money invested in community building goes a long way. The investment moneys come from a variety of sources, including a Treasury Department community development program launched under President Clinton and other sources such as banks, insurance companies, and foundations—in other words, a true partnership between government and the private sector.

Companies that seek investments from a community development fund must go through the same kind of rigorous scrutiny as any firm in search of venture capital funds. The main difference is that small companies that hire low-income workers or operate in depressed communities are favored in the selection process. Thus, unlike mainstream venture capital funds, which often focus on high-tech businesses in industries perceived as "sexy," community development funds will support manufacturing and service companies that generally have trouble attracting investors.

An example of the kind of company that can benefit from the community development fund movement is Ryla Teleservices, an Atlanta firm that provides call center services to financial and other firms. Ryla was founded by Mark Wilson, an African-American entrepreneur with experience in the call center field, with the specific goal of hiring, training, paying, and promoting call service workers more professionally than is usually the case. "I wanted to make sure they would feel respected and needed," Wilson has said. The idea was that treating workers with dignity would improve service quality, reduce turnover, and ultimately increase profits.

It's a fine idea, one that our experience in the hospitality business has shown to be sound. But it's not the kind of high-tech concept that normally attracts venture capital. Enter SJF Ventures, a community development fund in Durham, North Carolina. SJF investigated Ryla, studied its business plan, did its own market research, and decided to invest $700 thousand in the firm in exchange for an equity stake. Today, Ryla employs about 160 people and is hoping within the next year to double its 2003 revenues of $4 million.

The community fund movement is being nurtured by the Community Development Venture Capital Alliance (CDVCA), an organization with over 100 member funds. CDVCA offers training programs for venture capital professionals, consulting services, research and communication programs, and a central fund that offers seed money and co-investment capital to help community venture funds launch and grow new projects. A sampling of businesses being supported by CDVCA members includes:

- Niman Ranch, a California producer of beef, lamb, and pork that supports small family farms that raise livestock following strict codes of ecological and humane practice. Niman's packing plant is located in an Enterprise Zone in East Oakland, where about 90 formerly low-wage employees are now earning an average of over $12.50 an hour, as well as enjoying full health coverage, 401(k) membership, and other benefits. The growth of Niman ranch has been supported by $400 thousand in investment funds from Pacific Community Ventures in San Francisco.

- Allegheny Child Care Academy (ACCA), a string of 40 day care centers in Pennsylvania that employs over 800 people—one quarter of them former welfare recipients—and serves 3,200 children. ACCA's recent expansion was made possible by a $1 million investment from the Sustainable Jobs Funds (based in Durham, North Carolina) and the Future Fund of Pittsburgh. Not only does ACCA directly employ many inner-city residents, but the services it provides (including serving children three meals a day at no additional cost to parents, maintaining extended hours to accommodate parents who must work late, and offering computer and Internet access to preschool clients) help remedy one of the biggest obstacles to economic independence—lack of adequate child care for working parents.

- Cuddledown of Maine retails comforters, pillows, featherbeds, and other luxury items made with goose down. Founded in 1973, the company had grown to about $1 million in sales by 1988 when it was purchased by Christopher Bradley, who hoped to enter a new phase of growth. To make this possible, the company secured financing from CEI Ventures, a community fund in Portland, Maine, which has invested a total of $550,000 as well as helping Cuddledown recruit and hire a chief financial officer. Today, Cuddledown has sales of $22 million annually and employs 82 people who receive excellent wages and benefit packages in an otherwise depressed, economically struggling community.

The community venture movement is a great example of the multifaceted benefits of private-public partnership. With modest help from government sources, the community venture funds are able to help businesses that otherwise might fold or fail to grow. The businesses in turn employ people who need jobs, supporting families and helping to build thriving communities. Individuals who might have been dependent on handouts become self-supporting, and local, state, and federal tax revenues increase. At the same time, the private investors who provide capital to the funds benefit from the relatively high returns they enjoy.

Most of the companies that benefit from community venture funds are too small to attract attention from the mass media; they operate below the radar of Wall Street. Yet, small family businesses have always been at the heart of American economic growth. And the cumulative benefits that thousands of companies like these bring to rural or poor urban communities around the country are almost incalculable. They deserve support.

Even more modest—yet powerful in the aggregate—are the kinds of enterprises being fostered by the worldwide "microlending" movement. Launched by visionary economist Muhammed Yunus, founder of the famous Grameen Bank in Bangladesh, and especially active in regions like Latin America, Africa, and the Indian subcontinent, microlending provides loans as small as $100 to "microentrepreneurs" who are struggling to support their families through tiny business enterprises. These borrowers—largely female, often illiterate, and extremely poor—may need the money to buy a sewing machine, to put up a roadside stand for selling produce, or to buy sacks of flour for making tortillas. Microlenders free these poor but hard-working business people from reliance on loan sharks by lending them small amounts of money at fair interest rates. It's a privately managed movement that receives crucial support from the public sector—government, business, and philanthropy working in partnership.

One of the brilliant innovations of the microlending movement is its use of the technique known as *peer lending*. Local groups of microentrepreneurs—all the women in a particular village, for example—join forces and assume mutual responsibility for the borrowing of each individual member. This unique form of partnership creates a peer support network that helps each of these small business owners to navigate tough times, solve financial problems, and maintain the determination to overcome difficulties. As a result, repayment rates to microlenders are highly comparable to those enjoyed by conventional bankers who lend much larger sums to bigger companies with more significant collateral.

Groups like Acción International have helped to spearhead the microlending movement. Over the past 30 years, Acción has grown to the point where it served, either directly or through partner programs, over 740,000 clients around the world (including the United States) in 2002. Once again, the microlending movement wouldn't exist without private/public partnership. Acción is funded by a wide range of sources, including foundation grants, individual donations, and funds from public organizations such as the World Bank and the U.S. Agency for International Development (USAID).

THE KINDS OF PUBLIC/PRIVATE PARTNERSHIPS I'VE CITED IN THIS chapter—welfare to work, community venture funds, and microlending—all focus on economic development. But similar partnerships could help America tackle other seemingly insoluble problems in our society. Consider these examples:

- *Health care:* In the long run, some form of public-private partnership will probably be needed to resolve the intractable problems of rising health care costs, the plight of some 40 million uninsured Americans, the burden of insurance costs on businesses, and the dilemma of "rationing" health care without harming those most in need. All the parties involved, from insurance companies and HMOs to health care providers and pharmaceutical companies, must be willing to work together for the benefit of America's citizens, perhaps sacrificing some level of profit so that the neediest can be served. Only government has the clout to play the role of honest broker to make sure that the solutions devised spread the benefits and the costs fairly.
- *Education:* President Bush's No Child Left Behind Act has been one of the more controversial achievements of his administration.

Supporters say it places an appropriate burden of responsibility on schools that fail to teach; opponents say it creates mandates for testing and improved results without providing funding to support them or to help schools overcome the social problems that often underlie poor achievement. Perhaps one missing link here has been the failure to involve such private sector resources as local business organizations, which have such a major stake in the quality of education, as well as contributions from teachers' unions, parents groups, and other concerned stakeholders. The right solutions will come about when the educational system is reformed in an atmosphere of partnership, not treated as a political football.

- *Environment:* For too long, debates about the environment have pitted business leaders against "green" advocates, with the former generally advocating fewer or weaker regulations and the latter calling for more and tougher rules. Depending on the party in power, the pendulum has swung back and forth between these two poles, creating uncertainty and continuing rancor without guaranteeing the results all parties seek—a clean environment and a healthy economy. Some of today's most innovative economic thinkers have developed promising strategies for achieving both objectives through creative public-private cooperation, such as the use of trading markets for air and water rights. These partnership-style solutions deserve more attention than they've received.

There's an old saying that war is too important to be left to generals. In today's complicated world, public policy is too important to be left to politicians alone. The best ideas and the most powerful resources from every sector of society—academia, small business, community organizations, private foundations, and major corporations as well as government—must be brought to bear on the most difficult challenges we face. Business leaders need to keep an eye on the bottom line. But they also need to participate in the national debate as caring corporate citizens if they want a world in which they and their employees can live and thrive.

Kate Carr

Kate Carr is the president and chief executive officer of the Elizabeth Glaser Pediatric AIDS Foundation, a worldwide leader in the fight against pediatric AIDS and other serious and life-threatening diseases afflicting children.

Under Kate's leadership, the Foundation has expanded its work beyond the United States through the international Call to Action Project and taken a leadership role in establishing a national pediatric research agenda, as well as promoting global education, awareness, and compassion about children with HIV/AIDS.

Before joining the Foundation in 1998, Kate held a number of positions in politics and government. She served at the Democratic National Committee under the late Ron Brown and was finance director of the Democratic Senate Campaign Committee. After two years as a special assistant to President Clinton, she helped to launch the Welfare to Work Partnership.

Kate's multifaceted background has served her well since joining the Foundation. Perhaps the most important skill she exercises on a daily basis is the ability to create and nurture partnerships among a wide range of people and organizations—health care providers, not-for-profit groups, government agencies, universities—for the benefit of children around the world.

When we spoke with Kate by phone on March 22, 2004, she explained that the emphasis on children is one of the features that makes the Elizabeth Glaser Pediatric AIDS Foundation unique. "Among the many important things our founder Elizabeth Glaser did was to keenly focus us on the needs of children. Children aren't well represented in Washington, DC," Kate notes. "They can't buy a plane ticket to meet with their congressman or write a check to hire a lobbyist. One of our jobs is to provide them with the voice they need."

There are many research institutions, hospitals, and university centers that focus on health care issues. The Foundation looks for gaps in what is being done, especially as related to children. Kate offered this example: "Most people don't realize that three quarters of the most commonly prescribed drugs have never been tested on kids. As a result, health care providers have relatively little knowledge about proper dosages for children, unexpected side effects, and so on." The Foundation has worked with other organizations such as the American Academy of Pediatrics to change this situation. In the fall of 2003, their efforts met with success. A new law signed by President Bush in December requires that all new drugs with pediatric applications be tested on children.

It's obvious that successful lobbying requires partnerships across party divisions. We asked Kate about this. "Actually, lobbying is a very small aspect of our work. But we've always sought bipartisan support for our cause, dating back to our very first fund-raising event in 1989. It was co-hosted by conservative Republican Orrin Hatch and liberal Democrat Howard Metzenbaum. We've found that people are ready to respond when you ask them to rise above partisan or ideological differences on behalf of kids. And that applies not just to politicians but to business leaders, labor leaders, and ordinary citizens."

The global AIDS pandemic is an enormous adversary that no single organization could hope to conquer. One of the Foundation's key roles is to catalyze the creation of partnerships that focus the resources of government, private foundations, and other institutions on specific aspects of this challenge.

One example is the Glaser Pediatric Research Network, one of the first projects Kate tackled after joining the Foundation. "Research into childhood illnesses can be very hard to organize," Kate explains. "The kids who are the subjects of the research are often relatively few in number and may be widely

(Continued)

spread out geographically. That makes it hard for a single insti-
tution to successfully study and track their progress. We needed
a way to bring together the best minds to solve these kinds of
problems—a new kind of research partnership. The Foundation
brought together representatives from five of the nation's greatest medical research institutions: Harvard, UCLA, Baylor College of Medicine (Houston), UC San Francisco, and Stanford. It
took two years for us to craft an agreement covering such important and complex issues as intellectual property rights, data
sharing, and so on. But now the five centers are engaged in eight
collaborative studies funded by the Foundation, covering a variety of illnesses from osteoporosis and childhood obesity to pal-
liative care for children who are terminally ill."

The partnerships launched by the Foundation extend beyond
research into implementation. The Call to Action project is one
of the most remarkable.

The impetus came in July 1999, with a study suggesting that a
drug called novaripine could help prevent women from passing
the HIV virus on to their newborn children. When novaripine is
administered to an infected mother at the onset of labor and to
her baby within three days of birth, the rate of transmission—
normally as high as 35 percent—is cut in half. The outlook im-
proves further when additional steps (such as foregoing breast
feeding) are included.

Kate Carr explains, "Within a month of this initial study, the
Foundation's board decided to invest one million dollars to start a
series of demonstration projects. We wanted to test how a regimen
including drugs like novaripine could reduce the HIV transmission rate in a variety of settings, including developing nations. By
the following February, we'd funded such projects in Thailand
and several countries in Africa."

This was just the start of the effort. In 2000, the newly
formed Gates Foundation provided a grant of $15 million,
which permitted the Glaser Foundation to expand the effort into

implementation projects in 17 countries. More recently, the U.S. government has stepped up to the plate. In September 2002, the Foundation entered a cooperative agreement from the U.S. Agency for International Development (USAID) that will provide $100 million over the next five years, and in 2003 the Centers for Disease Control (CDC) created a similar agreement providing another $125 million.

The impact has already been enormous, as Kate explains. "Close to one million women in 17 countries from Russia, India, and the Caribbean to broad regions of sub-Saharan Africa have received prenatal care, counseling, and testing. If they test positive for HIV, we arrange access to medications like novaripine. And we're training not just physicians and nurses but traditional birth attendants to use the new regimen. As a result, thousands of babies have been spared the ravages of HIV infection."

The Elizabeth Glaser Foundation could never have achieved these results on its own. "Call to Action illustrates how a relatively small organization armed with the right idea can leverage assets from many resources—government, foundations, private companies, individual volunteers. When you bring together these forces behind a single goal, the multiplying effect is tremendously powerful. Each partner is crucial to the broader effort. But the combination is what enables us to accomplish so much."

CHAPTER 9

What's in It for the Owners?

Bringing Dollars and Sense to the Bottom Line

Society is a partnership in all science, a partnership in all art, a partnership in every virtue and in all perfection. As the ends of such a partnership cannot be obtained in many generations, it becomes a partnership not only between those who are living, but between those who are living, those who are dead, and those who are to be born.

—Edmund Burke (1729–1797)

THE PARTNERSHIPS WE'VE DISCUSSED SO FAR—WITH EMPLOYEES, WITH customers, with other companies, and with the community at large—are all important ingredients in the success of any organization. But there's one more partnership that's as crucial as any. That's the partnership with owners—the people who provide the money on which your organization is built.

In the capitalist system, owners are essential to both the existence and the growth of your enterprise. If the owners are happy, the investment money will continue to flow, salaries will get paid, products and services will be delivered, partnerships with outside people and firms will thrive, and the firm will have an opportunity to grow. If the owners are unhappy, the money will dry up, and soon every other activity of the organization will grind to a halt.

On the other hand, the *purpose* of a business is not simply to create short-term profit. If it were, it wouldn't matter what business you were in, and the kind and quality of your other partnerships would also be irrelevant. You could run the business in any way you liked, so long as profits continued to grow. (There may be some business people who think this way; there may even be some business leaders who operate organizations this way. I'm not one of them, and if you've read this far in the book, you're not, either.)

The purpose of a business is to create long-term value. The best way to do this is by creating products and services that offer good value to customers, provide rewarding career opportunities to employees, nurture economic growth, and help enrich the lives of our communities, our nation, and all humanity. And all of these goals require partnerships.

Business leaders have to be skilled jugglers, keeping several balls in the air at once. Yes, you've got to be profit-minded—which means operating your business with hard-nosed realism, demanding operational excellence, aggressive sales and marketing efforts, cost controls, and smart investment decisions. But you've also got to keep in mind the broader goals of the enterprise, and somehow maintain a balance among them all.

At Loews Hotels, we take our fiduciary relationship to our owners very seriously. They demand a good rate of return on their money, and we're determined to provide it. But we've discovered that the best way to achieve this is by maximizing *all* of our partnerships—not just one or two. Contrary to popular belief, the most successful businesses aren't run in accordance with a philosophy of "profit first, everything else last." In reality, when a company's relationships with employees, customers, the community, other businesses, and government agencies are strong and mutually beneficial, the bottom line inevitably benefits.

You may be wondering whether leaders in nonprofit organizations are exempt from today's unrelenting bottom-line pressures. Superficially, they are; the people who fund nonprofits aren't seeking financial profit from their donations. But in a larger sense, nonprofit leaders are in exactly the same situation as business executives. They too are competing for available money against thousands of other organizations.

And like investors, charitable donors expect the nonprofit organizations they support to be run with maximum efficiency and productivity.

No wonder many of today's most progressive nonprofits are recruiting top-flight business executives to lead them. For nonprofits, the bottom line takes a different form than it does at profit-making companies—but it matters just as much.

IN CONTEMPORARY CAPITALISM, OWNERSHIP CAN TAKE SEVERAL FORMS. In the case of Loews Hotels, there are several layers of ownership. Looking upward from my CEO desk, there are the "owners" to whom I report: the directors of our parent company, Loews Corporation, and the Loews shareholders who have ultimate control over the entire organization. Looking downward, there are the smaller company units for which Loews Hotels is responsible—the individual hotels, each of which is run as a separate business that must contribute to our bottom line. In addition, some of our hotels are owned, in whole or in part, by outside investors. Each relationship in this "ownership layer cake" is an important one that must be managed thoughtfully to maximize the success of the corporation as a whole.

Let's begin by looking at our relationship to our parent corporation. Being owned by Loews Corporation gives Loews Hotels a number of advantages—some fairly obvious, others less so.

We enjoy the benefits of being part of a publicly traded Fortune 500 company as well as the relative freedom of a small, nimble, entrepreneurial operation. It's an environment that gives the company managers a reasonably good shot at producing excellent profits for our owners (Loews Corporation and, ultimately, Loews Corporation's shareholders) while also building healthy partnerships with employees, communities, and our other stakeholders, to the benefit of all.

As part of Loews Corporation, Loews Hotels has the resources of a company with nearly $80 billion in assets behind us. We get our human resources, real estate management, information technology, and legal services from the parent corporation, which means we get better quality services than we could afford on our own. Best of all, we have access to a significant pool of Loews' capital for investments. It's an advantage that has stood us in good stead, especially during tough times for our industry—including the challenging period we are emerging from today.

Some other organizations in the hospitality industry are struggling right now because of the large burdens of debt they assumed to expand during flush times. This debt burden and the huge interest payments they must meet every month force them to manage quarter-to-quarter, making short-term decisions that may hurt their business over time.

At Loews Hotels, we're lucky to be able to take a longer term view. One reason is the sheer size and diversity of our parent company. Loews Corporation owns a variety of businesses that tend to react differently at various stages in the economic cycle. At Loews Hotels, our performance generally lags six months behind the ebb and flow of gross domestic product (GDP), simply because customers usually book their meetings and hotel space in advance. Thus, we suffered from the economic downturn of 2001 later than some other companies (and will benefit from the recovery more slowly). Because Loews Corporation owns a diversified portfolio of investments, the pressure on any one business to carry the load of profitability is lessened.

Our ownership status also has implications for the ways we grow—and don't grow. Growing through asset purchases can be challenging. Loews has an opportunistic investment philosophy, based on seeking out companies that have hidden or unrecognized value. We've established fairly high hurdle rates that must be achieved for a potential investment to pass muster, which means that we forgo some hotel purchases that might seem tempting. This is especially true today, with many large, well-capitalized investment firms (such as Kohlberg Kravis Roberts and the Blackstone Group) now active in the hospitality arena.

At the same time, being part of Loews Corporation enables Loews Hotels to do things that other chains can't do. The public/private partnership we created in Miami, for example, was possible only because of the combination of the availability of investment money from Loews Corporation and our entrepreneurial leadership style. Similarly, our three hotels in Orlando represent a development that Loews Hotels could have created only with the backing of our corporate parent.

Loews Corporation's sponsorship makes a huge difference when we need to raise capital in the debt market. Loews Corporation has strong partnerships with such great investment firms as Bank of Nova Scotia, Deutsche Bank, JP Morgan, and West LB, all of which have a specialty in financing the hospitality industry. As part of the corporation, Loews Hotels enjoys a number of concrete benefits that flow from these partnerships.

Here's a case in point. In September 2001, we were in the process of refinancing the Loews Miami Beach Hotel, using a particular kind of debt instrument known as collateralized mortgage-backed securities issued under the auspices of Deutsche Bank. Then the terror attacks of September 11 occurred. Activity in the debt marketplace almost completely shut down, and many proposed refinancings fell through. But ours went forward on time, because Deutsche Bank felt that the sponsorship of Loews Corporation would carry us through that difficult time. Sure enough, investor confidence in our solvency never wavered. We raised the needed capital at a time when others in our industry couldn't.

In some industries, being part of a larger corporate entity can have its drawbacks. My co-author Karl Weber points out that book publishers that are owned by larger media conglomerates have historically struggled to justify their relatively low rates of return as compared with businesses such as television and motion pictures. The conglomerates often end up selling the publishing houses, unable to realize enough long-term value in these low-yielding businesses.

Fortunately, this isn't a problem we've faced. Loews Corporation understands the hotel business. As you recall, Loews Hotels was the founding business of the company, which creates a sense of institutional memory and commitment to our industry that might not otherwise exist. This helps the parent corporation deal with the ups and downs of our performance realistically. During the current difficult business climate, for example, we've deliberately chosen not to focus solely on year-over-year performance, which has declined for us just as it is for almost every hotel company. Instead, we're measuring our performance against that of other major hotel chains, looking at such metrics as revenue growth and profit performance. If we are trending better than our main competitors, we reason, then we are doing a good job.

In the short term, profits may not be as high as we'd like. But when the upturn comes—as it inevitably will—we'll be positioned to take advantage of it and, we hope, outstrip the growth of our competitors. Having owner/partners like Loews Corporation who can afford to be patient takes a little pressure off us, enabling us to make better decisions for long-term value creation.

We sometimes hear from our friends in the investment banking community with offers to spin off Loews Hotels as a separate business. We

TISCH'S TIPS

Is your organization part of some larger entity? If so, have you examined the benefits and disadvantages you obtain from the partnership with your parent organization? Try listing these in two columns—one labeled benefits, the other labeled disadvantages. Then consider whether or not the benefits outweigh the disadvantages. If they don't, look for ways to increase the benefits, reduce the disadvantages, or both . . . or else consider whether it might be possible to break off the partnership in favor of independent existence.

haven't done it because we don't need access to capital or infrastructure assets. Being part of Loews Corporation is pretty comfortable for us, and for the foreseeable future that's where we intend to stay.

As I've explained, one level of ownership that must be considered in managing Loews Hotels is that of our parent, Loews Corporation. Now let's shift our point of view and consider how the owner partnership works at a lower level—that of the individual hotel.

Experience shows that many businesses get into trouble because of a disconnect between the interests and goals of the owners and those of the people who run the operations. We've heard the horror stories about self-dealing executives who enjoy enormous salaries, bonuses, stock options, and personal perks while neglecting the long-term health of the firm. Less spectacularly, many companies flounder when well-meaning managers of individual divisions or departments get out of synch with the overall strategic objectives of the corporation. Every organization must find a way to align the plans and actions of managers with the objectives of ownership—without unnecessarily stifling the managers' individual creativity.

This challenge is particularly acute at Loews Hotels. In some ways, Loews Hotels is not so much a single business as a collection of 20 businesses. Our chain includes 20 hotel properties, each with its unique economic environment, clientele, marketing potential, size and amenities, labor issues, and other business characteristics. Thus, the Loews Hotels' business plan is really built on at least 20 different budgets (not even factoring in the separate budgets for our home office and other service providers).

To further complicate matters, some of our hotels have third-party owners. As I'll explain in more detail later, these outside owners must be treated as partners, and their input on all major business decisions is vitally important.

After years of experimentation, we've found that this complex business system works best when we treat each hotel as an individual business unit with one decision maker in control. In the leadership structure we put together under President Jack Adler some five years ago, we made the general manager of the hotel the key point of account-ability. He or she is surrounded by an executive team of specialists in sales, marketing, operations, human resources, food and beverage, and other functions. And our talented home office team stands ready to pro-vide guidance, advice, and information to enhance the performance of the hotel. But the executive committee at the individual hotel remains the crucial link.

Our financial planning process reflects the complex balancing act we try to achieve among the individual needs of separate hotel proper-ties, the overall demands of the Loews Hotels' business, and the profit requirements of our owner/partners, including both Loews Corpora-tion and the third-party owners of particular properties.

From Labor Day through the end of the year, we create business plans for the coming year, working with the management of the individ-ual hotels, with third-party owners, and with expert guidance from our home office group. We present our plans once internally and then to the external owner/partners that we have at about half of our properties. After the Loews Hotels senior management approves the plans, they are rolled up into an overall budget for approval by Loews Corporation.

We've worked hard over the years to create a structure for this pro-cess that balances centralized guidance with decentralized control and initiative. Every line in our budgets requires thoughtful analysis and discussion. There's no cookie-cutter system for deciding which invest-ments will pay off and which will not. Again, there's a premium on having hotel managers in place with an intimate knowledge of the property, its customers, and the business environment. Being decen-tralized means that we give our GMs and their executive teams signifi-cant responsibility as well as authority to build the individual success of their hotels.

The fact that the ownership structure of our hotels differs from property to property adds one more twist to the challenge of aligning the interests of owners and managers.

Loews Hotels has outright ownership of about half of our hotels. In the other cases, we partner with outside owners. The three hotels at

TISCH'S TIPS

How do the planning processes at your organization balance centralization and decentralization? Are goals set in a truly consultative fashion? Or must lower-level managers simply accept objectives for profit and other metrics that are imposed on them? It takes a leap of faith to allow your employee partners to help shape the overall objectives of the organization—but if you do, the increased degree of buy-in and commitment they will exhibit in the coming year may surprise you.

Universal Orlando, for example, are owned 50 percent by Loews, 50 percent by Universal Orlando and the Rank Organization; the rights and responsibilities of each partner are spelled out in a detailed, complex contract. Several other properties, including the Loews Ventana Canyon Resort, the Don Cesar Beach Resort, the Jefferson, Loews L'Enfant Plaza, the House of Blues Hotel, and Loews Santa Monica Beach Hotel, are owned mainly or entirely by outside partners, with Loews serving as manager.

Where Loews has no investment stake in a property, major capital improvements must be funded by the owner, who assumes both the risk and the potential benefit. This can produce some tricky challenges for managing the partnership. The Loews Santa Monica Beach Hotel benefits from a very knowledgeable independent ownership group that recently initiated an $18 million renovation. In other cases, the property owner may focus on short-term profit, perhaps lacking the staying power to emphasize long-term value as Loews tries to do. The situation becomes especially difficult when ownership is vested in two or more partners who stop seeing eye to eye. Under these circumstances, it's sometimes hard to get decisions made. I believe that it's always better to make a decision—*any* decision—rather than no decision.

When the relationship of trust and shared goals breaks down, managing a partnership can be very difficult. But when the partnership is strong, the benefits are enormous. For example, it's extremely valuable to work with local partners who know the business climate, have relationships with key people in the community, and can help us steer clear of potential disasters.

As we noted early in this chapter, the need for long-term value creation is at the heart of the partnership with owners. Our chief responsibility to our owner/partners is to provide them with competitive rates of return on their investments. And one of the important challenges we must meet to achieve this is to clearly and intelligently define the businesses we want to be in.

Maybe this sounds obvious. But many companies have soared or crashed based on how they chose to define—or redefine—their businesses. During the 1980s, for example, IBM floundered in large part because it failed to challenge the traditional assumption that IBM was in "the computer business." As computer hardware became increasingly commoditized, margins shrank, and so did IBM's profitability. Today, the company is on firmer ground thanks to its new focus on "the information business," which has opened up a world of higher profit opportunities in consulting, services, and software.

In other cases, companies have struggled when they moved into businesses that were too far afield from their core interest or expertise, as Coca-Cola did when it bought Columbia Pictures. Smart strategic planning means striking a balance between the need to creatively redefine your business when required by changes in the economic environment and the importance of "sticking to your knitting." And the proper balance may shift from time to time and from one industry to another.

Finding this balance is especially challenging in today's hospitality business. Hoteliers are under increasing pressure to find new sources of revenue as some old sources dry up. For example, at an average-sized hotel, the telephone department used to produce some $200 thousand in revenues annually. No more. The increased use of cell phones and the Internet is drastically cutting the income generated by telephone usage.

Despite this pressure for new revenue sources, we at Loews Hotels try to stay close to our roots in hospitality, which means, in essence, providing rooms, food, and beverages. We are not necessarily involved in the many other related businesses that go on at hotel properties—although there are times when such involvement makes strategic sense.

The retail business is one example of our ongoing balancing act. We at Loews Hotels have sometimes operated the retail shops that exist on our properties, but we've increasingly come to recognize that we are not experts in choosing goods, stocking them, and managing retail operations. Perhaps we could develop this expertise if we chose. But it would take time and attention away from our core business. So strategically it makes more sense for us to lease out our retail spaces, and that's what we usually do.

Other examples of businesses we try to stay away from are providing audio-visual equipment and other business services, such as fax machines, computers, shipping, and others. These require technical knowledge that we'd rather not have to develop. Instead, we'll partner with companies that have made business services their specialty.

Another basic industry with enormous relevance to the hotel business is other forms of real estate. Here, too, we basically try to keep our hotel business separate from its inevitable link to real estate. This is another legacy from our company's historic roots. My uncle Larry Tisch, who did so much to establish the business philosophy of Loews Corporation, had strong reservations about real estate investment, especially because it is relatively hard to quickly "monetize" real estate—that is, to realize its cash flow value.

There are exceptions to this principle. For example, our Vanderbilt Hotel in Nashville includes an office complex, which in effect puts us in the local real estate business there. The building of such dual-purpose developments became popular in the late 1980s, and in this case it has proven to be tremendously successful. But we're generally not interested in applying the same model elsewhere.

Similarly, we've been urged at times to get into the gaming business. Actually, we once had a toe-hold in it: In the 1970s, before the recent boom in gaming, Loews Hotels owned the Monte Carlo Hotel, which included a casino. But over the years, this industry has become increasingly complex. Rather than compete with the experts in the field—people like Steve Wynn who have built great businesses around

> ### TISCH'S TIPS
>
> When was the last time you defined the nature of the business you are in (whether you work in a for-profit company, a not-for-profit group, or any other kind of organization)? Have you taken on functions, processes, and tasks that don't match your organizational expertise and fail to contribute significantly to meeting your goals? If so, look for ways to redefine your business to improve your focus on activities that are closer to the heart of your organization.

the economics of gaming—we've left casino ownership and management to others.

NO OVERVIEW OF THE QUEST FOR LONG-TERM VALUE WOULD BE complete without a look at the role of information technology (IT). Over the past 10 years, IT has been a major area of investment for most companies. There are signs that these investments are finally paying off. In fact, some economists, including Federal Reserve Chairman Alan Greenspan, now believe that much of our nation's growth in productivity during the 1990s can be attributed to process improvements made possible by IT.

As in so many other industries, IT is increasingly important in the hotel business. But it's easy to spend millions on IT investments without enjoying noticeable benefits. So we spend a great deal of time and energy on making wise decisions about IT spending.

One way to think about IT investments is on a spectrum, defined by the emergence of new technologies over time. A given company can choose to trail the market, buying only well-tested products at reasonable prices (but lagging behind its competitors somewhat in terms of capabilities). Or it can choose to lead the market, buying cutting-edge technologies at higher prices (but taking a risk on software or hardware that may not be fully proven).

At Loews Hotels, we try to position ourselves somewhere between the mid-point and the leading edge—what we sometimes call "the bleeding edge" because of the risk involved. If this sounds like another example of our conservative approach to investment planning, you're right.

One new wrinkle in IT for the hospitality industry involves the emergence of so-called "yield management systems." This refers to software programs designed to maximize revenues by adjusting prices in response to shifts in the supply and demand curve. Hoteliers have various ways to make these adjustments, including imposing or waiving length-of-stay restrictions, shutting off Internet access points to our reservation system, shifting the balance of group versus individual rooms, offering rate benefits to fill certain dates, and so on. It's complex stuff that can make a big difference in the bottom line for a hotel by filling every room at the best possible price.

Of course, software can only do so much. Running the system and making the key decisions about how to book rooms must be placed in the hands of one or more experts, known as *revenue managers*. This poses another choice between centralization and decentralization—and, as we usually do, Loews Hotels leans toward decentralization, putting the responsibility into the hands of a revenue manager who reports to the general manager at each hotel.

Giving 20 different properties this kind of independence produces some knotty challenges. Interpreting the extremely technical streams of data that the new yield management software generates is very tough. We're finding that it pays to closely scrutinize the revenue managers we hire, making sure they are technically capable as well as steeped in the complexities of our industry. A top-notch revenue manager generally has a hotel degree and training in sales or marketing in a hotel environment. But most important, he or she also has to know and love numbers.

It's a crucial job and one that we have to pay well to fill. We support the local revenue managers with guidance from the home office. We continue to try to provide more and more business intelligence to our local managers and are working now to develop a new database management system that will integrate our reservation system with our property management system to give us an in-depth understanding of our guests: who is coming in to each property, what revenues they are generating, what food and beverage income they are producing, and so on.

Nonetheless, the key decisions remain at the individual hotel. After all, the power to control prices and bookings is tantamount to the power to control profits.

WE'LL CONTINUE TO EXPERIMENT WITH THE PROPER BALANCE BETWEEN centralization and decentralization in the financial management of Loews Hotels. There will always be a tension between these two pressures in our organization, in part because we have ownership partners at several different levels. All of these owners have a rightful claim on a share of the value we create, and we therefore have a responsibility to produce solid streams of revenues and profits for all of them. And since these partners link up with us at different levels, we need to focus on long-term value at both the micro and macro levels—each hotel needs to generate its proper share of value, as does the entire chain of properties.

As a result, Jack Adler, the rest of our home office executive team, and I will probably always be tinkering with our leadership structure and our management processes, in search of the ideal way to achieve these somewhat disparate goals. Nonetheless, one thing seems clear: There's only so much we can do to impact value growth by manipulating spreadsheets and organization charts. The best way to grow value is to:

- Hire the best possible people at every level in the organization and give them all the tools they need to deliver great performance.
- Develop intimate connections with our customers and create products, services, and marketing approaches that respond to their needs and desires.
- Nurture healthy, mutually supportive relationships with the communities in which we do business, helping them to thrive as places in which to live and work and as travel destinations.

- Find ways to cooperate with other companies, both inside and outside our industry, to enhance our mutual profitability and strengthen the economy.
- Work constructively with all levels of government for the benefit of our country and its people.

In other words, when we do a great job of managing all our other partnerships—with employees, customers, communities, other companies, and government—our partnership with our owners will thrive, too.

PORTRAIT IN PARTNERSHIP

Sir Howard Stringer

Sir Howard Stringer is chairman and chief executive office of Sony Corporation of America and vice chairman of Sony Corporation. He's responsible for developing the strategic linkage between the entertainment and electronics businesses, and furthering the company's content businesses worldwide. He oversees Sony Pictures Entertainment (the parent company of Columbia Pictures), Sony Music Entertainment Inc., and Sony Electronics Inc.

Before joining Sony, Sir Howard had a distinguished 30-year career as a journalist, producer, and executive at CBS Inc. Under his leadership, the CBS Television Network became the first network to rise from last to first place in one season. He signed David Letterman to CBS, developed the award-winning news program *48 Hours,* and helped make *The CBS Evening News with Dan Rather* the dominant network evening broadcast of its day.

When we interviewed Sir Howard by phone on January 20, 2004, we asked him to consider how the Power of Partnership affected his work at Sony, He replied, "It depends very much on which part of our business we're talking about. For example,

(Continued)

Sony is very active in the arena where technology and content are converging, along with software, hardware, and entertainment companies. In that world, competition is fierce, and partnerships are relatively rare." What about Sony's motion picture business, we wondered. Isn't the production and distribution of films an inherently cooperative venture?

"Indeed it is," Sir Howard replied. "Producing movies requires a skillful blend of disparate elements contributed by people with different goals. It's a form of partnership, but one with many built-in tensions.

"Start with money. Producers, directors, and actors generally take up-front fees which the studio finances. As a result, the studio is usually the only participant who runs the risk of losing money. The production process becomes a battle royal to preserve the revenues so that the studio can make a bit of profit. How you manage the resulting tension determines your success."

The situation was quite different in Sir Howard's previous arena, the television industry. "As compared to a movie studio," Sir Howard explained, "The network has much more power over the process. The network can fire a producer or a director, or cancel a program. The only real control that a movie studio has over its creative partners is to refuse to work with the same artists in the future.

"The pendulum has swung a long way from the days of the old studio system, when movie actors and directors were completely dominated by the studios. I wouldn't want to go back to that system, even if it were possible. But the pendulum needs to swing back a little in the other direction."

We asked Sir Howard whether he'd developed any techniques for managing the tensions built into the movie-making partnership.

"A studio executive," he told us, "must be both inspirational and motivational. Now that the old days of the studio tycoon giving orders and firing people are gone, relentless communication and evenness of temperament are key. The goal is to help all the partners in the process recognize that, at bottom, our goals are identical—to create great movies that also make money for everyone."

We commented that perhaps the old stereotype of the studio executive pounding his fist on the table was a bit outdated. Sir Howard agreed. "Sometimes being explosive can work—at least for a time. But only while you're very successful. The minute things go wrong, nobody gives you a helping hand. In the last four years, we've seen the downfall of leaders in many businesses who behaved like imperial CEOs."

He went on in a thoughtful vein. "The unwritten social contract that used to govern the relationship between the lowest- and highest-paid employees of the corporation blew apart in the late 1990s. The stock market bubble of the 90s put too much focus on the share price. For some CEOs, operating the company became secondary to making deals and boosting the share price, mainly for the benefit of the executives themselves. As a result, many business leaders lost their ability to motivate their people. The deal-centric CEO quickly became the egocentric CEO.

"This must change," Sir Howard concluded. "The great company is still a shared experience. It's an ideal that took a beating in the 1990s, but one that is still valid today."

CHAPTER 10

New York Rising

The Power of Partnerships in Time of Crisis

*Successful sports teams are never built on only one person.
Even transcendent stars like Michael Jordan or Babe Ruth need
strong supporting casts—and the proof that they're true leaders
is that those other players were better around Jordan or Ruth
than they would have been otherwise.*

— Rudolph W. Giuliani
Mayor of New York, 1994–2002

NEAR THE START OF THIS BOOK, I POSED THIS QUESTION: CAN THE
Power of Partnerships really work in today's ultra-competitive world,
where many organizations are struggling simply to survive? When
people feel threatened, don't the primitive instincts of fight or flight
take control, overwhelming the idea of cooperation in a mad scramble
for self-preservation?

You might think that the hard-nosed and realistic answer to this
question is yes. But I know it isn't so. I've seen the Power of Partnership at work in the city I love best—New York—during the toughest
year in anyone's memory: the year that followed the horrific events of
September 11, 2001.

The aftermath of the terrorist attacks that destroyed New York's
World Trade Center and took nearly three thousand lives posed a

number of overlapping challenges, some of which our nation is still grappling with. Two of these challenges directly affected me and the organizations I serve. One was a short-term humanitarian crisis, as thousands of New Yorkers and visitors to the city needed immediate assistance, both physical and psychological, to cope with the tragedies. The other was a longer term business crisis, as an already-wobbly national economy was pushed further into recession by the confidence-shattering effects of the attacks. The lessons in partnership that I and countless other Americans learned during this time of testing are deeply relevant today, and they will be for years to come.

Just as every American of an earlier generation remembers where they were when they heard the news of John F. Kennedy's assassination, everyone today recalls what they were doing on Tuesday morning, September 11, 2001. I was at home in my apartment on New York's upper east side. I was feeling lousy. I'd spent the previous day in bed, fighting off a flu bug and a temperature that had climbed as high as 102 degrees. But that morning, I was determined to feel better. I was due downtown at the American Express building, next to the World Trade Center, where the Travel Business Roundtable would be holding an 11 A.M. news conference to announce its new partnership with the World Travel and Tourism Council. This was an event I didn't want to miss.

A few minutes after 8:30, I was eating some toast, scanning the four newspapers I have delivered every morning— the *New York Times,* the *Daily News,* the *New York Post,* and the *Wall Street Journal*—and wondering whether I was well enough for the big meeting downtown. As I read, NBC's *Today Show* was playing in the background.

Then, at 8:42 A.M., everything changed. Katie Couric broke in with disturbing news: A small plane had crashed into one of the towers of the World Trade Center in lower Manhattan. (That was how the initial attack was originally reported.) Suddenly, like millions of other Americans—and especially New Yorkers—my attention was riveted to the television. As the morning's events unfolded, I sat with my eyes glued to the TV set. I watched as first one tower, then the other collapsed in a column of smoke, dust, and rubble.

Maybe you experienced the same jumble of thoughts and feelings I did in those terrible moments. Concern for the victims, fears for our country, anger at the terrorists, and worries about how our world was changing jostled for my attention. I quickly considered all the people I knew who might be downtown that morning, some in the World Trade Center itself. Many of my friends and family members routinely attended business meetings in the Twin Towers. The spectacular Windows of the World restaurant, with its views of the New York skyline, the harbor, and the Statue of Liberty, was a favorite spot for early morning conferences and conversations. Maybe someone I cared about was trapped in one of those buildings, desperately seeking a way out.

My phone started ringing. One of the first calls came from Emily, a close friend who worked in the west forties, not far from Times Square. "Jon," Emily said, "Have you heard the news? What do I do? I'm scared." She sounded it.

"We're all scared," I replied. "Just come up here as soon as you can." She set off on foot and made the 40-block walk in an hour or so. We spent the rest of the morning together. Somehow, at a time like that, it helps just to be near the people you care about. I quickly checked the whereabouts of family members. All were okay.

My mom and dad were in Denver, where they'd traveled via private aircraft to watch the New York Giants get beaten by the Broncos on Monday Night Football the previous evening. I knew they'd be trying to fly back—especially now, with their home city under attack. But air traffic around the country was being shut down. I had no idea how soon I'd see my parents again. It was disconcerting, at a time when we all felt the instinctive urge to be with those we loved.

(Later, I heard the whole odd story of what happened to my folks. At the time of the attacks, they were actually on the runway at Denver's Centennial Field, waiting for permission to take off for New York. Finally, they were ordered to return to the gate, where they learned what had happened. Although virtually all air travel was suspended around the country for almost a week, my parents made it home just two days later. My Dad is a clever guy. He phoned the head of security for Loews Corporation, who, like most corporate security chieftains, had been on the phone with his government contacts. It turned out that the Federal Emergency Management Agency needed a favor: They had four key workers stranded in Denver, with no way to reach the emergency in New

York. Was there any way Loews could help? Of course! On Wednesday night, Mom and Dad ferried the four FEMA workers to New York City on one of the few nonmilitary planes that was permitted to fly.)

As soon as I knew the people I cared about were all right, the bigger picture emerged. Naturally my primary emotion was the same stunned horror and shock that everyone else felt. But as a business leader, I had other worries, too. Our national economy, which had already been showing signs of faltering, was now in serious trouble. And the industry I belong to, travel and tourism, might be hit hardest of all. Here were four wide-bodied aircraft being used in an act of war—two against the Twin Towers, one against the Pentagon in Washington, DC, and one plowed into a field in Pennsylvania, with terrible loss of life. What could be more devastating to any business than having one of your proudest symbols used as a terrorist weapon?

It was clear that travel would be shut down completely for a time, and that even once the airways were reopened, many people would be afraid to fly. The implications for our industry would be devastating. And the city I know and love best, New York, now reeling from one of the most horrific assaults in history, would be hit especially hard.

By noon that Tuesday, it was clear that thousands of people had lost their lives. Gradually, I realized that many more—perhaps millions— might also lose their livelihoods. This would be a long-term crisis that I and other industry leaders had an obligation to tackle.

IN A TIME OF CRISIS, MOST PEOPLE REACT ACCORDING TO DEEPLY MARKED personal habits. In the immediate aftermath of the terror attacks, the courageous firefighters, police, and emergency workers instinctively did what they have been trained to do: They rushed into the danger zone. Doctors, nurses, psychologists, counselors, and social workers immediately set up trauma centers where the injured and the terrified could be comforted.

As a business leader, I spend my days looking for opportunities to bring people together to solve problems and grow our business. So my natural instinct on September 11 was to start organizing a response to

> ## TISCH'S TIPS
>
> Has your organization ever faced a time of crisis? It need not be a moment of national tragedy like September 11; it could be anything from a fire or accident, the sudden death of an important leader, or a serious, unexpected problem with the services or products you offer. How well did you handle the crisis? Were you able to call on support from partners throughout the community? Every organization needs a crisis preparedness plan. And no such plan is complete without a set of strong partnerships that you know you can count on when a crisis strikes.

the crisis, first on behalf of the Loews Hotels' family, then on behalf of the larger business community to which we belong. And my way of doing this was, as usual, to find ways to create partnerships that could multiply the power of our efforts.

To begin with, we had to address the immediate aftermath of the tragedy. At the time, Loews owned two hotels in New York. One of these, the Metropolitan, was right across the street from a firehouse and a police station. We'd always had great relations with the firefighters and the police; our kitchen often sent them meals and snacks to keep up their spirits throughout the day and night. I checked with our manager at the Metropolitan to make sure our employees were okay—thankfully, they were—and asked her to do everything she could to support the uniformed services. "We're already on the case," she assured me.

For the next several days, the Metropolitan turned into a refuge for the rescue workers. Like many New York firehouses, the station across from the Metropolitan was devastated on September 11, 2001; 11 of their firefighters were lost in the collapse of the towers. There's no way to soften a blow like that, but we helped as best we could. Friends and family members of the police and firefighters streamed into the neighborhood; we put them up in our hotel rooms. We provided sheets, blankets, towels, shampoo, and soap to the rescue workers and to hundreds of people left stranded or homeless by the attacks. In the days that followed, our kitchen and restaurant workers put in extraordinary hours cooking thousands of meals for the rescue workers, firefighters, police, and building crews searching through the rubble at Ground Zero.

Hundreds of other businesses and countless individuals contributed in similar ways. Words like partnership, community, and teamwork are scarcely adequate to describe the outpouring of love and caring evoked by the tragedies of September 11.

On the day of the attacks, traffic into and out of the city was halted, and there were no flights leaving New York or any other American town. So we knew that Loews and all the other New York hoteliers would have to house thousands of stranded people—not just tourists and travelers but native New Yorkers and suburban workers who couldn't get home. This was the second priority we tackled as that horrible Tuesday unfolded.

After spending the afternoon on the phone with dozens of friends, colleagues, and acquaintances, trying to nail down the facts about what was happening and to formulate plans for keeping the Loews operations running smoothly, I walked over to the Regency Hotel (which is close to our home office headquarters) for dinner. I'd invited everyone I knew, realizing that thousands would have nowhere else to go—and that everyone would want to be together at a time like this. Emily and I found the dining room completely packed. Nearly all of the city's restaurants were closed, except for the ones in hotels. So hundreds of hungry visitors had gravitated to the Regency, looking for something—anything—to eat, as well as a little respite from the overwhelming sense of tragedy and confusion. Here was a minibusiness crisis that needed immediate attention.

We mobilized everyone we could grab from the Loews staff—marketing executives, accountants, salespeople. They were all to set work in the kitchen or in the dining room. I helped bus tables and deliver baskets of bread. We served hundreds of dinners at the Regency that night—many more than normal. Most important, our dining room became an informal community center for stranded visitors and their New York friends. We set up video monitors around the room so people could track the news. Many stayed there late into the night, talking about what had happened and comforting one another.

The next day, Wednesday, I was asked to attend a meeting of city business leaders. Because the city's emergency command center had been located in one of the buildings destroyed at the World Trade Center, the city took over the police academy on the East Side. As you can imagine, security was drum-tight. I've never seen so many police officers in one place.

When I walked in, the first person I saw was Sunny Mindel, Mayor Rudolph Giuliani's director of communications. I've known Sunny for almost 40 years. As I'd seen on the news, she and the mayor had almost been killed the day before when a downtown building collapsed around them. As I greeted Sunny, the mayor suddenly appeared. "Jon, how are you?" he asked.

"Never mind that," I replied, "What's important is, how are *you*?" The mayor was already emerging as the leader the city and indeed the nation were turning to for strength and reassurance. It was obvious that he'd hardly slept the night before. He was haggard and drawn. But he simply gave me a big hug and said, "I'm okay. And *we* are going to be okay." It was obvious who he meant by *we:* He meant New York and all its people.

When it comes to politics, Rudy and I have disagreed. But at this moment, the connection between us felt deep and important.

The meeting began. Its setting was weird. A big room had been commandeered and hastily outfitted with furniture and equipment. Wires were hanging everywhere. A bunch of old-fashioned black phones from a generation ago had been dug out of storage and hooked up for communication purposes. The place felt held together with duct tape. But the group that assembled around the big table included 50 of New York's most influential business and political leaders: people like my friend Bill Rudin of Rudin Management, whose father Lew, the great real estate developer, was dying at the time (at his memorial service a few days later, the list of speakers would begin with Bill Clinton); Andy Lack, then president and chief operating officer of NBC, who went to the same prep school as I did; Joseph Spinnato, president of the Hotel Association of New York City; Charles Gargano, chairman of the New York State Economic Development Corporation; Brian McLaughlin, president of the New York City Central Labor Council; Steve Spinnola, head of the Real Estate Board of New York; Deputy Mayor Joe Lohta, head of operations for the city; and Bob Harding, deputy mayor for economic development.

When Fire Commissioner Thomas Von Essen, Police Commissioner Bernie Kerik, and Mayor Giuliani arrived at the table, all of us stood and applauded.

The mayor started by briefing us on the challenges New York would now be facing. After discussing the human casualties and the disruption of services caused by the attack, he remarked, "I'm worried about the fact that millions of feet of office space was destroyed or damaged yesterday. Some of it can be repaired, but it will be unusable for several months, at least. We've got to find homes for the companies that occupied that space. If they flee the city, even temporarily, they might be tempted to move out for good. New York doesn't need that kind of economic blow right now. Does anyone have a suggestion?"

"What about using hotel space for temporary offices?" I suggested. "Our hotels have been jammed with stranded travelers. But today people are beginning to leave the city, even if it means a long drive home to Chicago or Florida. The hotels are starting to empty out. And with everybody spooked by these attacks, our business is going to be down for a while. Why not use empty guest rooms, ballrooms, and meeting rooms as office space?"

An informal partnership was quickly set up to make it happen. The Real Estate Board of New York served as a clearing house, compiling information about companies that needed space and the hotels that could accommodate them. Many businesses ended up taking advantage of the hotel offer. For example, Starwood made a deal to provide space for displaced workers from Lehman Brothers, the big financial firm, at the Sheraton Manhattan Hotel at Seventh Avenue and 52nd Street. Lehman moved in for six months rather than uprooting their workers from New York. The city kept a bit of its vital tax base intact at a time when a financial hit would have been devastating.

For an hour, the assembled business and political leaders swapped ideas about how to solve the enormous problems New York was now facing. The tone of the meeting was remarkable: The skirmishes over turf, control, and prerogatives that usually arise when members of the public and private sectors get together were virtually absent. We knew we were rallying behind a cause that was bigger than any of us—the city we all loved. The meeting ended with a simple pep talk from Rudy:

If you are the leader of a business or other organization, do you have an open channel of communication to public sector leaders in your community? Public/private partnerships are always important, but never more so than in troubled times. Don't wait until then to develop a good working relationship with government leaders in your town or state; look for opportunities to work together on behalf of the community today. The partnerships you build now will stand you in good stead if you ever face a time of crisis.

"Hang in there, folks. We need you more than ever. And let us know how we can help. We're in this together."

The next day, we convened an emergency meeting of the executive committee of NYC & Company, of which I was a member.

As you've seen, NYC & Company is a classic example of an effective private-public partnership. Its mandate to promote New York City as a visitor destination is a challenging job at the best of times. In the aftermath of September 11, our belief in the power of partnerships to sustain the morale and economic fiber of our community would be tested as never before.

Among those who attended the emergency meeting was Christopher Knabel, manager of the Regent Hotel, located just a block from Ground Zero. I was shocked when he walked in. The usually dapper Christopher was covered in dust. "Sorry," he said, "We've been digging out from under the debris. Haven't had a chance to change." I felt for Christopher. He'd worked for Loews at the Regency Hotel before taking over at the Regent just three months before September 11. He'd experienced a tough summer; because of an economic slowdown, downtown hotels had been struggling. Now Christopher was literally near the center of the worst disaster in the city's history. The Regent's majestic ballroom had become a triage area and a makeshift barracks and mess hall for police and firefighters.

The Regent wasn't the only hotel damaged in the catastrophe. The Marriott World Trade Center collapsed, and two of its employees were killed. The Marriott Financial Center, a block south of ground zero, was badly damaged in the attack and didn't reopen for over a year. An Embassy Suites, which had just opened right near the downtown offices of American Express, was also shut down until late in 2002. And during the days after the attack, the Millennium Hotel was thought to be in danger of collapse. (TV news had been showing footage from inside the Millennium—eerie, ghost-town images of rooms inches-deep in dust, shredded paper, and other debris.) It too remained closed until late 2002.

On a broader scale, nearly every travel-related business in New York was suffering. Theatres had been shut down, and no one knew whether audiences would return when the curtains rose again. Professional sports were on indefinite hiatus. Thousands of restaurants and other businesses in the city were closed.

Now we were gathered as an industry for the first time since the catastrophe: hoteliers, restaurateurs, tourism promoters. Danny Meyer, president of the Gotham Hospitality Group, which runs several great New York restaurants, was there. So was Ellen Futter, president of the American Museum of Natural History. Jed Bernstein, president of the League of American Theatres and Producers, represented the Broadway stage.

It was clear that the problems we faced were extraordinary, and that an extraordinary effort would be needed to overcome them. We decided to create a special task force to handle the aftermath of the terror attacks. We dubbed it *New York Rising*, and I was asked to serve as its chair. Our job was to find ways to tell the nation, and the world, that New York was open for business. We had to persuade native New Yorkers to return to their normal lives, and visitors to return to the city.

This was no longer just a matter of civic boosterism or business promotion. Supporting New York was now a matter of patriotism. The sooner New York got back to being its vivid, raucous self, from the downtown dance clubs to the posh boutiques on Madison Avenue, the better we'd frustrate the terrorists' dreams of crushing America's spirit.

New York Rising began meeting for breakfast at the Regency Hotel once a week. The mood of these gatherings must have been reminiscent of the power breakfasts among city leaders that had led New York through the fiscal crisis of the 1970s. We came up with a series of plans to revitalize the battered New York economy. Nearly all involved partnerships between the private and public sectors, as well as partnerships among groups of individual businesses that normally engage in intense rivalries.

Communicating the message of New York's resilience through advertising was one part of the equation. That took money, of course, and we got it through contributions from several sources. New York State provided $20 million for advertising; the city produced a smaller amount; and the Port Authority of New York and New Jersey, the public/private corporation that manages our airports, tunnels, bridges, and other pieces of the travel infrastructure, put up another $20 million.

The ads themselves were great. Several were hilarious, featuring New York icons such as comedian Billy Crystal, Yankee great Yogi Berra, movie maker Woody Allen, and even statesman Henry Kissinger, all acting out their "New York fantasies." (Kissinger ran the bases at Yankee Stadium, Yogi conducted the New York Philharmonic, and Woody Allen somehow turned into an expert figure skater, cavorting on the ice at Rockefeller Center.) For another unique ad, the casts of all of Broadway's top shows gathered in Times Square to sing the theatre anthem, "There's No Business Like Show Business."

Partnership in action: The assemblage of advertising, production, and show-business talent that quickly came together in support of our efforts was a mind-boggling example of how generous people will be

TISCH'S TIPS

Have you ever been asked to build a partnership on behalf of a worthwhile cause? When you are, think big. Seek out the most talented, effective, powerful, noteworthy people and organizations and try to enlist them on your team. The worst thing they can say is no—and you may be pleasantly surprised to discover that the biggest and busiest people in any field are often the most generous.

when the need is real and you reach out to them, not on the basis of ego or financial gain, but simple caring.

New York Rising created several successful marketing programs built around partnerships among various business sectors. One was our "Spend Your Regards to Broadway" promotion: Collect receipts totaling $500 or more from New York retail shops, and get two free tickets to a Broadway show.

Another was a spinoff from an older NYC & Company program, which we'd called "Paint the Town Red." It was a discount travel package that allowed a visitor to call NYC & Company and buy Broadway tickets, arrange a hotel room, and reserve a table at a restaurant with a single phone call. Now we created a patriotic variation called "Paint the Town Red, White, and Blue," offering similar packages at three attractive price points.

We pushed ahead on other fronts as well. We heavily promoted local events like the New York City Marathon. We convinced organizations like the American Society of Travel Agents and the American Society of Association Executives to move their annual meetings to New York.

Sometimes, I imagine, we pushed a little *too* hard in our eagerness to boost New York. One day during the fall of 2001, I got a call from Marc Morial, then the mayor of New Orleans and president of the U.S. Conference of Mayors, a national organization. "We all want to see New York bounce back," Marc said. "What can I do to help you?"

"How about moving next year's Super Bowl game from New Orleans to New York?" I replied. Marc chuckled, then demurred. I wasn't surprised. Mayors ardently pursue Super Bowl games—and the hundreds of millions of dollars in economic impact they generate. They don't give them up lightly. But I was ready with a back-up plan.

"All right, then," I said, "So why not hold the next meeting of the Conference of Mayors in New York City?"

Marc liked the idea. Every previous winter meeting of the Conference of Mayors had been held in Washington, DC. In January 2002, the group broke precedent. After two days of sessions in Washington, the entire meeting shifted to New York for two days. I got to address the Conference, speaking about my two favorite topics: the Power of

Partnership and the vital importance of travel and tourism to our national economy. The Conference has since created a tourism task force that is actively supporting the industry on Capitol Hill and in America's 50 statehouses.

All in all, NYC & Company did a great job of maintaining business in New York. Remarkably, we managed to keep *all* of the major contracts that were on the books—not a single convention or meeting fled the city in the aftermath of the attacks. Travel and tourism was still hit worse than any New York industry other than finance, but the damage was minimized by the partnerships we forged.

What we accomplished was important in business terms. We helped prevent the inevitable downturn from becoming a full-blown local depression. And by the visibility and effectiveness of our efforts, we raised the consciousness of civic leaders concerning the importance of travel and tourism for the city's economy. Formerly, most New Yorkers thought of tourism as a nice sideshow on the local business scene, far less significant than finance, publishing, advertising, apparel, and other industries. Now that has changed. At a conference of business leaders in January 2003, called to brainstorm solutions to the latest phase of the municipal financial crisis, Mayor Michael Bloomberg declared travel and tourism was the industry that could create the new jobs we needed to help lead the city back to economic health.

All of this is very important. Yet, I think what we accomplished during the months after September 11 was even more significant in human terms. By reminding the world of the special role of New York as America's greatest city, and appealing to New Yorkers to demonstrate yet again the indomitable spirit they have shown in so many times of crisis, we played a role in boosting national morale in a time of trauma. The healing of New York led the way for our country.

None of this could have been accomplished without the creation and mobilization of many partnerships, involving businesses, government agencies, nonprofits, and thousands of individual citizens. And it all happened quickly, as people drew together under the pressure of events. The aftermath of September 11 suggests to me that partnership is more than a management tool or a leadership technique—it's a deep-seated human instinct that comes to the fore whenever people feel threatened or in need.

AS THE FIRST ANNIVERSARY OF SEPTEMBER 11 APPROACHED, I TALKED with Cristyne Nicholas of NYC & Company and others about how our industry ought to recognize the date. We came up with the idea of holding a commemorative breakfast. Fittingly, it was held at Christopher Knabel's Regent Hotel, near Ground Zero.

Our partner in this event was Local 6, the union for hotel and restaurant employees, whose president and business manager is Peter Ward. It was important, we felt, to give the front-line workers of our industry the recognition they deserved. After all, during those harrowing days following the attack, they were the ones who couldn't get home to their families; they were the ones working exhausting hours in kitchens and dining rooms, the ones offering comfort, food, and shelter to firefighters, emergency workers, and bereaved families. So we invited Local 6 to draw up the guest list. It included hundreds of housekeepers, bellmen, waiters, cooks, porters, and other hospitality employees—as well as the board and members of NYC & Company.

Partnering with Local 6 enabled us to host an event that brought together all the constituencies most affected by the events of September 11—an important step in the ongoing process of healing.

TISCH'S TIPS

Have you ever had the job of organizing an event to commemorate, celebrate, or otherwise mark an important turning point in the life of an organization or a community? It's an important responsibility. When you must tackle such a task, think outside the box. Don't honor only the obvious stars or leaders; pay tribute as well to the rank-and-file employees, volunteers, and supporters who are essential to the success of any broad-based partnership.

On the morning of September 11, 2002, some 500 people gathered in the Regent's ballroom. The breakfast began with the hymn "Amazing Grace" sung by the ARC Gospel Choir, a 36-person a cappella group made up of gifted singers who also happen to be recovering victims of drug or alcohol abuse (talk about inspirational stories). I said a few words. Joe Spinnato gave a moving speech. And Tom Valenti, a talented New York chef who owned and ran the famous Ouest restaurant (and today also owns Cecsa), spoke about the Windows of Hope Foundation, which had been raising money for the families of food and beverage workers killed in the terror attacks.

When the breakfast events were over, we lingered to watch the official commemorative events from Ground Zero on big-screen televisions set up in the ballroom. We exchanged handshakes and hugs and kisses, and shed a few tears. We spent the rest of the day in somber reflection—until the evening, when the tone shifted to one of renewal. NYC & Company sponsored a candle-lighting ceremony in Times Square, highlighted by a stirring rendition of "God Bless America" led by Broadway stars Paige Price and Marilu Henner. Then, with a group of friends, I took in a preview of the new hit show *Hairspray*. NYC & Company had arranged to give away several hundred tickets to several of the hottest Broadway shows—just another way to emphasize our theme: New York is rising.

LOOKING BACK ON THE HORRIFIC EVENTS OF SEPTEMBER 11, OUR CITY and our nation are still working to recover from one of the most traumatic events in our history. New York has been battered. Fear of terrorism and global security continue to dominate the headlines and the national consciousness. And some of us are still haunted by the faces of the friends we lost.

But we've survived—as individuals, as a city, and as a nation. And I'd submit that we owe that survival in large measure to the spirit of partnership that arose, almost spontaneously, in the hours after the calamity struck. We have been able to minimize the physical, economic, and psychological damage suffered by all our people because of the ways we've pulled together in subsequent months. This includes not just the efforts of business and political leaders in New York, but also the support we've received from others around the country and the world.

Tough times like these are when the Power of Partnerships is truly tested and proves its lasting value. But that spirit of partnership will be available in times of crisis only if you've laid the foundation for it in all of your daily behaviors, in good times and bad. If you truly hope to tap into the Power of Partnerships on behalf of your organization, its stakeholders, and the communities you serve, then you need to start living and working in accordance with that broader vision—the sooner the better.

One of the most eloquent spokesmen for this philosophy of life was the late John W. Gardner, who served our nation as president of the Carnegie Foundation, secretary of Health, Education and Welfare under President Johnson, and founding chairman of Common Cause, the widely respected citizens' advocacy group. In his essay "The American Experiment" (1999), Gardner wrote about the opportunity created by times of trial and challenge:

> Those who have not succumbed to the contemporary disaffection and alienation must speak the word of life to their fellow Americans. . . . We do not want it said that after a couple of great centuries we let the American Experiment disintegrate.
>
> When the American spirit awakens it transforms worlds. But it does not awaken without a challenge. Citizens need to understand that this moment in history does in fact present a challenge that demands the best that is in them.
>
> Most Americans welcome the voice that lifts them out of themselves. They want to be better people. They want to help make this a better country.
>
> Awaken them to what they can do for their country, the country of their children and their children's children.

These stirring words are as meaningful today as they were when Gardner first penned them. And here's another quotation from Gardner that's a special favorite of mine—nine words he used to sum up what he called the Democratic Compact:

Freedom and responsibility,
Liberty and duty,
That's the deal.

Those simple words describe the kind of partnership that underlies our dream of a truly civil society—a society in which all people have the opportunity to achieve their fullest potential. No matter what our field of endeavor—whether we are business people or politicians, educators or homemakers, health care workers or artists, scientists or clergy—bringing this world a little closer to the realization of that vision should be the ultimate goal of all our efforts.

In the final analysis, that's what the Power of Partnerships is all about.

PORTRAIT IN PARTNERSHIP

Jane Rosenthal

Television and feature production executive Jane Rosenthal cofounded Tribeca Films with actor/director Robert De Niro. Housed in De Niro's Tribeca Film Center in New York, this production company has turned out a steady stream of distinctive films, from dramas like Martin Scorsese's *Cape Fear* (1991) to comedies like *Analyze This* (1999). A mother of two, a Democratic Party fund-raiser, and a sometime children's book author, Jane is also a cofounder of the Tribeca Film Festival, which has become one of the great New York experiences since its creation in 2002.

We caught up with Jane between meetings on the morning of March 19, 2004, as she simultaneously worked on the 2004 edition of the festival, preproduction development of the sequel to her hit comedy *Meet the Parents,* and the Las Vegas production of a show based on the music of anthem-rock group Queen fresh off

(Continued)

a two-year run in London. We asked her to explain how the Power of Partnerships had helped create the Tribeca Film Festival.

"Bob [De Niro] and I had occasionally talked about the idea of a film festival for New York," Jane told us. "But my attitude had always been that the world didn't need another film festival. The events of 9/11 changed that. After the terrorist attacks, New York and specifically lower Manhattan needed something to lift our spirits and to create a new memory—to send the message not only that had we survived and were fine but that we were ready to revitalize our community and become stronger than ever."

The immediate impetus, Jane explained, was a sobering visit to a favorite hangout in Little Italy. "About a month after 9/11, my husband Craig Hatkoff and I went to a place on Mulberry Street for dinner. We were shocked. The neighborhood didn't feel like New York any more. It was deserted. The store owners were practically crying in their windows."

Most people would have reacted by feeling sad, and perhaps talking about how "*someone* ought to do something." Jane and Craig came up with a plan. "We wondered, what would happen if we asked 10 couples to come downtown and join us for dinner? And what if we asked each of those 10 couples to invite 10 other couples? We figured this could make a difference in the lives of the restaurant owners and workers—people whose families and livelihoods were at stake. We came up with the motto, 'Have a meal, save a job.' And we started making phone calls."

The plan snowballed—"became viral," in Jane's words. Five hundred friends and friends of friends showed up for dinner. They met downtown and spread out, patronizing restaurants in Little Italy, Chinatown, and the Wall Street area. Later a second dinner was held, this time drawing 700 people.

Jane had discovered a new mission. "I became obsessed with getting people back downtown, into these wonderful downtown neighborhoods, where every nationality, religion, and ethnic group is represented. You can travel around the world within a few blocks of New York. And these neighborhoods were now in jeopardy. I spent a lot of time talking with my husband Craig and my business partner Bob De Niro about what we could do to bring even more people into downtown. That's when we realized that we could use the power of film to bring people to Tribeca."

That phrase, "the power of film," evokes a powerful memory for Jane. "When Bob and I started the Tribeca Film Center, one of our first things we did was to host a fund-raiser for Nelson Mandela's African National Congress. At the time, Mandela was on his first visit to New York, having just been freed from prison. To our amazement, he knew all about the movie people he met—people like Bob and Spike Lee—and he threw his arms around them. He explained how watching their movies had kept him alive in prison."

Now the power of film would be brought to bear on post-9/11 New York. "We created the first Tribeca Film Festival in just under three months. It took an amazing collection of partners to organize everything from legal permissions to corporate sponsorships. The number of details that needed to be coordinated was overwhelming. And because we'd never done anything like this before, we found ourselves inventing the festival as we went along.

"I remember calling Bob in the middle of our planning and saying, 'I hear there's a new *Star Wars* picture almost ready. Can you call George Lucas about showing it at the festival?' Bob called George and learned that the movie wouldn't be ready till May 9, which was several days after our festival was scheduled to close. So we changed the dates of the festival! *Star Wars: Episode II—Attack of the Clones* became one of our highlights."

In the end, launching the festival required the efforts of over 1,300 volunteers, along with extraordinary cooperation from a wide array of institutional partners. New York City Mayor Michael Bloomberg and Governor George Pataki quickly lent their support; the festival's press conferences and opening ceremonies were held at City Hall. New York's famously combative labor unions, from the Teamsters to the movie projectionists' union, bent over

(Continued)

backward to waive rules and facilitate quick decisions, and the local community boards and police precincts pitched in with plans for traffic control, street closings, and visitor safety.

Jane recruited her friend Jennifer Maguire, a former executive at CNN, to run the festival. (She is still in charge two years later.) She brought from the TV news business her energy, organizational skills, and determination, along with two slogans that everyone quickly adopted: "'No' isn't an option," and "Never go to black."

The third slogan that became a rallying cry for all the partners associated with the festival was a more somber one: "Look left." It referred to the former site of the World Trade Center, a gaping, smoking hole in the fabric of New York that happened to be located just a few steps to the left of the Tribeca Film Center. Jane explains, "At times when we were working 16-hour days, it felt like insanity, and we'd sometimes begin to ask ourselves, What are we doing this for? When that happened, someone would say, 'Look left.' That reminded us what we were doing and why."

In May 2002, the first Tribeca Film Festival brought 150,000 visitors to downtown Manhattan and generated over $10 million in revenues for local merchants. The 2003 festival was even more successful, attracting 350,000 people and pumping $47 million into the downtown economy.

"The good news," Jane says, "is that downtown is now on its way to recovery. We're into the rebuilding phase—thank God. People are pulling their lives together. But the community is still counting on the festival.

"Maybe the biggest compliment we received came from a city council member who told me, 'You know, the merchants downtown look forward to the festival like they look forward to Christmas.'"

Thanks to Jane Rosenthal and the dedicated partners she has recruited, the people of Tribeca should be enjoying Christmas in May for many years to come.

Twelve More Tips

A Recipe for Personal Success

It's true that you can be anything you want, but it is far easier when your ambition is complemented by the ambition of others.

—Kurt Vonnegut Jr. (1922–   )
American novelist

WHEN I TRAVEL AROUND THE COUNTRY, SPEAKING ABOUT THE POWER OF Partnerships, I'm often asked for personal career advice—especially by young people facing today's daunting job market. In these final pages, I want to briefly depart from the partnership theme to offer my thoughts about what you can do to maximize your prospects for success.

In this connection, the lessons I have to share inevitably trace back to the wisdom I absorbed from my family when I was growing up.

The death of my uncle Larry Tisch, in November 2003, was a tough time for our family. Because we're prominent in the business world, especially in our hometown of New York, this rite of passage was a public event, witnessed and written about in all the papers and covered in the electronic media.

All of this might have added up to a traumatic, painful time. We found it very emotional but also uplifting. In our sadness, we drew together as a family and found ourselves looking backward with fresh appreciation at the wonderful things my Uncle Larry created in partnership with his brother—my father—Bob.

There's that word *partnership* again. And although I've used it a lot in these pages, it could never be more appropriate than when describing the relationship between Larry and Bob Tisch. Each has been a dynamic, innovative business leader. Separately, they'd have been highly successful. But as partners, they reached a level of achievement that personifies the best of the American dream.

In part, their shared success was due to their complementary talents and temperaments. Larry was primarily a "numbers guy," Bob a "people guy." Between the two, there were few problems they couldn't solve. They made that simple plan work effectively for more than 50 years, and the enterprise they built is still going strong today, a fact that says volumes not so much about the talents of the younger generation that is now running the show as about the firm foundations that Bob and Larry established.

It was painful to have to say goodbye to Uncle Larry. But for all of us, the time of intense grief gave way to a kind of afterglow—a protracted period during which we shared recollections of what made Larry Tisch such a special person.

He was a brilliant business thinker. If you ever met Larry Tisch and got to talking business with him, within five minutes he would probably understand your business better than you do—that was the quality of his mind. But his greatest strength was his unwavering belief in the basics, whether in business or in life. He always sought the simple solution to the most complex problem—and most often, he found it. And at rock bottom, there was integrity, which he always recognized as the one indispensable ingredient.

Because of those simple yet elusive qualities—belief in the basics and reliance on personal integrity—Larry Tisch was able to live his life without regrets. He never looked back, never wasted time or energy complaining about bad luck or having second thoughts about a deal that didn't work. He believed that if you stuck to your principles, you'd be successful—if not in the short term, then over time. And history has proven him right.

The passing of one of our family's founders has caused all of us in the younger generation of Tisches to renew our focus on one of life's big questions: How do we pass along the values and strengths of our family to the next generation?

The most important thing is to be conscious of those values yourself and to try to live them in your own choices. Beyond that, as parents and role models, we need to think about how our words, actions, and assumptions impact our children. In a family like ours that has been so deeply blessed over the years, we need to impress on our children what's really important in life.

The early years of the twenty-first century are a very different time from when I grew up. It's a celebrity-conscious society in which fame, power, and wealth are publicized and held up as symbols of all that's worthy. Those of us who believe there's more to life need to convey that message to our children. I try to do this, in part by my words—reminding those I'm close to how fortunate we are, and never to take any of our advantages for granted—as well as by my deeds—acknowledging others and always treating them with dignity and respect.

If our children live by those lessons, I'll be very proud of them, no matter whether they grow up to work for Loews Corporation or follow other career paths.

MY FAMILY MEMBERS AREN'T THE ONLY PEOPLE I HOPE TO INFLUENCE IN a positive way. I try hard to be a worthwhile role model for the many Loews Hotels employees whose lives I touch, and who have contributed so much to the success of our business over the years. I take advantage of every opportunity I can to serve as a mentor to younger Loews Hotels employees. I meet with them, one on one, in small groups, and in large gatherings, as often as possible, and we all learn a lot from these encounters.

One of my ways of sharing my ideas about success has been through the original "Tisch's Tips"—a collection of simple suggestions that represents my own interpretation of the family values I inherited. These ideas may not be earth-shattering in their creativity or brilliance, but they've played an important role in my own career, and I suspect that others can benefit from them. Here they are. I hope you'll find them helpful in thinking about your own future endeavors, whatever business or profession you may be in.

✓ Never Start a Paragraph with "I": *Copernicus Proved It—The Universe Doesn't Revolve around You*

Getting wrapped up in your own importance is one of the biggest mistakes anyone can make. Today's media sometimes portray successful business executives as self-absorbed, spotlight-hugging egotists. It's a terrible image—and many of the business people who have lived that way have found themselves falling from the heights of power and fame into well-deserved ignominy.

In the classic movie *Citizen Kane,* Orson Welles plays a brilliant, charismatic, and intensely egotistical businessman. Early in the film, the young Kane has taken over a newspaper. Eager to demonstrate his idealism, he pens a "Declaration of Principles" to be printed on the front page of the paper, under the watchful eye of his best friend, the cynical Jed Leland (played by Joseph Cotten). As he writes, Leland offers a sardonic criticism: "That's the second straight sentence you've started with 'I.'"

The movie proves Leland right. Kane's idealism proves to be no match for his egotism. Within a few years, he converts the newspaper from a crusading force for good into a personal plaything, and his bitter friend Leland sends him back the original copy of the "Declaration of Principles" torn into tiny shreds of paper.

When writing letters, e-mails, or business reports, avoid starting paragraphs with the word "I." If you habitually violate this rule, you send the unmistakable signal that *you* are more important than the reader. Don't believe it! Your business career is not about you—it's about the worthwhile things you can accomplish through partnerships with others, things that will benefit *all* the parties concerned.

✓ Listen Carefully: *You Never Learn a Thing While Your Mouth Is Open*

Plenty of business people take courses in public speaking. There are "media coaches" who will train you to appear witty and eloquent on TV, and organizations like Toastmasters that will help you master the art of giving speeches and presentations. All of this is fine. But I wonder why we don't put equal stress on the art of listening. If we did, the world in general would be much better off.

Being a good listener means more than simply hearing the words another speaks (although that's an essential starting point). It also means paying attention to the underlying feelings, the unspoken concerns, the deeper desires of the person at the other end of the communication line. Sometimes there's a gap between the literal meaning of the words you hear and the inner thought that drives those words. Learn to be sensitive to the difference if you hope to be an effective leader *or* follower.

When you are engaged in a difficult negotiation or a conversation that's fraught with the potential for misunderstanding or anger, it's especially important to be a good listener. One technique that helps is to show you've heard and understood your partner by echoing back their concerns *before* presenting your own point of view. Doing this defuses tension by demonstrating your readiness to take your partner's needs into account. It's a way of showing respect—something everyone craves and deserves to have, in business and in life.

✅ Make It a Win/Win Situation: *You Can't Have It All—Where Would You Keep It?*

The most effective business partner is not the person whose sole motivation is to maximize the benefits to himself or to his organization, nor is the best negotiator the person who makes sure he grabs every dollar on the table. Instead, the key to long-term success is making any partnership and any negotiation into a victory for everyone involved—because only if everyone benefits will the relationship last and flourish.

Implementing this rule doesn't simply mean not being greedy (although the willingness to leave a little for your partner is certainly one aspect of it). It also means having some psychological insight and empathy into your partner's needs. Always ask yourself: What will make my partner successful in his boss's eyes? (*Everyone* has a boss. Even a company CEO must report to a board of directors.) Then try to find a way to help him achieve that goal.

If you operate in this way, you'll have laid the foundation for a long-term, mutually beneficial partnership. Your partner will become an ally, and perhaps a friend; later, when you are in a bind, he'll be more willing to help you out because of the consideration you showed him in the past.

Are there people who will try to take advantage of you? A few. But that's no reason to abandon the philosophy. You'll soon learn the identities of the win-at-any-price people in your business, and you can avoid them thereafter. The great majority of people will appreciate the shared-benefits approach, and they'll be happy to provide you with all the help and support you need to achieve your career goals.

✅ Do Your Homework: *What You Don't Know Can Hurt You*

One of the biggest factors in career success is being a constant learner. There are many sources of insight, information, and knowledge, ranging from courses and seminars to books, magazines, and newsletters. Whether you hope to climb the ladder in any organization or simply contribute more in your current position, take advantage of the sources and devote a few hours of your evening and weekend time to sharpening your knowledge base.

Start by becoming an expert at your own trade or craft. Are you involved in bookkeeping, accounting, or finance? Master the important formulas, the rules and regulations, and know exactly when and how to apply them. Are you in marketing or advertising? Study the proven techniques of persuasion and the newest media technologies, and strive to understand what makes them effective. Are you involved in the arts or the sciences? Keep current with the latest scholarly writings and critical theories in your field. Seize every opportunity to watch, talk with, and learn from the professionals who are the leaders of your industry. This is one vital aspect of doing your homework.

Another is investing time and effort in learning about the people and companies that inhabit your playing field, including partners, potential partners, customers, competitors, investors, and others. Are you interviewing for a new job? Devote time to learning about the company—its history, financial status, biggest hits and misfires, and current challenges. Are you negotiating a contract between your organization and another? Run an Internet search on your negotiating partner and investigate how they've handled previous negotiations. Are you hoping to land a new client or customer? Read every article you can find about them in search of clues as to what makes them tick.

Get to know your own organization and its industry backward and forward. Learn to read a balance sheet and a profit and loss statement, and develop a sense of the key factors that influence the bottom line. Use your computer to experiment with "What if?" questions, so that you'll know which tactics can be used to improve your organization's financial condition—and which tactics are risky.

Finally, know yourself. Figure out what you are good at and where your talents are lacking. After you've done all you can to improve your weaknesses, take steps to surround yourself with others who complement you. Remember, you don't have to be all things to all people. Instead, build partnerships with colleagues who can make you more effective.

All of this may sound like hard work. It is! The truth is that I don't know anyone who has become successful in any field without working hard. Many of the most successful people have less raw talent than their competitors—but they simply outwork them.

☑ Be Media Savvy: *Your Fifteen Minutes of Fame Is Coming—Are You Ready?*

In these pages, I've talked a lot about the element of showmanship in every business, including my own world of travel and tourism. The truth is that, in the twenty-first century, the media is infiltrating every walk of life. As the world grows smaller, as organizations become more transparent, and as partnerships become increasingly important, leaders who are able to communicate their point of view in a clear, winning fashion have a definite edge over others.

In the early stages of your career, you may not be called on to serve as a public spokesperson for your organization. But as your experience and responsibilities grow, so will your visibility. Be prepared. Devote time to studying how the media intersect with organizations in your field, and make notes as to which people and groups do the best job of advocating for their own causes. Think hard about the image you want to convey, both personally and at an organizational level, and work on honing the messages you send until they are concise and compelling.

Look for opportunities to shine a positive media spotlight on your organization and its contributions. This doesn't have to involve staging elaborate stunts or spending millions of dollars; it can be as simple as phoning a local reporter with information about a program, service, product, or event that is truly relevant to that reporter's audience. As you've seen from the examples in this book, great publicity can make a small- to mid-sized organization look like a giant in the world's eyes. The person who develops an instinct for capturing such attention can be an enormous asset to her organization.

☑ Be Creative: *Learn to Think Upside-Down, Inside-Out, and Sideways*

Most people and most organizations are competent. That's the price of admission to today's competitive arena. The people and groups that rise to the top are those with a little something extra—a spark of originality, energy, freshness, and verve that I call *creativity*. As famed designer Todd Oldham (known, among other things, for his brilliant work for Target Stores) puts it, "Creativity = Good Karma." He's right.

Don't be intimidated by the word *creativity*. In the world of business or nonprofit enterprise, creativity doesn't require the artistry of a Pablo Picasso, a Toni Morrison, or a Steven Spielberg. The creative edge can be something as simple as borrowing a technique, a strategy, or a process from one field and applying it to another. In 2003, Democratic presidential hopeful Howard Dean revolutionized party politics by showing that the Internet could be used to raise millions of dollars in campaign funds from grass-roots contributors. Dean and his team didn't invent the Internet or any of the electronic tools they used to promote the candidate; they just applied preexisting technology in a new way. Although they didn't win their party's nomination, their creativity will influence politics for decades to come.

If you are gifted with a strong esthetic sense, by all means apply it to whatever field of endeavor you're in. You don't have to be an artist, composer, or designer to do so. If you work in retailing, take a good look at your store and figure out how it can be made more dramatic, colorful, interesting, or appealing. If you help run a social service agency, study the room where clients wait to be served—can it be made more attractive, thereby boosting the morale of clients and staff alike?

If you're a school teacher, look for ways to incorporate music, art, drama, film, and television to make your classroom a more exciting and rewarding place.

One of the most valuable techniques for everyone to master is the art of brainstorming—a way of tapping the benefits of partnership in the service of creativity. (The Loews Hotels' Good Neighbor Policy was the product of a brainstorming session.) The basics are simple: Gather your smartest and most energetic colleagues in a room with some big pads of paper and felt-tipped markers. Then throw out the question or challenge of the day and invite your partners to pour out ideas, which you capture in phrases or sentences on sheets of paper posted around the room. To keep the ideas flowing, follow a few basic principles: Don't judge or criticize—when brainstorming, there are no bad ideas; bounce freely from one topic to another; draw connections among ideas, logical or illogical; and encourage stealing, combining, and modifying of other people's ideas. If the well of inspiration begins to run dry, toss out a provocative question—the weirder the better: "Can we turn this topic upside-down, inside-out, or sideways? What if we woke up tomorrow and found everything we assumed to be true was false?" Sometimes the most brilliant insight emerges in response to the most bizarre or irrelevant notion.

As we've seen in this book, creativity has the power to unlock doors—to help smaller organizations out-compete those with bigger payrolls and marketing budgets. There's room for creativity in every field. Make it your business to help that creativity flourish in any organization you touch.

✅ Empower Others: *You Can't Perform a Symphony if You're a One-Person Band*

One of the crucial arguments in support of the Power of Partnerships is the simple truth that, if you try to do everything yourself, the amount you'll do will be severely limited. All great achievements come from the combined efforts of many people in support of a larger cause—in a word, from partnerships.

Most people accept this reality. But many overlook an important corollary: To create an effective partnership, you must be prepared to empower others. That doesn't mean simply assigning tasks to people, or, worse yet, ordering them around. Empowerment means what it says—giving others the power to accomplish things on their own.

When you empower others, you give up some degree of control. The goals should be agreed on, but the empowered partner can choose her own way of pursuing those goals. Empowerment means letting others have the resources and tools they need to run their own show. It also means making sure they have access to the information and knowledge they need to make smart decisions.

If you are in charge of a project, you must empower the people and groups you rely on to make the project happen. If instead you try to turn those people into mere instruments under your control, they will come to resent you, and ultimately may even sabotage your efforts. True empowerment is the only successful partnership strategy for the long term.

However, this doesn't mean offering no advice, guidance, or over-sight, nor does it mean tolerating sheer incompetence or unwillingness to work. As with most things in life, empowerment is a balancing act—finding the right middle ground in which you offer your partners the help they need as well as the freedom they want. Is it easy? Not always. But the art of effectively empowering others is a vital one for any as-piring leader to learn.

☑ Reinforce the Brand: *Build the Legend of You*

When you hear the word "brand," you probably think of great com-pany names like those advertised on television—Coca-Cola, McDon-ald's, IBM, and so on. But in reality, every organization—even every individual—has a "brand name" that deserves to be defined, enhanced, promoted, and continually reinforced. A brand encapsulates what you and your organization stand for, and few things have a greater impact on your success or failure than the strength of that brand.

On the organizational level, reinforcing the brand name involves important elements, including deciding what kinds of products or ser-vices you want to provide, and then making sure that the quality of your offerings is as high as possible; linking that high quality to the name of your organization as frequently and powerfully as you can; enhancing the public perception of your brand through advertising, marketing, public relations, and other techniques; looking for opportunities to extend the brand into compatible areas; and developing visual, tactile, auditory, and other materials that continually remind people of the brand name in a pleasing, positive style.

Organizations need branding specialists to oversee this process. Even more important, however, are the daily efforts of everyone associated with the organization to maintain the brand name's appeal by providing high-quality products and services. Whenever you're on the job—every time you answer the phone, write a letter, serve a customer, package a product, answer a question, or sweep the floor—you are either enhancing or harming the value of the brand name, depending on the quality of the work you do.

And much the same is true on the personal level. Think of your own name—"Nancy Smith," "Pedro Feliciano," "Howard Ng"—as your brand. Everyone who comes into contact with you develops an opinion, positive or negative, about that brand. Taken together, these hundreds of opinions amount to the *brand image* you have among people in your field. And everything you do will either improve or damage that image.

When you think about it this way, every day, every hour, every minute of your life is important. Are you reinforcing your own brand—strengthening your image as a professional, caring, honest, thoughtful, creative, motivated person—or hurting it?

☑ Take a Job, Any Job: *Don't Be Afraid of Starting at the Bottom—You'll Have Nowhere to Go But Up*

Today's job market is a tough one, especially for young people getting ready to enter the work world. The gains in productivity of the 1990s have been beneficial to business, but they mean that many companies have learned to do more with fewer people. As a result, reaching that first step on the career ladder is now harder than it has been in years.

If you're in this quandary, my advice is: Take a job, any job. The best way to enhance your future value is simply to work. It almost doesn't matter what industry you find yourself in or what your specific assignment may be. Any paid job (and many unpaid jobs, including volunteer work and internships) provide you with a host of valuable opportunities: to learn from more experienced employees; to study an organization from the inside out; to hone your skills at communication, planning, and organization; and to learn more about yourself, your abilities, your interests, your likes, your dislikes.

Don't be afraid of getting sidetracked by taking a job that is irrelevant to your long-term goals. Few people today will work in one career for an entire lifetime. The job you consider irrelevant today may prove to offer important background knowledge that will be relevant to your third or fourth job, 15 or 20 years from now. (My years as a TV producer in the 1970s have proven to be profoundly relevant to my work in hospitality.) Some of the people you encounter in your first, "dead-end" job may turn into lifelong friends, mentors, and guides. And who knows? As your personality and interests change and grow, you may find yourself fascinated by a field you expected to dislike.

Take a job, any job. The worst thing that can happen is that you'll want to try something different in six months or two years—and in the meantime, you'll have learned (and earned) a lot more than you would have if you'd sat at home playing video games!

✅ Pay Attention to Detail: *Perfection Is in Trifles—But Perfection Is No Trifle!*

One of the lessons I've learned over and over again is that it doesn't take much to make or break a relationship. It's as true in life as it is in business.

In my world of hospitality, small details can have a profound impact on a guest's perception of a hotel. Think of a single eyelash—is there anything smaller that's still visible to the naked eye? But an eyelash in the wrong place—say, on the rim of a drinking glass in a guest's bathroom—can be enough to turn an enjoyable night in a hotel into a disaster. That's why Loews Hotels (like other fine hotels) establishes strict guidelines for cleanliness as well as for the many other services it provides. Tiny details? Yes—but so important.

How does the importance of details impact your career? In a hundred ways. Take the simple act of applying for a job. There are dozens of tiny details that can sabotage you: a typo on your resume, a small stain on your blouse or necktie, telling a tasteless joke during the interview, misspelling someone's name. (My co-author and I would love to have a dollar for every time someone has written to us as "John Tish" or "Carl Webber." We are *not* positively disposed when we start reading those letters!)

Some people are naturally obsessive about details—they are the Felix Ungers of the world (as you'll know if you've ever seen the *Odd Couple*). Others consider details boring, stupid, and fussy—call them the Oscar Madisons. You probably know by now which category you belong to. If you're a Felix, congratulations! (Although you can probably afford to loosen up just a little.) But if you're an Oscar, beware! Maybe your carelessness with details hasn't tripped you up so far, but it will someday.

Slow down, take a deep breath, and pay attention. The details you focus on today may save your reputation tomorrow.

✅ Network, Network, Network! *You've Got Something in Common with Everybody*

In some circles, networking has gotten a bad rap. People sometimes associate it with insincere smiles and phony friendships. They think that a networker is someone who wants to know you only in order to *use* you.

As you can guess, that's not what I mean by networking. Think of networking within the broader context of partnering. Partners work together for a common goal; they set aside individual interests in pursuit of shared objectives; they look for tasks and projects that can benefit everybody concerned. That's the way networking should be practiced.

Considered in this light, networking means getting to know a wide array of people from many walks of life, and looking for opportunities to link those people in interesting, creative, and constructive ways. The networker is the kind of person who sends a friend a clipping from an obscure magazine, because he remembers the friend's special interest in the topic. The networker offers a helpful reference or contact to a friend who has just launched a new business or is seeking a new job. The networker gladly gives an informational interview to a young person interested in breaking into the industry—along with a little concrete advice about how to improve her resume or sharpen her interviewing skills.

To be a good networker, you need to care about people—not in the artificial, smarmy style of the fake networker, but with genuine feeling. And you need to set aside your own goals and objectives in favor of helping others.

Will you ultimately benefit from the networking you do? Of course—the old saying about "casting bread upon the waters" is still true today. But if you try to network with selfish motives, people will sense your insincerity and reject it. Be real, or don't bother.

✓ Be Good to People: *It's the Golden Rule, Stupid!*

In a way, this final tip encapsulates all the others. It sounds simple, but in practice it can be truly challenging. "Being good to people" means more than living up to conventional rules of etiquette, corporate codes of conduct, or legal requirements. It means thinking about the *other* person's point of view and treating her the way you'd want to be treated if you were in her shoes. It takes time, effort, empathy— even a bit of imagination, since it involves escaping, at least for the moment, from the little world of your own desires, needs, expectations, and entering into another person's point of view.

It's no coincidence that this last tip is so close to what has come to be called the Golden Rule—"Do unto others as you would have them do unto you"—or that, in one form or another, the same principle is at the heart of all the world's great religions. There's something basic about human nature that calls upon us to live by this rule.

When you follow this principle, your career is likely to thrive. At the same time, you'll be doing your part to improve the world in which you live. And that's a form of personal success that's more important and more satisfying than fame or fortune.

SOURCES

Chapter 1   The Power of Partnerships

Material on history of Loews Hotels in Miami Beach, including quotation about Morris Lapidus from *The New Yorker,* from:

> *Golden Opportunities: 50 Years of Loews Hotels.* Bethesda, Maryland: CustomNEWS Celebration Publishing, 1996.

Material on new hotel project from:

> Miami Beach Convention Center Online. Available from www .miamibeachconvention.com.

> "Beach Hotel Plans: Some Fit, Some Don't," by Peter Whoriskey. *Miami Herald,* March 9, 1994. This article and all other articles from the *Herald* are available from http://nl.newsbank.com.

> "And Now, It's Showtime for Pricey Hotel Plans. The Prize: South Beach Mega-Resort," by Anthony Faiola. *Miami Herald,* June 28, 1994.

> "Top Plan for S. Beach Resort Has Deco Spirit 16-Story Hotel Praised for Its Design," by Anthony Faiola and Peter Whoriskey. *Miami Herald,* June 30, 1994.

> "Loews Wins Battle To Build Beach Hotel," by Anthony Faiola. *Miami Herald,* July 22, 1994.

> "Best for Miami Beach." *Miami Herald,* July 25, 1994.

> "Back to the Beach," by Anthony Faiola. *Miami Herald,* July 31, 1994.

> "Bargains in the Sunshine State," by Robert Lenzer with Stephen S. Johnson. *Forbes,* March 25, 1996. Available from www.coralcreeklanding.com /bargains.htm.

> "Powerful Families Bid for Beach Hotel Casino Not Required, They Say," by Anthony Faiola. *Miami Herald,* March 1, 1994.

> "Loews Miami Beach Hotel Ready for Grand Opening," by Cynthia Corzo. *Miami Herald,* March 5, 1999.

"Loews Miami Beach Hotel Exceeds Profit Projections." City of Miami Beach Press Release, April 27, 2001. Available from www.ci .miami-beach.fl.us/newcity/press/press01/pr042901.htm.

Material on the Welfare to Work Partnership from:

The Welfare to Work Partnership. Available from www.welfaretowork .org.

"President's Welfare Reform Package Strengthens Families: Remarks by the President [Bush] to Welfare-To-Work Graduates." Available from www.whitehouse.gov.

"Miami Area Hotels Form Coalition to Help Welfare Recipients Find Work," by Gregg Fields. *Miami Herald,* February 16, 1998.

"Jobs Hard to Come by as Welfare Deadline Approaches," by Connie Prater, Mimi Whitefield, and Gregg Fields. *Miami Herald,* June 10, 1998.

"New Miami Beach Hotel Begins Hiring in August," by Dale K. DuPont, *Miami Herald,* July 2, 1998.

Background material on Rodney Carroll from:

No Free Lunch: One Man's Journey From Welfare to the American Dream by Rodney J. Carroll with Gary Karton. New York: One World/Ballantine Books, 2002.

Chapter 2   Now Who's Boss?

John F. Kennedy quotation from address in the Assembly Hall at the Paulskirche, Frankfurt, West Germany, June 25, 1963.

"Loews Hotels Chairman Performs Housekeeping, Other Duties for Reality Show." *Miami Herald,* February 17, 2004.

"The Best Hotels for Families," by Felicity Long. *Parenting* magazine. Available from http://www.child.com/living_in_style/family_travel /best_hotels.jsp?page=1.

Background on Jeffrey Zucker from:

NBC Online: "Jeffrey Zucker" NBC Executive, Biography. Available from www.nbc.com.

Chapter 3   A Family Business

Gerald Early quotation from Preface to *Daughters: On Family and Fatherhood,* by Gerald Early. New York: Perseus Books, 1994.

Background information on Loews Hotels and Loews Corporation from:

Golden Opportunities: 50 Years of Loews Hotels. Bethesda, Maryland: CustomNEWS Celebration, 1996.

CNA available from www.cna.com.

Background information on New York Giants from:

"Turning $500 into a $573 Million NFL Team," by Monte Burke. *Forbes,* August 29, 2003. Available from www.forbes.com/2003/08 /29/cz_mb_0829giants.html.

NY Giants Team Online: "Front Office" and "Wellington Mara." Available from www.giants.com.

Background information on travel and tourism industry from:

"Media and Minister's Briefing, Third Global Travel & Tourism Summit, WTTC's TSA Research and Special Report on SARS," World Travel & Tourism, May 15, 2003, Algarve, Portugal.

TIA Online: "Fast Facts: Economic Impact." Available from www.tia.org.

"United States Travel & Tourism: A World of Opportunity—The 2003 Travel & Tourism Economic Research," World Travel & Tourism Council. Available from www.wttc.org, 2003.

WTTC Online: "Tourism Satellite Accounting." Available from www. wttc.org.

Other sources:

"Feinstein's at the Regency Kicks Off the Fall 2001 Season." Loews Hotels Press Release, October 31, 2001. Available from www.loewshotels.com /aboutus_pressroom_full.asp?press_id=75&hid=8.

"Gone with the Wind Atlanta Premiere," by Larry Worthy. *About North Georgia.* Available from www.ngeorgia.com/feature/gwtwpremiere .html.

Background on Mark Morial from:

American Council for Technology Online: "Marc H. Morial," Biography. Available from www.fgipc.org.

National Urban League Online "About Us: History of the National Urban League." Available from www.nul.org.

Chapter 4   The Employee Comes First

Information on Henry Ford, Thomas Watson, and Edward Filene from:

Management by Peter F. Drucker. New York: Harper & Row, 1974, p. 338–342.

Background information on American Apparel from:

"Made in the U.S. of A.?" by Linda Baker. *Salon.* Available from www.salon.com.

"No Sweat: Dov Charney Is Not Only Ensuring That Conditions at His American Apparel Clothing Factory Are Good, He's Also Making a Profit. Here's How He's Surprising the Industry," by Chris Warren. *Southwest Airlines Spirit,* November 2003, pp. 44–48.

Background information on Emeril Lagasse from:

Emeril Lagasse Online. Available from www.emerils.com.

Chapter 5   Turning Customers into Partners

Detail on Eleanor Roosevelt margarine testimonial from:

Ogilvy on Advertising by David Ogilvy. New York: Vintage, 1985, page 109.

Background on Starbucks from:

Pour Your Heart into It: How Starbucks Built a Company One Cup at a Time, by Howard Schultz and Dori Yang. New York: Hyperion, 1997, Chapter 18.

Background on Charles Schwab from:

> *Clicks and Mortar: Passion Driven Growth in an Internet World,* by David S. Pottruck and Terry Pearce. San Francisco: Jossey-Bass, 2000, Chapter 10.

Background on Ben & Jerry's from:

> *Ben & Jerry's: The inside Scoop: How Two Real Guys Built a Business with a Social Conscience and a Sense of Humor,* by Fred "Chico" Lager. New York: Crown, 1994, Chapter 13.

Details on Harley Owners Group from:

> "About H.O.G." Available from www.harley-davidson.com.

Background on NASCAR from the following:

> "NASCAR Business at the Green Flag," by Rick Horrow, February 10, 2004. Available from CBS.SportsLine.com.

> "How to Woo NASCAR Fans," by William Schneider. *National Journal,* December 16, 2003. Available from www.theatlantic.com.

Background on JetBlue from:

> "Johnny Jet's Q & A: JetBlue's David Neeleman." Available from www.johnnyjet.com.

> New York New Media Association Online: "David Neeleman," Biography. Available from www.nynma.org.

Chapter 6   Being a Good Neighbor

Friedman quotation from:

> *Capitalism and Freedom* by Milton Friedman with the assistance of Rose D. Friedman. Chicago: University of Chicago Press, 1962, page 133.

Background on Merck from:

> *Built to Last: Successful Habits of Visionary Companies* by James C. Collins and Jerry I. Porras. New York: HarperBusiness, 1994, Chapter 3.

Background on Tom's of Maine from:

The Soul of a Business: Managing for Profit and the Common Good, by Tom Chappell. New York: Bantam Books, 1993, Chapter 10.

Background on outreach programs in hospitality industry from:

"Please Won't You Be Their Neighbor?" by Marla Misek. *Lodging HR,* September 2003, Vol. 5, No. 6., p. 1.

"A Question of Competence." *Lodging HR,* September 2003, Volume 5, Issue 6.

"Is Time Money?" by Ari Karen & Keith A. Halpern. *Lodging HR,* September 2003, Vol. 5, No. 6, p. 3.

Background on President Jimmy Carter and river blindness project from:

The Carter Center Online. Available from www.cartercenter.org.

Merck Online: "Merck: Corporate Responsibility: Policies and Performance" Available from www.merck.com.

Chapter 7　E Pluribus Plenty

Hightower quotation from *Cullen Hightower's Wit Kit.* Available from www.conservativeforum.org.

Background on Hard Rock Hotel from:

Hard Rock Online: "Hard Rock Hotel: Orlando, Florida." Available from www.hardrock.com.

Background on House of Blues from:

House of Blues Online: "About HOB [House of Blues]." Available from www.hob.com.

Background on travel and tourism organizations from:

PCMA Online: "Professional Convention Management Association [PCMA] History." Available from www.pcma.org.

ASAE Online: "Meet American Society of Association Executives [ASAE]." Available from www.asaenet.org.

AH & LA Online: "About American Hotel & Lodging Association [AH & LA]." Available from www.ahma.com.

TBR Online: "About Travel Business Roundtable [TBR]." Available from www.tbr.org.

WTTC Online: "About World Travel & Tourism Council [WTTC]." Available from www.wttc.org.

Background on NYC & Company from:

NYC & Company. Available from www.nycvisit.com.

Background information on Paul Tagliabue from:

"Guiding Might: NFL Commissioner Paul Tagliabue Wields Power Wisely from the Top of Pro Sports' Most Successful League," by Dennis Dillion. *The Sporting News*, December 31, 2001. Available at www.findarticles.com.

Chapter 8 Beyond the Ballot Box

Thoreau quotation from "A Yankee in Canada" (1853), in *The Writings of Henry David Thoreau*, Vol. 5, p. 17. Boston: Houghton Mifflin, 1906, Vol. 5, p. 17.

Details on New York City tourism from:

"Marketing New York City in the 21st Century." Presentation by NYC & Company, New York City, Fall 2003.

Background on passport issue from:

"State Dept. Says Few Countries Can Meet Machine Readable Passport Deadline," February 3, 2004. Available from www.usinfo.state.gov /topical/pol/terror/texts/04020305.htm.

Details on international travel promotions from:

"Media and Minister's Briefing, Third Global Travel & Tourism Summit, WTTC's TSA Research and Special Report on SARS," World Travel & Tourism online, May 15 2003, Algarve, Portugal.

Details on economic impact of world travel from:

"Tourism Satellite Accounting," WTTC Online. Available from www.wttc.org.

Background on Welfare to Work from:

Welfare to Work Partnership Online: "Business Resource Group." Available from www.welfaretowork.org.

"Liberal Lessons from Welfare Reform," by Christopher Jencks. *Prospect*, July 15, 2002. Available from www.prospect.org/print /v13/13/jencks-c.html.

"Bush's Blunder," by Mark Greenberg. *Prospect*, July 15, 2002. Available from www.prospect.org/print/v13/13/greenberg-m.html.

"The Next Step for Welfare Reform," by Jennifer L. Noyes. *American Outlook Today*, January 7, 2004. Available from www.welfarere-former.org/index.cfm?fuseaction=publication_details&id=3166.

"Marriott International's Pathways to Independence." *PR Newswire*, May 3, 2001. Available from www.findarticles.com/cf_dls/m4PRN /2001_May_3/73995710/p1/article.jhtml.

New Democrats Online: The Democratic Leadership Council's Online Community: "Earned Income Tax Credit." Available from www .ndol.org.

"The Earned Income Tax Credit," by Pamela Friedman. *Welfare Information Network*, April 2000, Vol. 4, No. 4. Available from www.welfare-info.org/friedmanapril.htm.

"Human Services Federal Issues Overview," National Conference of State Legislatures. Available from www.ncsl.org.

Background on Philadelphia project from:

"New Convention Hotel Slated for Philadelphia," *Seattle Daily Journal of Commerce*, April 17, 1997. Available from www.djc.com/news /re/10023247.html.

"New Purpose, Old Style: As a Loews Hotel, the PSFS Building Fills a Lodging Niche," by Tom Belden. *Philadelphia Inquirer*, April 5, 2000.

"Its New Life as a Hotel: PSFS Reincarnated as the Loews Hotel," by Jenice M. Armstrong. *Philadelphia Inquirer*, April 5, 2000, business section.

"Loews Gets the Royal Treatment," *Metro*, April 6, 2000.

"Bright Light in Big City: Loews Enhances a Philadelphia Landmark," *Philadelphia Inquirer*, April 6, 2000, Editorial page.

Background on community venture movement from:

"Capital for Companies That Aid Communities," by Anne Field. *New York Times*, October 16, 2003.

CDVCA available from www.cdvca.org.

Background on microlending from:

"Microlending Offers a Superior Alternative to Massive Immigration," by Brenda Walker. *MichNews.com*, December 28, 2003. Available from www.michnews.com/artman/publish/article_2100.shtml.

"Profiles in Microenterprise," by Betsy Brill. *New Village Journal*, No. 2. Available from www.newvillage.net/Journal/Issue2/2microlending.html.

Accion Online available from www.accion.org.

Background information on Kate Carr from:

Elizabeth Glaser Pediatric AIDS Foundation Online. Available from www.pedaids.org.

Chapter 9 What's in It for the Owners?

Burke quotation from:

Reflections on the Revolution in France, by Edmund Burke, 1790.

Background on Sir Howard Stringer from:

Sony Online: "Howard Stringer," Biography. Available from www.sony .com.

Chapter 10 New York Rising

Giuliani quotation from *Leadership,* by Rudolph W. Giuliani with Ken Kurson. New York: Miramax, 2002, p. 107.

Background on John Gardner from:

John Gardner Center Online: "John W. Gardner (1912–2002)" Available from www.gardnercenter.stanford.edu.

"The People's Architect," by John H. Richardson. *Esquire,* March 2002, Available from www.rockwellgroup.com/printer.php3?page=press /esquire.html&article=0.

Background information on Jane Rosenthal from:

Tribeca Film Festival Online. Available from www.tribecafilmfestival .org.

"Jane of All Trades," by Meryl Gordon. Available from www .newyorkmetro.com/nymetro/movies/features/5963.

INDEX